CW00539048

# How Railways Changed Britain

## *A New Social and Economic History*

Edited by David St John Thomas

RAILWAY & CANAL HISTORICAL SOCIETY

*In memory of David St John Thomas*
*Writer, Historian, Publisher*
*1929 — 2014*

First published 2015
by the Railway & Canal Historical Society

www.rchs.org.uk

The Railway & Canal Historical Society was founded in 1954 and incorporated in 1967.
It is a company (no.922300) limited by guarantee and registered in England
as a charity (no.256047)
Registered office: 1–2 Vernon Street, Derby DE1 1FR

Uncredited illustrations are by the contributors or from their collection

ISBN 978 0 901461 63 6

Designed and typeset by
Malcolm Preskett
Printed and bound in Great Britain by
Berforts Information Press
www.bookprinting.co.uk

Cover illustrations
Front
*upper: Ramsgate Harbour station, 1924 (National Railway Museum)*
*lower: Virgin Pendolino at Atherstone, 2008. © Rail-Online*
Back
*upper: Normanton station and hotel, 1845 (engraving by A.F.Tait)*
*lower: Intermodal freight train on way to a sea port, 2011. © I4lcocl2.Dreamstime.com*

# Contents

# Contributors

**Peter King**

Dr Peter King graduated in chemistry from Leicester University. He then practised as a solicitor for some years. He took an interest in local history in the area where he lived. This led him into studying the charcoal iron industry, first locally and then nationally. This was the subject of his doctoral thesis, completed in 2003, and he is now an Honorary Research Fellow in the School of History and Cultures at the University of Birmingham. He has published about three dozen academic articles mostly on the iron industry and related subjects. This has included such transport history subjects as early railways and river navigations, including papers for the last two early railways conferences and articles on Andrew Yarranton for two biographical dictionaries.

**Malcolm Reed**

Malcolm Reed's lifelong interest in railway history is reflected in his authorship of several books and articles in this field. This has been combined with a career in transport planning and administration, most recently as Director General of Strathclyde Passenger Transport Executive and then as the first Chief Executive of Transport Scotland. Since his retirement from the Civil Service in 2009 he has been an adviser to Virgin Trains.

Malcolm is a member of the Railway Heritage Trust advisory panel, and has previously served as a member and vice-chair of the Railway Heritage Committee and represented the PTEs on the advisory committee of the Railway Safety & Standards Board. He was appointed CBE in 2004 for services to the transport industry, and is a Fellow of the Chartered Institute of Transport & Logistics, the Chartered Institution of Highways & Transportation, and the Institution of Railway Operators.

**Tony Kirby**

Until taking early retirement, Tony Kirby was Co-ordinator of Strategic Planning at Anglia Ruskin University. He is a former President of the

Cambridge Antiquarian Society and Chair of the Cambridgeshire Records Society. His publications include *An Atlas of Cambridgeshire & Huntingdonshire History* (ed. with Dr S. Oosthuizen, 2000), *Anglia Ruskin University 1858–2008: A Celebratory History* (2008), articles and reviews in local history and railway journals, and commentaries on OS maps for Alan Godfrey Editions. Brought up in rural North Yorkshire, his interest in railways and the urban landscape was first sparked by journeys to visit relatives in the very different industrialised West Riding (although at the time, 'copping' 8Fs and even the odd Beyer-Garratt at Normanton and 'Scots' at Keighley took precedence).

For some years he was a member of the Rail Users' Consultative Committee for Eastern England and is currently involved in a Heritage Lottery-funded project investigating the oral history of the railway community in Cambridge.

### Philip Scowcroft

Philip L. Scowcroft, a retired solicitor in local government service, has been writing and talking about transport history topics (and much else) for many years – indeed for most of the fifty years he has been a member of the Railway & Canal Historical Society. In this he has made a speciality of excursions and holidays, also of transport connections with sport and cultural matters, and is grateful for the opportunities afforded by the Society in pursuing this. In particular a long-held admiration for the works of David St John Thomas persuaded him to have a shot at writing a chapter on Railways and Leisure for this co-operative book.

### Andrew Jones

Andrew Jones is an amateur historian and writer who focuses on nineteenth- and twentieth-century social and economic topics, and, professionally, has over thirty years experience working for one of the UK's major banking groups. His deep-rooted interest in railways goes right back to childhood memories of catching trains from a gas-lit station on the West Highland Line (in the 1970s) and is such that he has never learned to drive (and always prefers the train to the plane).

Andrew has had a few articles published on-line and in (non-railway) society publications covering a variety of railway and postal/telecommunication history subjects. He lives in Linlithgow, Scotland and is currently studying for an MA in local history through the Open University.

## Andy Brown

Andy Brown has a Degree in economics from Trinity College, Cambridge and a Masters in British history from Birkbeck College, London.
His interests lie in economic history of the industrialisation of Britain especially the impact of railways. More specifically his research encompasses the role of the state in Britain's railways and railway company management practices and performance and he is investigating the Great Central Railway and its constituents in this context. He has written a short article in *Back Track* on railway fares in 1850. Andy is employed in the change management function of a large bank in London and is married with one child.
His interests beyond railways include food, travel and watching cricket.

## Gordon Biddle

Gordon Biddle is a founder member and a Vice-President of the Railway & Canal Historical Society and the author of twelve books on the history of waterways and railways, the latter with emphasis on architecture and engineering. They include *Britain's Historic Railway Buildings: a Gazetteer of Structures and Sites* and, with Jack Simmons, *The Oxford Companion to British Railway History.* In 2012 Prince Michael of Kent presented him with the Transport Trust's Lifetime Achievement Award for recording historic railway and canal infrastructure. A retired surveyor, he is also a Vice-President of the North West Region of the Inland Waterways Association and a Fellow of the Royal Society of Arts.

## David Hodgkins

David Hodgkins CB studied history at Cambridge where he specialised in the development of the British economy in the first half of the nineteenth century. He then worked in the Ministry of Labour, Treasury, Department of Employment and the Health and Safety Executive. He wrote a number of articles on aspects of the transport history of Derbyshire. Since his retirement he has written *The Second Railway King, the Life and Times of Sir Edward Watkin,* and edited *The Records of the Cromford and High Peak Railway* for the Derbyshire Archeological Society and *The Diary of Edward Watkin* for the Chetham Society, both with substantial introductions, as well as articles, particularly on the business aspects of railways. He is now engaged in writing a biography of George Carr Glyn, the banker and chairman successively of the London & Birmingham and London & North Western railways.

# Preface

> What are needed are sound books of a more ambitious nature,
> and particularly perhaps books that cannot be written by a single
> author. For example, an economic and social history of railways
> with thematic chapters would be a real treasure, but a venture of
> the kind that it is difficult for commercial publishers to take on.
> The problem with such joint works is that they tend to take a
> long time to come to fruition.

SUCH was the clear message from David St John Thomas, author and
publisher, when in 2010 he became chairman of the Railway & Canal
Historical Society Publications Committee. His enthusiasm for this type of
railway history should have caused no surprise, as it dated back to at least
1960 when he wrote what proved to be a groundbreaking work.

In later reviewing the achievements of his publishing house David & Charles,
he commented: 'The series of which we were proudest was the Regional
History of the Railways of Great Britain, which began with my own volume
on The West Country. Setting the railways against the economic and social
background, it contained more about agriculture, tourism, industry and
population changes than any other non-academic title then available.
In five hardback and three paperback editions, sales exceeded 40,000
– an astonishing figure for so serious a work.'

David always regarded this volume as the most deeply researched of all his
many railway titles. It inevitably influenced how he wished the R&CHS venture
to take shape. By late 2011 arrangements had been agreed with most of the
contributors who were advised in characteristic style: 'The book should
certainly be about changes the railways effected rather than just plain railway
history. It is not to be an erudite academic work, but a distillation of what
many contributors will long have absorbed into their memory without
necessarily recalling when. The emphasis should be helping a broad audience
understand what it is all about.'

David was certainly right in his prediction that a joint work might take a long time to come to fruition. Yet steady progress had been made by 2012 when I was invited to join the Publications Committee and a year later was asked to become its chairman. Like David I have been both an author and publisher, and have also written two volumes in the 'Regional Railway History' series. The prospect of seeing through a work with a social and economic theme did not therefore cause too many palpitations, especially as David continued to give advice and assistance.

It therefore came as a profound shock to learn of his death in August 2014. Matthew Searle commented in an obituary in the *R&CHS Journal*: 'David's contribution to transport history as author, publisher and Society member has been immense and, as with everything he did, was undertaken with infectious enthusiasm, imagination and great charm.'

One of my prime roles in taking over the editorship of this book has been to try and achieve a reasonable consistency of approach. One of David's final requests was to keep notations to an absolute minimum and only include brief details of further reading. He did not define 'brief', but this has involved contributors in making deletions that were not always what they might have wished. I am grateful for their forbearance. In the case of chapter 6, Andy Brown's list was extensive and its relevance went well beyond his own chapter. It clearly made sense that this should be retained as a selective bibliography in the concluding pages.

It is a matter of great regret that David did not see this book in print. It was the last title with which he was involved and I hope it forms a worthy memorial to his endeavours.

*David Joy*

# Introduction

## *David St John Thomas*

E
VEN those of us who are familiar with the story sometimes find
ourselves amazed by the speed and scope of what the coming of
railways did for Britain – and later for the world. Railways were
a thoroughly British invention. There is a long history of freight
(mainly coal) carrying lines before what is generally assumed to be the first
line: the Liverpool & Manchester, a public passenger and goods-carrying line
opened in 1830. The date is convenient, for historians regard a generation as
thirty years, and I love saying that the generation 1830–1860 changed things
more rapidly than any other.

Consider. In 1830, nobody travelled faster than a horse. Parliament was
unreformed. Streets were mainly unlit, sewerage pouring down their middle,
and cholera reigned. Newspapers had changed little from the libellous sheets
of the previous century, and only had local circulations. News of naval battles
were passed along the south coast by semaphore signalling posts not open
at night and sometimes wiped out by poor visibility by day. The great majority
of children had little education. Though timed in half minutes at the glorious
end of their existence, mail coaches were still slow and, worse, had limited
accommodation, making it impossible to travel at short notice. Few ordinary
people attended the funerals of even close relatives further than walking
distance away.

With astonishing speed, the railway changed all this. Only thirty years
after the opening of the Liverpool & Manchester, the largest English towns
without a railway were Weymouth and Hereford, and they didn't have to
wait much longer. Compare this with the decades it took to develop our
motorway network.

9

With the railway came the telegraph giving instantaneous news. Over large slices of the country national newspapers were delivered at breakfast. What was at first referred to as 'railway time' was adopted nationally.

Far more important, attitudes changed. With their mighty power of creative destruction, old ways were swept aside and people's expectations broadened. In 1830 many people living near the sea had never seen it. By 1860 annual if short visits to it were commonplace. But possibly the most important thing the railways did to unify Britain was to carry millions to the Great Exhibition of 1851, the first truly national event.

It was also thanks to railways that national brands were created. To mention one example, the great Quaker brands of chocolate depended on trains for their existence and popularity – helped by widespread advertising including on the risers of station steps. And remember, stations were great trading places even for those not travelling by train.

Almost wherever they went, railways cut the price of coal (much more used than in later generations) by half and doubled the price of milk. It became cheaper to produce milk in the countryside than within London and, similarly, workers could be brought in cheaply from a wide area. The suburbanisation of Britain was only made possible by trains, and began surprisingly early.

There were inevitably casualties as Britain became more standardised. The spread of the humble Peterborough brick spoilt the appearance of villages where only local materials had been used. But then many local industries were wiped out, some traditional mills closing the very day that trains arrived from the outside world. Centralisation became the theme and was not always for the best. Village shops had to contend with the new-fangled mail-order, another railway first.

Though to many villagers the expresses passing by them may have seemed to have scant relevance, the railway revolution was at its greatest in the countryside. The steam locomotive was the most modern thing in the valley and it brought with it the first civilians to wear uniform – signalmen are still often called bobbies – while even the bosses weren't gentlemen like parsons and teachers but ordinary people who worked their way up the ladder. Promotion by rank was among the many changes wrought by railways.

Above all, with their creative destruction the railways changed attitudes. Things no longer had to be as they always had. Innovation was in the air. Everything became possible if only given priority. Decisions were for taking, including whose funerals one attended – and then, soon, what holiday one might take and which cities and cathedrals to visit. Changing where one lived became an everyday occurrence. People began to think and behave very much as we do today.

Some argue that the biggest change was the invention of the car, but motoring simply followed on from the prime change: that man was no longer restricted to the speed of a horse. Yes, many railways had their day and ceased to be but the revolution they wrought was not the less for that. For example, there are villages (North Tawton in Devon is a good example) where the arrival of trains killed the local mill and source of employment, and development stopped dead. Virtually no new homes were built for nearly a century.

Especially for those who know their architecture, dating buildings from early in the centre to later around the periphery is interesting. As one travels south from London the same applies to whole suburbs. Which reminds one that hundreds of once-busy suburban stations were closed as trams, buses and cars destroyed their business inevitably based on the sparsity of services. Plymouth alone boasts fifty closed suburban stations which were only viable when the alternative was walking to work but none the less had their busy innings.

Though I've written much about the history of railways, even I am amazed afresh by how fast they spread and how greatly they changed Britain. This book celebrates that change in a different way, with contributions by a team of specialist contributors. Nothing can ever be the final word on so important a subject, but working the ground in a new way helps one think again. Indeed even the table of contents can make one dizzy when considering all that there is to say. I'm grateful to the contributors whose pooled knowledge and enthusiasm is boundless.

Railways had profound influence but were a world of their own, not part of anything else. They had their own technology in abundance but little of it was useful to other industries. A railway was ever a railway but it turned life upside down.

A final thought. In my youth nearly everything published on a village or town was of a literary or religious nature. That dated from the Victorian days when trade was 'not quite respectable'. To one well-known writer who had shown me his draft I suggested he mention the opening of the railway, probably the most important event in the area he was covering. 'No', he said. 'That's everyday, not about what people are interested in: literature and religion.' Happily perspective is better today but one still comes across old local history titles that don't deign to mention 'mundane' things such as trade and transport.

# CHAPTER 1

# Before the Main Line

*Peter King*

THE popular view is that the first railways date from the 1820s. In fact railways had already existed in some form for over two centuries. On the other hand, most people's experience of railways concerns passenger transport and in that sense the popular view is largely correct. The long preceding period concerns what would today be referred to as mineral railways, but in terminology of the time, called waggonways (mainly in northeast England), railroads, footrails, or railways. This chapter will explore these two centuries and more, looking at the technology of these early railways. They were almost always horse-hauled. Ox-haulage is occasionally mentioned, and in the early nineteenth century locomotives began to be introduced. The main exception is where no haulage was needed because they were self-acting inclined planes (funicular railways).

The track began with wooden edge-rails with a flanged wheel *(see plates 2 and 3)*. In the 1760s, the rails began to be shod with cast-iron plates. Later still cast-iron L-shaped tramplates of various designs began to be used with unflanged wheels, but this was proved less efficient, because the grooved track tended to collect grit or dirt. This removed the basic advantage of the railway, which is to provide a smooth surface for the wheels to run on.

This chapter will begin by looking at other forms of transport before the main line railway, at roads, rivers, and canals. Of course none of these were entirely replaced by railways, but the ability of locomotive-hauled railway trains, to achieve much greater speeds and provide a smoother ride than horse-powered transport elsewhere, provided them with a technological advantage, which lasted for most of the nineteenth century; until this was in its turn eroded by twentieth-century vehicles powered by internal combustion engines and using pneumatic rubber tyres on tarmac roads.

## Some principles

BEFORE turning to the detail of railways or even transport infrastructure generally, it is useful to look at some general economic principles underlying the choice of transport. The first issue is the value to weight ratio of the goods carried. Valuable light-weight (or rather low density) goods could profitably be carried great distances by road, even from remote parts of England and Wales to London. Conversely dense cheap goods (such as coal and grain) can only be carried significant distances by road if the merchant can, in practice, add transport costs to his prime cost and still achieve a profit at the destination. A possible exception to this was perishables, such as fish, where speed was essential. For grain this meant that the destination had to be where there was a shortage of locally produced products; otherwise transport costs would eat up the gross profit. Coal could profitably be carried by land, away from the coalfield, into country where there was no coal to mine, but only for a certain distance. Eventually competition from locally-grown firewood would make coal an unprofitable commodity. On the other hand, wood might also be in great demand locally, for example if there was a local charcoal-fuelled ironworks.

This principle applied mainly to road transport. Transport on navigable rivers was much cheaper. In the late seventeenth century, carrying a ton of iron by road cost about eight (old) pence (3.33p) per mile. For example, in 1668, Philip Foley's accounts show 15 tons of iron from Brewood (Staffs) to [Wolver]Hampton for £3.15.0 – probably 7½ miles. On the other hand, in 1669, the freight for pig iron from Broad Oak, near Newnham on Severn (below Gloucester) to Bewdley was only five shillings (25p) a ton, an amount that would have allowed it to be moved by land a mere 7½ miles. With pig iron worth £5 or £6 per ton, transport costs were a significant, but not an overwhelming, consideration. With coal worth a few shillings a ton at the pithead, transport costs were much more important: coal was sold in many towns in south and east England at 24–33 shillings per London chaldron of 28cwt (17–23 shillings per ton). Where river and coastal transport was available, coal could be sold profitably in towns and cities many miles from the pithead. This meant that the coal had a good market. Newcastle coal went down the Tyne in keels and was then loaded on to coasting colliers that shipped it to London and other ports on the east and south coasts of England. Coal from Neath was sent to Devon, Cornwall, and Ireland. Ireland was also Whitehaven's major market. Coal from near Nottingham was presumably sold along the river Trent. Severn trows took coal from Broseley in Shropshire to Shrewsbury, Bridgnorth,

Bewdley, Worcester, Tewkesbury and Gloucester, also up the Warwickshire Avon to Pershore, Evesham and Stratford. Before William Sandys improved the river up to Stratford in the 1630s, the fertile Avon valley suffered from a shortage of fuel.

The ability of these riverine coalfields to market coal at considerable distances meant that coalowners had a ready market for what they mined, though of course not an unlimited one. This is in marked contrast with landlocked coalfields where – with their more limited market – coal was probably cheaper. Certainly landlocked coalfields attracted industries that required coal in a way that riverine coalfields do not seem to have. Near Stoke-on-Trent, this was pottery. At Sheffield it was cutlery, with a nailmaking area just to the north and a scythemaking one just to the south. The Black Country (west of Birmingham) manufactured iron, brought up (or down) the Severn or by land from Derbyshire or Staffordshire, into nails, locks, hinges, and a wide variety of other iron goods. Birmingham had a reputation for being a source of metalwork but, by the mid-eighteenth century, it was concentrating on more sophisticated products where the use of coal was a less significant factor. It used the stamp, the press, the lathe, and the drawbench to make buckles, buttons, watch-chains and other goods collectively known as 'toys', but other iron goods were still made in the Black Country to the west.

At Birmingham, the move away from coal may have been an eighteenth-century development, but the industries of the landlocked coalfields can commonly be traced back into the sixteenth century. The pattern continued and has to some extent persisted until recent times. The area around Stoke is still known as the Potteries, though that industry is in severe decline; the Black Country still for metal-bashing; and Sheffield for steel and cutlery. All of these industries first developed when their coalfields were still landlocked. The contrast became less stark in the in the eighteenth century, when Ambrose (later Sir Ambrose) Crowley began his 'factories' making iron goods at Winlaton and Swallwell near Newcastle (using local coal to manufacture goods from imported Swedish and Russian iron); and Abraham Darby settled at Coalbrookdale to make cast-iron pots with coke-smelted iron.

Another issue concerns friction; perhaps that is not quite the right term: it is about the smoothness of ride. On a potholed road, the horse has continually to pull the cart or carriage up a slope out of the holes. On a smooth road this is less of a problem, but the size of the load may still be limited by the horse's ability to pull it up hills. On a railway, the rails provide a smooth surface, and the use of embankments and cuttings can ease the gradient. A barge floating on a canal or river has an even smoother ride, but canals have difficulty going up hills and are therefore impracticable in hilly country.

As long as traffic is limited to walking speed, canals were probably a more efficient form of transport than railways, followed in turn by roads. Rivers cannot usually be quite as good as still-water canals, as barges must be hauled against the current when going upstream. This can be measured by the load that a horse could draw. A pack horse could carry 240lb (slightly over 2cwt). A pair of horses could draw a wain loaded with a ton of goods. A road waggon was limited by an Act of 1662 to 1½ tons in summer and a ton in winter, drawn by five horses (increased to six in 1696). Newcastle waggons running on rails carried a Newcastle chaldron of coal, a measure that grew from 15 bolls (33cwt) in 1660s to 24 bolls (53cwt) in 1797. These had a single horse, but were as far as possible built with a steady descent so that the horse was mainly employed to take the empty waggon back to the pit. A canal barge on the Droitwich Canal took 30 tons of salt; and a Trent and Mersey narrow boat with one horse 20–30 tons of goods.

The main-line railways were of course locomotive-hauled. They had an advantage of speed that was not available to previous generations. Increases of speed were not really feasible on waterways, because the wash behind the boat is liable to erode the banks, meaning that even in these days when canal barges have engines, they are still generally limited to walking speed. Furthermore, their ability to go uphill, even if the gradients could only be gentle, enabled railways to develop a much more widespread network than the canals were ever able to.

## Roads

ROAD transport is very ancient. An important feature of Roman rule was the construction of a road network. Parts of this remained in use into medieval times (and today) but usually only where they led in a direction that later people still wanted to go. If a medieval town was away from a Roman road, travellers would naturally head off the old road, forming a new route going more directly to the town. Later accounts sometimes portray medieval roads as dreadful, but people apparently managed to get about on them without great difficulty. Mechanisms existed for repairing bridges. Occasionally tolls were imposed to repair specific lengths of medieval road, but not often. From 1555, each parish was required to work four (soon increased to six) days each year on repairing the roads of the parish, probably codifying an ancient obligation.

A Commonwealth Ordinance (continued by statute in 1662) provided for the levying of a highway rate, but this was onerous for a small parish with a major road through it. In 1663 temporary tolls were imposed on the Great North Road in Hertfordshire, Cambridgeshire and Huntingdonshire, to enable a capital sum to be raised to improve the road used by traffic bringing

**A Tyneside coal waggon on a gravity run down to a staith in 1773, with the driver sitting on the brake. A staith for loading coal on to a keel is in the background.**

goods to Ware at the head of the navigable river Lea. In the 1690s, unusual measures (involving tolls) were found necessary to keep certain main roads in repair, such as the road from Reigate to Crawley and two ascents of the Cotswolds from Gloucester.

The system was gradually extended as more and more roads became turnpikes. Much of the road from Bristol to Birmingham was turnpiked in the mid-1720s; most of that from London to Oxford by 1720, and thence to Birmingham mostly by 1730; Watling Street (as far as Dunchurch) by 1723, but improvement of its continuation to Chester (not along Watling Street) was only authorised in 1741. Most turnpikes were the result of local initiatives, by which Parliament was asked to authorise improvement of specific roads, initially the great arterial roads, sometimes those radiating from a particular city or town, otherwise just one or more local roads needing improvement.

The great age of turnpike creation began in about 1740, when enterprise was no longer devoted only to major arterial roads, but to a great many locally significant roads. Almost all the roads of the modern A- and B-class network (other than modern bypasses) were once turnpikes.

A pack horse can go virtually anywhere, but it can only carry a small load. A wain or cart can carry more, and wheeled vehicles gradually replaced pack horses as roads were improved. Scheduled carriers' services operated from inns in the outskirts of London to towns and cities all over England by the eighteenth century. Services for passengers operated in the same way, using stage coaches. The Post Office had its own mail coaches (which did not have to pay tolls on turnpikes). However road traffic was limited to the speed of horses. Attempts were made in the early nineteenth century to uses locomotives on highways but these were abandoned apparently because the engines proved unreliable, perhaps partly because the going was not smooth enough.

## Navigable rivers and canals

ANOTHER form of early transport infrastructure was the navigable river. Use of rivers must go as far back as men had boats, but the Romans certainly used rivers. Most of their legionary fortresses were on navigable rivers: York on the Ouse, and Wroxeter beside the Severn. Caerleon and Chester are also ports, and the tiles made at Holt presumably reached the legionary fortress at Chester down the river Dee. Certain of their land drainage cuts seem to have been navigable.

The great rivers of the realm were placed under the king's peace by the laws of Edward the Confessor, with the lesser rivers under the peace of the county. A series of medieval statutes authorised the king to issue commissions to remove obstructions to navigation culminating in the Statute of Sewers 1531, which brought together the two themes of navigation and land drainage. However, the judges decided in the 1610s that there was no power to force creation of a new navigation. This required statutory intervention, as grants by order of the Privy Council (such as to William Sandys for the Warwickshire Avon) were a dubious foundation. The problem was ultimately a constitutional one, as to whether the crown could, for the public good, deprive a subject of his freehold property, even with compensation.

A variety of navigation schemes were promoted in the seventeenth century with varying degrees of success. The pattern developed of an undertaker improving the river. A body of commissioners was also appointed to fix the compensation payable to landowners for land taken. Schemes varied between being a resounding success and a complete failure, the latter sometimes because the works were inadequately constructed or proved much more expensive than initially estimated. The river Wey in Surrey ran into financial difficulties partly because there were two competing groups of owners, one acting under legislation declared void at the Restoration and the other under post-Restoration Letters Patent of questionable validity.

The Warwickshire Avon's navigability was confirmed by a clause in the Act for the rivers Stour and Salwarpe, but needed substantial expenditure to restore navigation above Evesham. Sandys undertook works on the river Wye, but the tolls were inadequate to cover maintenance, so that Windsor Sandys failed to pay his rent and by 1675 his rights reverted to the county. Further legislation was needed to authorise further works in 1695.

The Dee below Chester and the Don above Doncaster were improved by local interests in the early eighteenth century but, with so many people involved, incorporation became necessary. On the other hand, the Kennet and the Upper Avon Navigations remained as unincorporated syndicates, who shared the revenue generated. The naturally navigable Severn had no locks, but fishweirs had periodically to be regulated (most recently in 1575). The Thames had many mills which had to live with the pre-existing navigation rights. They generally had a flash lock next to the mill – a weir that could be dismantled to allow the passage of a vessel but with a severe effect on the power available to the mill.

When the Burcot Commission improved the section of the river below Oxford in the 1620s, they seem to have introduced pound locks (with two pairs of gates). William Sandys adopted pound locks on the Avon in the 1630s so that, by building a lock next to each mill, vessels could pass the mills with only a minimal loss of the water available to power the mill. This became the norm and was applied on the Worcestershire Stour, the Welland, and all subsequent navigations.

In a sense the first true canal navigation was the Sankey Navigation (up to St Helens), approved in 1757, which was formally to make the Sankey Brook navigable, but was more of a canal. The Duke of Bridgewater's scheme for taking coal from his mines at Worsley to Manchester became the first true canal in Britain, and was subsequently extended to Runcorn and then further into Cheshire.

This was followed by further still-water navigations, authorised in the 1760s for creating links between river systems across the watersheds of England – the Trent and Mersey Canal; and the Staffordshire and Worcestershire Canal (which linked it with the river Severn); then a series of canals linking these with the Thames at Oxford (completed in 1790). These differed from river navigations in being artificial and having no (or usually very little) current. However they were wholly different in concept, in that they connected the country internally across the watersheds. Rivers ran towards the sea, whereas canals could take traffic out of one catchment into the next. They united England commercially in a way that nothing except roads had done before.

There was a boom in approvals in early 1790s including canals across the Pennines, and the Kennet & Avon Canal, linking London and Bristol by inland navigation. However some of these took a long time to complete and a few never were. One of the more ambitious schemes was the Grand

Junction Canal, whose objective was to take a canal from Braunston on the Oxford Canal right into London. This was authorised in 1793, and partly opened in 1797, a branch being added to Paddington in 1801 and its extension, the Regent's Canal to the docks at Limehouse, authorised in 1812 and opened in 1820. Many of these canals were promoted as useful for the transport of agricultural products and no doubt they were useful for that, but their staple commodity was almost invariably coal. When the Birmingham Canal Navigation was opened from Wednesbury the price of coal (hitherto brought by road) dropped from 15–18 shillings per ton to four shillings in May 1770, though that low price did not hold. The main traffic on the Leominster canal was coal from the southern part of Wyre Forest Coalfield (around Mamble), but the capital to build the great tunnel needed to connect it with the Severn was never forthcoming, and the canal remained unconnected with the national network throughout its life.

## Early railways

As stated, the earliest railways had wooden edge-rails. In the late eighteenth century the rails were of cast iron often with a groove for the wheel to run in, so that the flange was on the rail, rather than the wheel. However the earliest main-line railways reverted to edge rails, but made of wrought iron and later steel. Nevertheless the earliest railway-like transport system, with the exception of a few ancient curiosities, was the *Leitnagel Hund*. This did not depend on the use of a flange at all, instead planks were laid along the mine passage with a gap between them, and the truck – *hund* (German for dog or hound) or *truhe* (box or chest) – had a guide pin that pointed down between the planks to keep the truck going in the right direction. The word *hund* could be derived from the Magyar *hintó*, meaning a carriage. If so, this points to an origin in the mines of Hungary, which at the time included Slovakia and Transylvania. The system was widely used in central Europe in the early sixteenth century, and may go back to the fifteenth or even the fourteenth century.

The system was introduced to England by German miners working for the Company of Mines Royal, who opened mines in Cumbria. The capital came partly from an Augsburg merchant house; the manager Daniel Hockstetter came from there; and miners were recruited in southern Germany and Bohemia. Documentary evidence indicates they used 'small rowle wagons bound with iron' in copper mines at Caldbeck, Newlands, and Grasmere. The first of these is near the significantly named Silver Gill at Caldbeck, where investigation has yielded the remains of some plank rails and possible sleepers. The system may also have been used at the company's silver-lead mines at Talybont near Aberystwyth.

**'Coal wagon way', a self-acting inclined plane railway, drawn in 1754 by R.R. Angerstein near Coalbrookdale. The arrangements at the bottom seem improbable: it is more likely that the wagon was unhooked from the chain and taken along a quay, but perhaps Angerstein failed to observe that.**

From T. and P. Berg (eds), *R.R. Angerstein's illustrated travel diary, 1753–1755*, 2001

## *The first edge railways*

THE *Leitnagel Hund* had some of the characteristics of a railway, but differs from them in that neither wheels nor the rails were flanged. The first true railways were English. Their function was to carry coal from the pit (or adit) down to a navigable river (or less often to a highway) to be transported to a distant place. Several candidates have been put forward as being the first. However, all the earliest documented examples have a definite start date, with the exception of one servicing the mines of James Clifford near Broseley in Shropshire, which has no clear date of construction. As Clifford was mining coal by 1575, the funicular railway, by which coal was let down from mines to trows (barges) operating on the river Severn, is likely to have preceded the others. Nevertheless, William Brooke was working his coal mines in Madeley, on the other side of the Ironbridge Gorge, where similar problems would have arisen, but that is only known because Arnold Bean of Worcester owed Brooke money when he died in 1579.

Most of what we know of Clifford and his local rivals comes from Star Chamber litigation in the 1600s by Clifford against Wilcox (the lessee of

Clifford's demesne lands at Broseley) with Wilcox's son-in-law William Wells. They constructed a rival railway, in order to mine on land owned by James Lacon of Willey, who otherwise had no access to the river Severn and thus to the market offered by towns along its banks. Clifford's railway may have been of the kind drawn by R.R. Angerstein when he visited the Coalbrookdale area in 1753, a rope-hauled system where a laden truck pulled an empty one back up the hill *(see figure, p.21)*. Such a railway had to divide where the trucks would pass. Some of the conflict related to Clifford's men not allowing Wilcox's and Wells' men to use Clifford's wharf. Wells and his men retaliated by removing something described as 'tilting rails' – perhaps the points for the passing place – to prevent Clifford using his, thus preventing him working the mines. This was clearly a bitter dispute, only ended by the deaths of Clifford and Wilcox, for Wilcox's lease died with him. Wilcox's and Wells' railway was ox-hauled. There were a number of mines along the side of the gorge in the succeeding period and each apparently had an associated railway. Some mines were pits, but some were 'insets' – mines operated through an adit, and in these cases the railway extended underground to the coalface.

The railway, which was until recently regarded as the first, ran between Strelley and Wollaton Lane End bringing coal down from the Strelley pits to the main road. The initiative was that of Huntingdon Beaumont who worked pits just west of Nottingham leased from Sir Percival Willoughby and Sir Philip Strelley. Willoughby in 1604 granted the right to drain the Strelley coals through Wollaton and also to carry coals 'along a passage maid with railes', probably ending at Wollaton Lane End, whence coal was taken in wains to Nottingham and to the river Trent for shipment downstream. Beaumont was a scion of the owners of the significantly named Coleorton, where the family had long worked their coal. Archaeological evidence indicates this to have been a particularly early example of a mine worked by the pillar and stall method – rather than from bell pits – as early as the mid-fifteenth century. Beaumont also leased mines at Bedlington in Northumberland from the Bishop of Durham in 1605 and, by the time his lease was renewed in 1608, he was certainly using rails to bring coals down to the shore. None of Beaumont's enterprises seems to have made a profit and he died in debt in 1624, but it was alleged in 1636 that Edward Delavale had removed the rails, probably to serve his own mines.

## Newcastle

ULTIMATELY the area where waggonways were most prevalent was around Newcastle. It is not clear how quickly waggonways were established there. Previously, transport was by wains, with four wheels drawn by two horses, which could carry about a ton. By the Restoration, waggons were carrying 15 bolls (about 33cwt); from 1700 19–20 bolls (42–44cwt) and from the 1750s, 24 bolls (53cwt). At Gateshead, Old Trunk Quay was at the end of the Old Wain Trunk Way, operating in the 1620s. In 1633 Thomas Liddell as owner of Ravensworth colliery still had a wainway leading to a staith at Dunston. The copyholders of Whickham complained to the Durham Chancery Court that they had authorised a way 7yds wide, but that the heavily rutted wainway had spread to 24yds wide (which the court reduced to 16yds). Their opponents, the Grand Lessees, who had a lease of mines on the bishopric estates, seem to have made the earliest waggonway to the Tyne as a response to the court order. Certainly, by 1622, stables for 'waggon horses' existed.

Three other waggonways were built before the Civil War. One at Benwell, north of the Tyne, probably dates from the end of the 1620s and remained in use into the early nineteenth century. The Winlaton Way could be almost as old. By the latter part of the seventeenth century three different waggonways were made, all reaching the Tyne at Stella, of which the Stella Grand Lease Way predates the Civil War. This represents a trend to the exploitation of collieries in the west of the coalfield. Stella was about the highest point to which the Tyne was easily navigable. One of the three, the Chopwell Way, became (in the late 1680s) the earliest to carry non-colliery related goods – lead and lead ore from the north Pennine leadfield. The Ravensworth family had a waggonway down to Team Staith by 1669. A little further east, others ran from Gateshead Fell and Fawd collieries down to the Tyne, the latter perhaps existing by 1656. Those running to the north side of the Tyne were generally a little later. One of the earlier ones was made by George Liddell and William Cotesworth from their Heaton colliery, but they had to petition the crown about this in 1724 because Newcastle Corporation refused them a wayleave, to prevent Alderman Richard Ridley's Byker colliery suffering competition.

As in Shropshire in about 1605, the provision of wayleaves was a matter of great contention. A landowner could hold his neighbour to ransom for the right to pass over his land. This provided a coalowner with a choice between paying a rent – often a substantial royalty – for a way or finding a route around the obstruction, over the land of some more amenable neighbour. Competition was perhaps most intense for routes through Whickham (west of Gateshead), where several rival routes were established by rival coalowners. This is related to the operations of a series of monopolistic cartels which began with a cartel of some of the largest producers called the Coal Office, a marketing partnership that sought to exclude non-members from the coal trade. Their efforts were resisted by Jane Lady Clavering who in 1712 built the first Western Way, whose route was not wholly satisfactory due to an uphill pull. When rivals succeeded in obstructing this, she obtained a more satisfactory route in partnership with Elizabeth Lady Bowes in 1721.

The Coal Office dissolved but Cotesworth and Liddell entered into an alliance with the Montagus (relative newcomers to the area) who built the Tanfield Way in 1724 (replacing the Dunston Way of 1692). They then persuaded George Bowes (recently of age) to join them as the Grand Allies: the parties would jointly exploit their extensive coal reserves and jointly use the waggonways. This again obstructed the Western Way but the Clavering group responded with a third Western Way down the left bank of the river Derwent. This led to a long period of stability in the exploitation of coal reserves south of the Tyne. These were some of the longest waggonways exploiting coal a significant distance from the river. Branches were made leading to new collieries as they were opened, for example over the Causey Arch. The period 1735–65 was one of great prosperity for the duopoly of these two waggonways. George Bowes died in 1760 worth £600,000; and Edward Wortley Montague in 1775 worth £750,000. In the next generation, heiresses fell prey to noble fortune-hunters, some of whom increased the vend thus damaging profits.

Collieries further east were also worked, but there the coal was much deeper. This meant that significant expenditure was needed on pumping out drowned mines, sometimes by means of a water-powered 'coal mill', but more usually after 1717 using a steam engine. Collieries were also worked even further south using waggonways leading to the river Wear but, with a couple of exceptions, they were all built well into the eighteenth century. This was the result of Sunderland being improved as a port, particularly after the Harbour Board (established in 1717) employed Joseph Robson to cut a channel through the rocky bar there in 1759. Rope- or chain-controlled inclined planes, which had long been used in Shropshire, did not appear on Tyneside until the 1780s. In the same period, an improved brake allowed a man to take two waggons down together. Iron rails were introduced to the area about the same time but, with a few exceptions, all waggonways remained edge railways. In 1819, when locomotive haulage was being considered for the Western Way, two-thirds of its rails were still wooden, as were one third for the Tanfield Way in 1828.

## *Elsewhere*

WAGGONWAYS were built in other places in the north of England but in much smaller numbers. Most of those in the north of England derived from Newcastle waggonways. Sir John Lowther of Whitehaven had a 'coalway', a sort of guided cartway running on balks of wood, from 1683 but his son Sir James had waggonways, made in the 1730s, from his Saltom Colliery in 1735 and from Howgill colliery in 1738. Coal was then loaded directly on to ships at Whitehaven, using particularly large staiths, to supply coal to Ireland. One from Sheffield Park to Sheffield was unusual in that the destination was a town rather than navigable water. Other waggonways were made to take coal down to the navigable Aire, Calder, and Dun, after these were respectively made navigable; and to serve collieries in the north of Ireland.

Shropshire railways (or railroads) form a separate tradition from Newcastle waggonways. The waggons were smaller because the mines were often insets (rather than pits). The railway often started at the coalface and a smaller waggon meant that only a narrow adit had to be made through dead ground. The descent to the river down the side of the Severn gorge was precipitous, and the descent was controlled using a self-acting inclined plane, something not used near Newcastle until the late eighteenth century, but probably in Shropshire for its first railway. Wilcox's & Wells' railway to Calcutts may have been down Birch Batch. Its terminus was later called Jackfield Rails, and it remained in use well into the nineteenth century.

A longer railway, ultimately from John Wilkinson's New Willey Furnace of 1757, went down Tarbatch Dingle to Willey Wharf but was probably built in the 1700s to serve coalmines and remained in use in parts for some 300 years, though from 1862 it led to the Severn Valley Railway, rather than a river wharf. North of the Severn, the lords of Madeley had railways at Madeley Wood when they let their mines in 1692. The establishment of new coke-fired furnaces in the 1750s and the associated expansion of mining led to the provision of further railways, the longest running from Ketley (near Watling Street) to Coalbrookdale Wharf on the Severn, so that by about 1775 Abiah Darby (the widow of Abraham II) stated that the Coalbrookdale Company had 20 miles of railways.

Other railways ran to landsale wharfs on Watling Street. In all, five gauges of railway were in use in the area, with those wholly above ground probably of a similar size to those at Newcastle.

The railways of this tradition were fewer in number and often shorter than at Newcastle. The 'footrail' at Amblecote, built by Andrew Yarranton and others in the 1660s to take coal down to the Stour navigation, has the distinction of being the first to be authorised by statute *(see plate 1)*. Other river navigation Acts enacted just after the Restoration have a similar clause, though not necessarily implemented. Railways near Neath (from 1697), in Flintshire (1740s), south Lancashire (1750s), and Scotland (1780s) seem to have been derived from the Shropshire system.

A system of inclined planes was later used to carry boats between different levels of canals. The Ketley incline had a rise of 73ft, where tub boats were carried in cradles on two sets of tracks. As most of the traffic was downhill, this plane was self-acting. The Windmill and Hay inclined planes on the Shropshire Canal raised vessels by a further 126ft and lowered them by 207ft respectively. This is no doubt why the tub boats used on the Shropshire canal system were smaller than the normal narrow boats, carrying a mere 5–6 tons – as much as the planes could manage. The Shrewsbury Canal also had an incline (at Trench) and slightly narrower locks than usual, which is why presumably these canals have not been revived in the past half century.

## Changing railway technology

THE early railways had wooden rails, fixed to sleepers with a wooden pin. The space between and around was filled with ballast. Outside the rails, ballast was laid nearly to the top of the rail to form a path for the waggon-men to follow. At Newcastle, this was probably sand ballast carried from colliers for their empty voyage back to Newcastle. The sleepers were 4–8in. square and somewhat longer than the gauge of the way. The rails were 4–5in. wide and high, perhaps with the width usually slightly exceeding the height. The rails might be 6ft long, pegged to the sleepers every 18in. with treenails of young oak 6–7in. long. The joints were above a sleeper, with adjoining rails merely butting up to each other. If a rail became damaged it could be turned over, as was done when Wilcox's and Wells' rails were hacked during the trouble between Clifford and them in Shropshire in 1605.

At Newcastle, the practice developed from the 1750s of having a 'double way', with a second rail fixed to the top of the first. This allowed more ballast to be laid above the sleepers, thus protecting them from being worn out by the horses' hoofs. This had the advantage that the joins between the rails did not have to be above a sleeper. In the older single way, the rail had to be replaced as soon as it began to wear significantly, perhaps once a year, but with the lower second rail below it, the upper rail did not have to be replaced until it had nearly worn through, so that the upper rails might last four years and the whole waggonway as much as ten years. The lower rail could be of fir.

### *Iron wheels*

THE claim that iron rails were used at Whitehaven as early as 1738 seems to be mistaken. It results either from one author inaccurately copying another or it is mistakenly derived from a reference to iron wheels, which were adopted there about that time. However the claim that it was an early user of iron wheels is correct. Iron wheels were first made at Coalbrookdale in 1729, when eighteen were supplied to the leading coalmaster Richard Hartshorne but, a coalowner at nearby Little Wenlock, J.U. Smitheman bought over 200 from 1732 to 1738.

At Whitehaven, Sir John Lowther had trouble with wheels made by John

Williams of Little Clifton Furnace for his Saltom waggonway in 1735, and showed a drawing in January 1736 to Mr Harrison of London – that is William Harrison, the Wealden gunfounder. However, the order for forty of them was placed with William Rawlinson of Backbarrow Ironworks in Furness, where they were no doubt cast by Isaac Wilkinson, the Backbarrow Company's ironfounder from 1735. Nevertheless Little Clifton was well-placed, with its association with a foundry on Old Trunk Quay at Gateshead, to exploit the largest potential market which was of course around Newcastle. It is not clear how far another alternative was used, such as a wooden wheel with iron spokes and an iron rim, patented by Elias Thornhill of Sunderland in 1731.

Iron wheels were also used on Ralph Allen's railway of 1731 for bringing Bathstone from Bathampton Down to Bath, 500ft below. Trucks were hauled by two horses on the level, but the steepest descent involved a drum, probably for a self-acting inclined plane. This is an early example of another use for early railways – the transport of stone, in this case in blocks of 5–6 tons. Other stone-carrying railways were often for limestone, which was needed for mortar, for fluxing for blast furnaces (or other metallurgical processes), or to sweeten acid lands. These were often feeders to canals, rather than navigable rivers. Indeed branch canals were occasionally built where a main purpose was to serve a quarry. This applies to the Caldon Canal with a railway from a quarry (1777), the Peak Forest canal and railway near Manchester (1796), and the railways from Ticknall and Cloud Hill feeding the Ashby-de-la-Zouche canal (1802).

## *Cast iron rails*

ANOTHER means of extending the life of the rails was to use iron plates. There are references to iron in relation to Newcastle waggonways as far back as 1692, but it is not clear how prevalent the practice was before the 1760s. In 1765, Gabriel Jars observed strips of iron at the joints between rails, evidently to reduce wear there, and a man was prosecuted in 1766 for stealing 60lb of iron. Often this may have been limited to curves and gradients, where the wear would be worst. In Shropshire, the partners in Horsehay Furnace shod their rails with the cheaper cast iron in 1767, but the practice was probably hardly adopted on Tyneside. This system was probably adopted for a railway at Landore, supplying Lockwood Morris & Co's copper works in 1776. Unfortunately the nature of the rails is not clear. Morris referred to 'cast-iron tram plates': in south Wales the term tram (or dram) road normally applied to a system with L-shaped flanged rails of cast iron, but the rail weight given seems too little for that. Other railways where iron plates were added included Alloa in Scotland (early 1780s); Neath (before 1791); Ravenhead colliery, Lancs (before Neath); and Mancot, near Hawarden, Flints (1793).

The next major development was rails made entirely out of cast iron. Here again, Newcastle was not the leader. Two systems were introduced. One continued to have flanged wheels and edge-rails, but now of wholly of cast iron. The other, with L-shaped rails, was introduced probably in 1787 by John Curr, the superintendent of the Duke of Norfolk's colliery at Sheffield Park, who published an account of them in 1797 with a system of hauling two wheeled corves at a time up the mineshaft. This had the advantage that the waggons could be taken on to an ordinary road, but the disadvantage that the rails tended to collect stones and dirt, causing friction. Plateways were made elsewhere. For example, the Derby Canal was fed by the Little Eaton Gangway (1796) from Smith Houses where several private tramroads from mines and other works led to it.

The greatest concentration of these cast-iron railways was among the ironworks in southeast Wales. Most were closely related to the operations of the coke ironworks, built along the rim of the coalfield. These brought limestone (for flux) down from quarries further north and coal and ironstone from the mines to the works and then took the iron down to a canal wharf. The blossoming of railways followed the provision of a series of canals all built in the early 1790s. The Canal Acts authorised the companies to build railways. If someone asked for a railway to be provided but the company declined, the applicant could rely on the company's powers to build one himself. The result was that the railways actually built were not precisely those shown on the initial canal maps.

Plymouth ironworks at Merthyr Tydfil was casting rails, perhaps for underground use by 1787. However, the first railways with edge-rails entirely of cast iron (if not Morris' at Landore) were probably ones linking Dowlais and Penydarren ironworks with the Glamorganshire Canal (opened 1792). Another candidate is Blaenavon, where a railway from Tyda quarry seems to have been abandoned before the Monmouthshire Canal opened in 1796. Because Richard Crawshay of the Cyfarthfa ironworks controlled the upper reaches of the Glamorganshire Canal, the three other Merthyr ironworks built a tramroad, opened by 1803, down the other side of the river Taff to a canal wharf at Abercynon. Further east, the Monmouthshire Canal Company (opened 1796) built feeder railways, leading to the canal. However, the western valleys (with no canal) were served by the Sirhowy Tramroad (opened 1805). This was partly built by the canal company and partly by a separate company incorporated for the purpose.

Though the initial railway to Dowlais probably had edge-rails, most subsequent railways in south Wales had L-shaped tramplates. There was a considerable variety of track design. Curr's original system had the tramplate morticed into a wooden sleeper. However, where stone was readily available, the iron rails were often mounted on stone blocks. During the 1790s, a chair was introduced so that the rail was fixed in the chair and the chair to the block or sleeper, instead of the rail having a projecting ear to be fixed down. Nevertheless, the use of stone blocks, particularly with edge-rails, had the difficulty that the gauge tended to spread with use. This could be counteracted by providing a tie bar, holding the rails together. Being supported at each end and possibly on a saddle at a point between, the rails were weak on the span between successive blocks or sleepers. This was counteracted by making the rail 'fish-bellied' – with a flange underneath to brace it.

## *Wrought iron rails*

EDGED rails also continued to develop. The Walker railway, east of Newcastle, seems to have had chairs and fish-bellied rails from 1798. The ultimate development of cast-iron rails was a design with a fish belly, patented in 1816 by George Stephenson and William Losh of the Walker ironworks. However these were in turn overtaken by wrought-iron rails. These were used at Tindale Fell near Brampton and at Walbottle in about 1808. Then John Birkenshaw, of Bedlington Ironworks near Morpeth, in 1822 patented a rolled-iron rail with a fish belly, produced using eccentric rolls, initially for a waggonway from Bedlington Glebe Colliery.

Cast iron is strong under compression but weak in extension, making it a less than ideal material for rails, but wrought iron is also strong in extension, and thus an inherently more satisfactory material. Birkenshaw and his master Michael Longridge successfully argued in favour of these rails to a committee of the Stockton & Darlington Railway, citing that the original cost for their rails would be less. This is presumably because less material was needed for the same strength with the inherently stronger material, as wrought iron was more expensive than cast. Stephenson supported the Bedlington proposal against the interests of his co-patentee Losh. The committee decided to use one-third cast and two-thirds wrought iron, but ultimately used 80% wrought. Other early producers of rolled rails included the Penydarren Works at Merthyr Tydfil and John Bradley & Co. of Stourbridge.

The 1805 Sirhowy Tramroad belongs to a new breed of increasingly long free-standing public railways. The first was the Surrey Iron Railway (1804) with its extension to Merstham (1805). The Oystermouth Railway of 1804 has the distinction of being the first to carry regular passenger traffic. In similar vein, the Gloucester & Cheltenham Railway (1811) connected the latter town to the Severn. However two railways leading from the Brecknock and Abergavenny Canal, itself an extension of the Monmouthshire Canal, were

particularly long. The Llanvihangel Railway (1814) left the canal near Abergavenny. This was extended by the Grosmont Railway (1818) and then by
the Hereford Railway (1829) to the Wye Bridge at Hereford, making a
total length of over 24 miles. The Hay Railway (1816/8) left the head of the
canal at Watton Wharf by Brecon and ran 24 miles to Hay-on-Wye and
Eardisley, whence another company extended it a further 14 miles to Kington
(1820) and ultimately to a quarry at Burlingjobb. The last two enabled
Welsh coal to reach relatively remote rural areas. They probably show the
inefficiency of navigation on the river Wye which had earlier enabled coal to
reach Hereford and Hay. All these railways also carried general goods. The
existence of the Kington Railway evidently enabled John Meredith of Kington
to expand his ironmonger's business. Raw materials brought by the railway
allowed him to introduce nailmaking to the area, and he built a foundry and
water-powered smithy.

Nevertheless, these railways represent a dead end, as they did not generally
become part of the national railway network. This also applies to the Stratford
& Moreton Tramway (1821), which used malleable fish-bellied rails. This was
a pioneer attempt to surmount the watershed between the Severn and Thames
catchments, but this remained a dream, as it was soon overtaken by much
more ambitious main-line schemes. Its envisioned extension southwards from
Moreton towards Oxford or London did not materialise, until the line was
leased by the new Oxford, Worcester & Wolverhampton Railway in 1847.
They rebuilt part for their line.

## Steam traction

A major factor in the development of the main-line railway was the adoption of
locomotive traction. The principle of the steam engine was invented in the
late seventeenth century. It remained a mere scientific curiosity until it was
developed into a commercially useful machine by Thomas Newcomen in,
or shortly before, 1712. Both this and the next major improvement, that of
James Watt – implemented in the 1770s, depended on the creation of a partial
vacuum by condensing steam. Watt made further improvements in the 1780s,
including the double-acting engine, in which work was obtained from both the
strokes of the engine, by also using the space above the piston. These stationery
engines were far too heavy to be locomotives. A breakthrough came when the
Cornish mining engineer Richard Trevithick powered an engine with what he
called 'strong steam' (pressurised steam). After a trial on a Cornish road,
he demonstrated the use of a locomotive on the Merthyr Tramroad, where it
hauled a train of loaded waggons from Penydarren at Merthyr Tydfil down to
the canal wharf at Abercynon. However, the engine was too heavy for the

cast-iron track and broke the rails, so that the locomotive was subsequently used as a stationery engine. Trevithick also demonstrated the use of the locomotive to the curious public on land off Euston Road in London, but he failed to develop his invention commercially.

The initiative returned to the north. Fears, over whether adhesion would be sufficient between iron locomotive wheels and iron rails, led John Blenkinsop to devise a sort of rack and pinion track for the engine built by Fenton Murray & Co. of Leeds for the nearby Middleton Railway (1812). This system was also used at Orrell in Lancashire, for the Kenton & Coxlodge Waggonway near Newcastle, and in a few other places. This was a technological dead-end, because the colliery railways at Heddon and Killingworth succeeded in using the locomotives, such as *Wylam Dilly* and *Puffing Billy* with the drive delivered through untoothed flanged wheels on cast-iron edge rails, to haul coal to the north bank of the river Tyne. Railways, such as these, were also the context for the cast-iron edge rails patented by Losh and Stephenson in 1816. Locomotives of several types were built in the north for use in south Wales shortly after their introduction.

# Conclusion

THE Stockton & Darlington Railway, the first main-line railway, was conceived as a typical Newcastle waggonway. The objective was to open up a new part of the coalfield by providing a route from it to the navigable water of the river Tees. However it brought together the best features of railways developed in the two preceding decades: it was established by a company with compulsory purchase powers; it used (though not throughout) Birkenshaw's rolled wrought-iron rails; and haulage was partly by steam locomotives (though horses were also used initially). The company soon found that a demand existed for passenger traffic. On the other hand, it relied on four inclines west of Darlington where it served Witton Park Colliery. It was intended to be a public railway, like a turnpike or canal, on which anyone (paying the toll) could carry his goods. In 1833 horse haulage was abandoned on the main-line route. Traffic control considerations made it necessary for the company to operate the trains itself, buying out the independent coach operators.

This railway provided the pattern for the Liverpool & Manchester Railway, which even more than the Stockton & Darlington was the forerunner of main-line railways. Nevertheless, the rails continued to be mounted on stone blocks, with chairs under the joints of the rails. The standard track design with sleepers and with fishplates joining the rails came later.

The Bridgewater Canal, linking collieries with Manchester and the navigable Mersey at Runcorn and thus with its port of Liverpool, was the forerunner of the canal era; for the Duke's success paved the way for the Trent & Mersey and Staffordshire & Worcestershire Canals, as well as the many that came after. In the same way, the Liverpool & Manchester Railway paved the way for long-distance main-line railways, Liverpool–Birmingham, Birmingham–London and so on. Until then, most railways had connected a source of coal or stone with a river, canal, or port or had provided a route for carrying it to a non-riverine town. In contrast, the new main-line railways connected one great industrial town with another, and faster speeds meant passengers soon became at least as important as goods. In this way, the railway entered a new era, but that subject must be left for the other contributors to this book to discuss.

## Further reading

This account is based on a large number of works, some of whose main content is not directly related to railways or even to transport. This list is accordingly far from comprehensive.

*Early Railways 2–5: Conference papers* (Newcomen Society 2003; and Six Martlets, Sudbury 2006–14)
C. Hadfield, Canals [A series of regional volumes] 1967–70

W. Albert, *The Turnpike Road System in England 1663–1840*, 1972
D.H. Aldcroft & M.J. Freeman (eds), *Transport in the Industrial Revolution*, 1983
C.J. Allen, *The Northeast Railway*, 1964
B. Baxter, *Stone Blocks and Iron Rails*, 1966
G. Bennett, A. Clavering & A. Rounding, *A Fighting Trade: rail transport in Tyne coal 1600–1800*, 1990
M.C. Duffy, 'George Stephenson and the introduction of rolled railway rail', *Journal of Mechanical Working Technology* 5,(3–5), 1981, pp.309–42
F. Fernyhough, *Liverpool and Manchester Railway 1830–1980*, 1980
D. Gerhold, *Carriers and Coachmasters: Travel and Trade before the Turnpikes*, 2005
C. Green, *Severn Traders: the West Country trows and trowmen*, 1999
A. Guy & J. Rees, *Early Railways 1569–1830*, 2011
D. Harrison, *The Bridges of Medieval England: transport and society 400–1800*, 2004
D. Hey, *Packmen, carriers and packhorse roads: trade and communications in north Derbyshire and South Yorkshire*, 2nd edn, 2001
M.W. Kirby, *The origins of railway enterprise: the Stockton and Darlington Railway, 1821–1863*, 1993
M.J.T. Lewis, *Early Wooden Railways*, 1970
R.A. Mott, 'Tramroads of the eighteenth century and their originator: John Curr', *Transactions of the Newcomen Society*, XLII, 1969–70, pp.1–23
E. Pawson, *Transport and Economy: the turnpike roads of the 18th century*, 1977
E. Pawson, *The Early Industrial Revolution*, 1979
F.S. Thacher, *The Thames Highway: I General History*, 1914: reprint 1968
B. Trinder, *Barges & Bargemen: a social history of the Upper Severn Navigation 1660–1900*, 2005
J. van Laun, *Early Limestone Railways: how railways developed to feed the furnaces of the industrial revolution in south east Wales*, 2001
T.S. Willan, *River Navigation in England 1600–1750*, 1936
T.S. Willan, *The Inland Trade: studies in English internal trade in the sixteenth and seventeenth centuries*, 1976

# CHAPTER 2

# The Generation that Changed the World

*Malcolm Reed*

## 'The Victorian Age was undoubtedly the age of the railway.'

S o wrote Michael Freeman, in his introduction to *Transport in Victorian Britain*, and indeed the expression 'the railway age' has sufficient currency to have been employed in the titles of several scholarly studies of this period. Because Britain's example of railway building was almost immediately followed elsewhere in Europe and in North America, the same expression has also found its way into international usage.

However, although the inherited view that railways were an extremely important element in the Victorian economy has survived the revisionism of more recent studies of this phase in economic history, the modern consensus is that railways, in Britain and elsewhere in the western world, were part of a wider process of change, rather than its sole or principal cause.

While precise quantification remains an issue, the railways' influence on the form and rate of economic change was certainly substantial, and mid-Victorian Britain would have been significantly poorer as a nation without this contribution. But the notion that railways, by themselves, were a unique initiator of economic growth in Britain has now been firmly discarded, a conclusion succinctly encapsulated by Patrick O'Brien in his comment in *Railways and the economic development of western Europe 1830–1914* that 'railways could carry forward but not propel rapid industrialisation'.

In Britain, this was true even of the three decades after the opening of the Liverpool & Manchester Railway in 1830, which demonstrated to a wider public the potential of the railway to provide speedy transport for passengers in addition to the established roles in carrying mineral traffic and in feeding canals that had encouraged the initial development of the technology. Over the ensuing 30 years, railways were transformed from a specialised and localised form of transport into a national passenger and freight network. By 1860, that network had grown to 9,000 route miles, and extended continuously from Aberdeen to Penzance (though with the contemporary inconvenience of a break of gauge in reaching the south-western extremities of Britain). This expansion, from just under 100 miles of public railway in 1830, reflected an average rate of annual growth that was never subsequently equalled in either total or percentage terms, and accounted for 45 per cent of the mileage that the Grouped companies inherited in 1923.

But growth in railway mileage, although spectacular, took place against a background of other striking changes in the national statistics. At the first national census in 1801 Great Britain had a total population of 10.5 million: by 1861 it had more than doubled to 23.1 million. The evidence that Britain's population, and therefore the country's economic structure, was already changing rapidly before the railway age began is confirmed by more detailed consideration of the chronology of these demographic shifts. There are no comprehensive official statistics before 1801, but various calculations of the population of England and Wales in the eighteenth century suggest a growth from an estimated 5.1–6.1 million in 1701 to 6.0–6.5 million in 1751, with growth within individual series ranging from around 300,000 to almost a million. All series agree that there was a significant upturn in the second half of the century, leading towards the 8.9 million recorded in the 1801 census for England and Wales, and many modern analysts attribute this increase to improvements in food supply and in medical knowledge which led to lower death rates at ages before and during the years of family formation. Contemporary social changes also assisted, by reducing some of the economic and familial obstacles to earlier marriage.

However, this population growth in the later eighteenth century, while striking enough to attract the attention of Thomas Malthus in his pessimistic 1798 study *An essay on the principle of population,* was small in comparison with that experienced in the new century. By 1901 the population of Great Britain as a whole had reached 37 million; that of England and Wales had increased by more than 3 million in each of the decades after 1871. But the size of these absolute increases reflected the levels that the base population had reached in the late Victorian era: the highest *rate* of inter-censal growth was experienced between 1811 and 1821, a period which included the final defeat of Napoleon at Waterloo in 1815. This second decade of the nineteenth century saw the kingdom's faltering emergence from a protracted, geographically-extended, and costly series of wars, yet the population of England and Wales increased by 18 per cent – an absolute growth in excess of 1.8 million. Proportionately, Scotland was not far behind, growing by almost 16 per cent on a much smaller base. In both countries, decennial growth rates remained below these levels for the rest of century, and in Scotland's case fell below 10 per cent in three of the decades after 1851.

Besides reflecting underlying changes in mortality and fertility, the nineteenth-century census figures also show the geographical impact of an industrial revolution that had been under way since the mid-eighteenth century, together with the relocations from the countryside, Ireland, and the Scottish Highlands that dramatically swelled the populations of the manufacturing and commercial towns. At the 1851 census, only a quarter of Glasgow's and Manchester's populations had been born in those cities; in Liverpool the locally-born proportion was even lower. The total population of Great Britain doubled between 1801 and 1861, but over the same period Liverpool and Glasgow each grew more than five-fold, to populations of 444,000 and 420,000 respectively. These cities were closely followed by Birmingham, Manchester, Leeds, and Sheffield, all of which experienced a quadrupling of their populations. In 1801, 16 per cent of the inhabitants of England and Wales lived in the six largest English cities: London (calculated on the boundaries of the later London County Council), Birmingham, Leeds, Liverpool, Manchester and Sheffield. By 1861 that percentage had increased to 22 per cent, a level that was only marginally exceeded in 1871 and 1891 before falling slightly at the 1911 Census. The change in Scotland was even more striking: in 1801 Edinburgh and Glasgow accounted for just less than 10 per cent of the total population; by 1861 that proportion had grown to 20 per cent, increasing to 26 per cent by 1901.

Substantial population growth also occurred in the counties of Glamorgan, Durham and Lanarkshire, where the rapid expansion of the extractive industries, especially coal mining, resulted in a more dispersed but equally significant increase in economic activity. In contrast, some of the more rural counties experienced growth of 50 per cent or less in their populations between 1801 and 1861 – as early as 1851, Britain had become an urban economy, with more than half of its population living in towns.

Cities with a longer-established and more traditional industrial and commercial base – such as Nottingham, Bristol, Norwich, and Coventry – also grew significantly as they too expanded and adapted, but in both absolute and proportionate terms their growth was less than that in those centres which were responding to new manufacturing processes or market opportunities. Even though greater London began the century with a population of just over a million and added almost another two million by 1861, its proportionate rate of growth during the nineteenth century was eclipsed by that of Birmingham, Liverpool, Manchester, Leeds and Sheffield. By 1861 the combined population of these five cities, which in 1801 had been equivalent to 30 per cent of greater London's, had grown to 50 per cent of that of the metropolis. As noted above, the London population comparisons are based on the later London County Council area, whereas the other cities' totals reflect the populations within their boundaries at the relevant census year. If the populations of adjacent areas which were subsequently incorporated are included, together with those of contiguous local authorities such as Salford or Birkenhead, then the balance moves further towards the great English provincial cities. Glasgow, slightly larger than Manchester in 1801, overtook Edinburgh in population size by 1821 and Liverpool by 1871: by 1911 it had become Britain's second city of more than a million inhabitants. On a much smaller absolute scale, but relatively even more impressive, Cardiff, with only 2,000 inhabitants in 1801, had more than fifteen times that number in 1861, and had grown to a population of 164,000 in 1901.

Clearly, the trends that drove these changes in the size and distribution of Britain's population had already begun before the emergence of railways as a national transport system. From their outset, these population movements reflected both the growth and the changing structure of production in what was still a largely labour-intensive economy. At the same time, an increasing population, supported by a growing total national income, added directly to domestic demand for the outputs of the newer industries as well as for those of more traditional sectors. As an example of the latter, the production of dutiable spirits in England and Wales almost doubled between 1801 and 1841, and we should not overlook the more basic demand created by the need to accommodate unprecedented population growth – the number of bricks charged with duty in England and Wales grew from 673 million in 1801 to 1,463 million in 1849, when the liability for duty (and therefore the collection of these statistics) ended. Although some of the associated building activity went to produce the slum dwellings of nineteenth century Britain, it also resulted in fine new architectural statements of civic and personal wealth, besides supporting the construction of the railways: it has been estimated that at the height of the boom of the 1840s about a third of the total national output of bricks was used in railway building.

Industrial change and output growth in Britain's economy in the nineteenth century has frequently been illustrated by reference to the great Victorian staples which created new wealth from exports – textiles, iron and steel, and coal. Within the textile sector, as cotton production gradually overtook that of woollens, and mechanisation extended from spinning to the weaving and finishing processes, the volume of raw cotton consumed by the British industry grew from just over 50 million pounds weight at the start of the century to 1,007 million by 1861. An estimated total British output of 243,851 tons of pig iron in 1806 (almost double the estimated quantity in 1796) grew to 3.8 million tons in 1860. The coal industry, on which both the textile and iron and steel sectors depended to drive their contemporary growth, also dramatically increased its output: although comprehensive British statistics did not begin until 1854, the shipment of coal from the ports of Newcastle and Sunderland grew by 77 per cent between 1801 and 1831, to a total of around 3.5 million tons. The overwhelming majority of this sea-borne output was accounted for by coastwise shipments to London and other domestic destinations. In 1854 the total output of the British coalfields was 64.7 million tons, with north-east England accounting for almost a quarter. By 1861 output had increased to 83.6 million tons, of which Northumberland and Durham supplied 19.1 million tons. Railed transport was crucial in supporting the local growth of production in most of the British coalfields, starting with the earliest colliery waggonways, which in north-east England were to become the technological progenitors of a national steam-powered network. Nevertheless, in 1861 London still received more than two-thirds of its coal by coastal shipping: 1867 was the first year in which a larger proportion arrived by rail.

The emergence of railways as a significant element of the British economy therefore took place during a time when Britain was already experiencing a fundamental transformation. Railways rapidly became an important element of that transformation, both through the effects of the transport services that they provided and through the demand that they created for other sectors: bricks have already been mentioned, and in the same constructional peak during the later 1840s the railways needed the equivalent of around 28 per cent of current domestic pig iron production to meet their requirement for rails. However, despite the pervasiveness of the image of the coal-fired steam train, the railways' direct demand for coal (beyond that embodied in the iron and steel and other materials used in permanent way, bridges, rolling stock, and other equipment) was no more than perhaps two per cent of national output in 1869.

So far as the railways' contribution as a provider of transport was concerned, it is one of the paradoxes of the early railway age that, although railway prospectuses emphasised the scope for profit from carrying goods, initially at least many of their promoters' freight traffic expectations were not realised. Taking as an example six companies that were authorised in 1836 – the Birmingham & Derby Junction; the Birmingham & Gloucester; the Manchester & Leeds; the Midland Counties; the North Midland; and the York & North Midland – their forecasts of annual goods revenue totalled £433,400. In fact their collective income from that source in 1843 was £287,100 – only two-thirds of the estimates – and only one, the Manchester & Leeds, earned more than its forecast.

There were some extenuating factors: the economy was in depression in 1843; the Birmingham & Gloucester's continuation to Bristol was not yet complete; and two of these companies (the Birmingham & Derby Junction and the Midland Counties) were engaged in price competition for traffic via Derby which was to lead to their consolidation, along with the North Midland, as the Midland Railway. But the same factors applied to passenger traffic, from which the six companies earned £553,700 in 1843, equivalent to 90.4 per cent of their original estimates; the Manchester & Leeds and York & North Midland significantly surpassed their 1836 expectations. Such experiences were not uncommon, and it was not until 1852 that total freight revenue on the British network exceeded that from passenger traffic.

A number of factors contributed to the relatively slow development of railway freight revenue. First, the organisation and methodology of goods traffic was demanding – the process of assembling, loading and unloading and then distributing a trainload of goods is complex in comparison with passenger handling, requiring specialised equipment, staff and accountancy. There was a view during the emergence of the first trunk lines that the task of managing the commercial side of the freight business should be left to the existing specialist carrying firms, such as Pickford's and Chaplin & Horne, which had developed their businesses in the canal and road transport sectors. This soon became a point at issue between the two companies that made up the London–Lancashire trunk line, the Grand Junction and London & Birmingham. The former, although providing facilities for carriers' traffic, also operated a goods business on its own account, while its southern partner left such traffic entirely with the carriers, creating problems for the through consignment of goods beyond Birmingham which were only finally resolved a year after the two companies (together with the Manchester & Birmingham) amalgamated in 1846 to form the London & North Western Railway.

One of the initial justifications for using the established carrying firms – the skills and experience which they brought from canal and road transport in managing the end-to-end consignment of goods over routes and modes with different ownership and separate charging structures – began to disappear after 1842, when the Railway Clearing House was set up as a means of apportioning revenue on through traffic over two or more companies' lines. It subsequently developed a wider role as an inter-company commercial and technical forum.

Despite this important development – in which the London & Birmingham had played a significant part – it was not until 1847 that the LNWR decided to bring the management of the goods traffic on its entire line into its own hands. Even then, goods handling in the company's London depots remained the responsibility of the carriers' staff until 1862, and road collection and delivery was only gradually brought in-house. While the LNWR and its largest constituents perhaps faced unusually acute challenges during the development of the route's freight traffic both before and after amalgamation, this initial reliance on third parties for at least a part of the goods business was far from unique – according to MacDermot's *History of the Great Western Railway*, that company also relied mainly on carriers at first, and it was not until 1849 the GWR appointed a goods manager. Such instances illustrate the organisational issues that early companies needed to resolve before they could exploit this part of their business to best effect.

A second reason why railway goods traffic developed relatively slowly was the limitations of early locomotives. Although the colliery waggonways of north-east England had provided the main test bed for the development of effective and – relatively – reliable steam locomotives, they were built for low-speed operation: quite apart from the still-experimental nature of a technology that had yet to prove itself conclusively against the alternative of cable haulage, the primitive cast-iron rails that were then available could not have withstood the impact of heavy unsprung locomotives and mineral wagons at much above walking pace.

The Rainhill trials of 1829 stimulated interest in higher speed, but the fleet-of-foot engines that were derived from Stephenson's successful *Rocket* for the Liverpool & Manchester Railway and its later trunk connections were light-weight machines, designed primarily for passenger service rather than the haulage of heavy goods trains. Although variants of the early mainline passenger designs were adopted for goods services, the development of satisfactory 'luggage' engines for the cost-effective movement of freight at the speeds needed on mixed-traffic lines was a protracted process, dependent on the emergence of longer boilers during the 1840s and the wider introduction of 6-coupled designs during the following decade. These motive power developments, together with improved rails and signalling, helped to underpin the rapid expansion of railway freight traffic during the 1850s: in 1852 goods train miles in Britain totalled 24.5 million, compared with 33.3 million passenger train miles; by 1861 the ratio was virtually at parity, with goods accounting for 49.5 million train miles and passenger services 49.6 million.

A third reason for the relatively slow initial development of railway goods traffic was competition from water transport: not only from barges on canals and navigable inland rivers, but also from coastal shipping, particularly as that sector also began to benefit from the application of steam power to propulsion. The importance of coastwise delivery of coal to London has already been mentioned: the fact that from the late 1860s more coal began to arrive there by rail had more to do with the development of supplies from the nearer inland coalfields to satisfy a growing metropolitan demand than with any change in the underlying economics of competing transport modes. The North Eastern Railway's huge mineral traffic – the largest of any of the British railways before the First World War – remained predominantly based on short hauls to coastal staiths rather than on long-distance overland transits. Indeed, in Northumberland and Durham the NER continued to share part of the seaborne trade with private colliery waggonways, the technical and organisational descendants of the local undertakings where George Stephenson had first learned his trade. In 1879 London received 3.5 million tons of coal by sea – half a million tons more than in 1867, when rail deliveries first exceeded those by coastal shipping.

Seaborne transport's ability to move bulk traffic relatively cheaply over long distances gave coastal shipping a continuing competitive edge, which, even before the building of the Manchester Ship Canal, could reach well inland, to riverine ports such as Gloucester, Selby or Grangemouth. In comparison, transport by canal did not have so great a cost advantage, because of the smaller carrying capacity of canal vessels and the indirectness and other limitations of some inland waterway routes. Only miniscule quantities of dutiable coal reached London by canal – a peak of 72,000 tons in 1844. Instead, the inland waterways in the London area (including the upper Thames) played a much more important role in the local distribution of coal that had arrived in bulk by sea.

So far as inland traffic was concerned, the canal network in much of central England had developed in parallel with the first phases of industrialisation, and in many areas the canals had directly influenced the locational pattern of the pitheads, mills, factories and warehouses which relied on the transport services they provided. This advantage persisted even after the railway network had grown sufficiently in extent to compete with canals for inter-regional traffic, particularly in places where the density of existing development made it less easy to build sidings to reach factories and mills which might already have a direct canal link.

**The Crumlin Viaduct across the Ebbw valley, opened in 1857 as part of the
Newport, Abergavenny & Hereford Railway's Taff Vale extension.**
From the lithograph published by Newman & Co, London

Canal building in Britain was however significantly more constrained by
geography than even the earliest railways. Although waterway engineers had
advanced their profession to a high technical level, demonstrating at sites such
as Pontcysyllte aqueduct, Standedge tunnel, and Foxton locks how far human
ingenuity could go in overcoming the constraints which the natural landscape
imposed on the level vertical alignment needed for water transport, such
achievements came at a substantial cost. Some of the pioneering railway
schemes – the Stockton & Darlington and Newcastle & Carlisle are examples
– arose as cheaper substitutes for canal proposals. Others, such as the
Liverpool & Manchester, were promoted to compete with existing but less
direct canal routes. Consequently, the railways were quickly able to extend
their reach beyond that of the existing inland waterway network, and also to
provide an alternative to the main east–west and north–south canal trunk
routes for freight traffic.

Gary Hawke's research, published in 1970 as *Railways and economic growth
in England & Wales*, has suggested that in mid-Victorian Britain the overall
difference between rail and inland waterway freight costs was relatively small,
and that (just as in the USA) it should theoretically have been possible, in
the absence of railways, to extend the canal network to achieve many of the
benefits which the railways were to provide to the economy in the form of
freight transport services. Inevitably the details of Professor Hawke's findings

41

have provoked further analysis, but his underlying point has not been substantially challenged: while undoubtedly important, the *value* of the freight transport services provided by the British railway system in the mid-nineteenth century was not crucial to national economic growth (although that growth would have been shaped differently in the absence of railways).

While it is easy to identify particular freight flows that were created by the speedy transport made possible by rail – for example, the supply of perishables such as fresh milk, fish, meat and vegetables to the major cities – it is important to keep these in perspective. Londoners' food requirements were met by the available means of transport and through the existing structure of the supply chain in 1801, when the population of the wider metropolis was already at a level that none of the other major British cities was to approach for another hundred years. The scale of London's own demands of course changed dramatically over the century, and would certainly have strained previous means of overland supply, but as early as 1841, before railways could have played any real part, the population of the greater metropolitan area had already nearly doubled, to 2.07 million.

No doubt there were dietary and environmental benefits as a result of the changes in food supply to London and the other great cities that the railways made possible but, however desirable, they were not so immediately crucial to the continuing viability of these cities' expansion in the way that the public health reforms of the early Victorian years were. And it is also necessary to recognise that some other impacts of the railways on the well-being of major British cities were less positive: as Dr Kellett's seminal work *The impact of railways on Victorian cities* showed, the demolition that accompanied the building of their routes into city centres, while often sweeping away slum property which could be acquired relatively easily, resulted in the displacement of the poorest families and the sterilisation and downgrading of adjacent swathes of inner-city property because of severance and the loss of amenity caused by proximity to railway activities. The same processes that reinforced city centre uses around sometimes architecturally magnificent main railway stations also created new slums along the approaches to these stations.

If the slow and clanking goods train of now far-distant memory was, in general, not in itself a fundamental cause of dramatic change in the economic structure of mid-Victorian Britain, but rather an example of more gradual progression and supersession, the opportunities provided by the rapid development of railway passenger transport were on a different scale. Those who used or watched the first steam-hauled passenger services were witnesses to the

**Paradise Row, Agar Town, London, with Kings Cross station in the background.**
From George Godwin, *London shadows: a glance at the 'homes' of the thousands*, 1854

inauguration of a transformational change: indeed, it was lack of compre-
hension of the technological scope of this change which caused the first two of
these spectacles also to be the public occasion of human casualties. These were
the unlucky keelman who, clinging to the outside of one of the wagons forming
the first train on the Stockton & Darlington Railway in 1825, fell off at speed
(15mph), 'dreadfully crushing' his foot when a wheel passed over it; and the
even more unfortunate William Huskisson MP. His fatal accident at Parkside
when he was run down by the *Rocket* during the opening of the Liverpool &
Manchester Railway on 15 September 1830 changed, in the words of his
memorial, 'a moment of noblest exultation and triumph that science and
genius had ever achieved into one of desolation and mourning … striking
terror into the hearts of assembled thousands'.

Although Huskisson is now chiefly recalled, if at all, as the first prominent
railway casualty, his accident was more significant in terms of its impact on the
politics of the day than because of its place in railway history. The aftermath of
the Napoleonic Wars was a troubled time in Britain, with economic depression
fuelling the social unrest that was most vividly demonstrated in the Peterloo
Massacre of 1819. Huskisson, who first became an MP in 1796, had long
ministerial experience, and through his political alliance with George Canning,
MP for Liverpool, was in close touch with the concerns and aspirations of
that city.

In 1823 he succeeded Canning both as one of Liverpool's two MPs and
also as President of the Board of Trade in Lord Liverpool's liberal Tory government, joining the cabinet later that year. At the Board of Trade he took forward

**The watering-station at Parkside, where William Huskisson suffered his fatal accident on the opening day of the Liverpool & Manchester Railway, 15 September 1830.**

From the engraving by T.T. Bury, published by R. Ackermann, *Coloured views on the Liverpool and Manchester Railway*, 1831 the progressive modernisation and relaxation of import and export regulations and duties, but in 1827 was unsuccessful in his attempt to modify the Corn Laws. These had been enacted in 1815 to protect post-war agricultural incomes from competition from imported grain by imposing a price threshold, below which imports were not permitted. Although Huskisson had originally been an advocate for this legislation, his association with Canning and his involvement with his new constituency were inclining him towards free-trade views. But besides the more abstract arguments of *laissez-faire* economists, spokesmen for the manufacturing areas and their labouring populations increasingly denounced the Corn Laws as unjust, artificially inflating the price of an essential food in order to line the pockets of farmers and landowners.

Lord Liverpool suffered a stroke in 1827 and the Duke of Wellington became Prime Minister in 1828, after the short intervening ministries of Canning and Goderich. But Wellington proved unable to hold together the various political interests that Lord Liverpool had ably moulded into a reforming cabinet: although proposals for a partial revision of the Corn Laws were approved by Parliament in 1828, later in the same year Huskisson (by then Colonial Secretary) resigned because of his opposition to the cabinet's position on a relatively modest measure of constituency reform. While Wellington's government did carry some progressive measures – the civic disabilities imposed on dissenters and catholics were relaxed, and in 1829 the Home Secretary, Robert Peel, established the Metropolitan Police – by 1830 his ministry was facing growing and orchestrated pressure for more thoroughgoing parliamentary reform. The victor of Waterloo was beginning to find himself the object of personal hostility in the country at large and especially in those large cities, such as Manchester, which had no seats at Westminster.

The general election which followed the accession of William IV in June 1830 did nothing to strengthen Wellington's waning political base. Huskisson's ill-fated attempt to take advantage of the Parkside watering stop during the Liverpool & Manchester's opening cavalcade by walking along the track to speak to Wellington seems to have been prompted by a wish for political rapprochement, which, if successful, would probably have given the Prime Minister the additional parliamentary support that he needed. Instead, just two months after Huskisson's death, Wellington resigned after losing a Commons vote on 15 November 1830. He was succeeded by Earl Grey, the leader of the Whigs and a long-time advocate of parliamentary reform, and after some vicissitudes the Reform Act was ultimately carried in 1832.

This extended the franchise and rebalanced the constituency map in a way which better – if still not completely – reflected the changing distribution of Britain's population. It was followed in 1835 by the Municipal Corporations

Act. Although that Act did not extend to Scotland or London, it swept away the existing archaic and unrepresentative structure of town corporations in England, replacing them with elected councils.

While the property qualification needed for voting meant that these measures amounted to only a limited extension of the franchise – even after 1832, perhaps only a fifth of adult males in England were entitled to vote in parliamentary elections – the reforms were the terms that the landed establishment was prepared to accept in admitting the moneyed urban classes into fuller participation in the governance of the nation. Bolstered by the intake of some fresh blood into parliament, the beginnings of a professionalised civil service, and the growing tide of informed debate on public policy issues, governments from the mid-1830s onwards began to engage more effectively with questions which directly impacted on the lives and well-being of the population – including the question of how the nascent railway system should be regulated in the public interest.

Not all of the reforms of the day were benign – the Utilitarian doctrines that underlay the New Poor Law ensured that the workhouse cast a long shadow across Victorian Britain. However, measures as diverse as factory safety and employment legislation, the Bank Charter Act of 1844, the sanitary and public health improvements which resulted from Chadwick's inquiries and the abolition of the Corn Laws in the face of the Irish potato famine laid the foundations for the mid-century 'age of equipoise' and paved the way for more far-reaching reforms from 1867 onwards. In response to the fundamental social and economic changes which Britain underwent during this period – changes in which the new railways were of course a very visible presence – the apparatus of government in Britain was able to adapt sufficiently to the challenges and stresses associated with these changes to overcome the threats that they posed to the orderly functioning of society and to 'the progress of the Nation'. The consequent enhancement of executive capability at both national and local government levels laid the foundations for a recognisably modern civil administration, overseen, with accidental symbolism, from the rebuilt Houses of Parliament, work on which commenced in 1840 following the destruction of most of the mediaeval Palace of Westminster by fire in 1834.

According to Samuel Smiles's account, in moving the gravely-injured Huskisson by train from Parkside to Eccles for medical attention, George Stephenson covered the 15 miles with his *Northumbrian* locomotive at an average of 36mph – a rate only previously approachable on horseback at full gallop, and 7mph faster than the average that had been achieved by the *Rocket* at the Rainhill trials the year before. Such speeds dramatically demonstrated the clear superiority of steam railways over horse-drawn road vehicles for passenger travel.

The years which saw the emergence of the steam railway in Britain also saw successful experiments with steam-powered road vehicles. However the turnpike improvements which began in the mid-eighteenth century, together with the initiatives of the Post Office to shorten mail transit times, had already greatly improved the speed of travel by stagecoach, from around 6mph in the early 1780s to more than 10mph on some of the fastest mail routes in 1830. This was probably close to the best that could have been achieved in regular service by the steam road vehicles of the time if their promoters had been able to overcome the opposition of turnpike trustees to their use. Even at these speeds, passengers still needed to devote half a day or more to making relatively short journeys: the journey between Liverpool and Manchester took around 3½–4 hours in 1830, and that between London and Oxford six hours, while about twelve hours was needed to travel from London to Birmingham.

Within six years of the opening of the Liverpool & Manchester Railway the fastest passenger trains were scheduled to take 75 minutes for the 30 miles between Edge Hill and Manchester, and the London & Birmingham offered a journey time of around six hours between its termini when it opened in 1837. As the L&BR's earthworks consolidated, schedules were progressively improved, and by May 1845 the fastest train was timed to take three hours for the 112 miles. Similar average speeds were being attained by the Great Western Railway, and maxima of over 50mph and even 60mph were not uncommon during the later 1840s: truly remarkable progress in less than twenty years, especially at that relatively early stage in the development of both railway motive power and infrastructure. The effects of this rapid transition from horse-drawn travel to the steam train were so far beyond the experience of any previous generations that the sense of a completely new dimension in travel was immediately apparent to passengers and observers, and quickly circulated more widely through the expanding print media of the time, which had been made affordable to a larger public by the parallel application of steam to printing processes.

Even while the system was in the initial stages of its geographical expansion, the early railways quickly affected journeys to and from destinations beyond those directly served by train. The Liverpool & Manchester's directors soon found that their line attracted passengers intent on travelling to the seaside by connecting coach services, making it necessary to strengthen trains on fine days. It became common for coach operators to switch to feeder routes when they lost trunk-haul business to a new railway: for example, as the Great Western's line from London was progressively opened in a westerly direction, connecting coaches to destinations such as Oxford and Cheltenham were established from the nearest railheads, together with road services bridging the gap to the railway's ultimate destination at Bristol.

In some instances the availability of a railway could divert passengers well away from traditional routes: when Joseph Pease MP, one of the founders of the Stockton & Darlington Railway, gave evidence to a parliamentary select committee in 1839, his itinerary from his South Durham constituency to Westminster involved travelling by coach to Preston and onward by train via Parkside and Birmingham to Euston. Despite the inconvenience of having to re-book en route for the different stages of the rail journey, he clearly preferred the long detour via Preston on the far side of the Pennines to the more direct route by coach along the Great North Road.

Higher-speed railway travel was initially confined mainly to those who could afford first-class fares: indeed, provision was made for the owners of private road carriages to have their vehicles conveyed on trucks attached to passenger trains. The experience of the poorer passenger in an open railway carriage was very different, though it must be remembered that stagecoach travel was also a luxury open to few, and the alternative of a hired post-chaise was even more costly. For most of the working classes, the horizons of a day's return journey had been restricted by walking distance or the range of conveyance by a farm or carrier's cart. For longer-distance travel, their alternatives to walking were likewise limited: stage wagons, cheaper, but far slower than coaches; or in some cases passage by canal boat or coastal vessel.

The low-fare passenger transport offered by carriers and stage wagons was generally provided in conjunction with their light goods and parcels traffic, and that business quickly succumbed when railway competition emerged. The loss of this cheap form of road passenger transport was one of the factors which encouraged Parliament in 1844 to enact that a penny-a-mile 'parliamentary train' should be provided daily in both directions on each railway. These trains were to be made up of covered vehicles and were to travel at an overall average speed of not less than 12mph while calling at every station. Although the requirement could only be imposed statutorily on lines which opened after the passage of the Act, the inducement of the removal of passenger tax on compliant third-class fares was sufficient to ensure its voluntary introduction on existing railways.

Cheap passenger fares were available on a number of lines before 1844, although generally for very basic accommodation, and mostly confined to the slowest trains. However, practice was far from consistent. The London & Greenwich Railway took a democratic approach at its opening in 1836, with only one scale of charges, but later in the year introduced a three-class fare structure, only to withdraw its third class in May 1837; it had reappeared by 1841. When the Grand Junction opened in 1837 it offered no third-class tickets on long-distance services, but cheap fares were available in open accommodation on the daily local train in each direction between its Wolverhampton station and Birmingham. Third-class passengers on the London & Birmingham Railway had to wait until 1840, when one daily train each way was provided for them, calling at all stations and taking around eight hours for the end-to-end journey. In the case of the Great Western, MacDermot describes an interesting transference of road transport practice that was mentioned in parliamentary evidence in 1840: the first provision for 'persons in the lower stations of life' on that line seems to have been made by a carrier on the railway, who allowed such passengers to travel with his goods traffic on the Great Western.

But if the qualitative improvements offered by railway travel were at first available mainly to the more comfortably-off members of society, railways had another significant advantage over horse-drawn road transport, and indeed over contemporary steam road vehicles: the sheer volume of passenger accommodation that they could provide. Stagecoaches could convey around twelve to fifteen passengers, with the majority enduring the rigours of an outside seat. While the earliest railway carriages were modelled on stagecoaches, the Liverpool & Manchester first-class vehicles which set the standard for most passenger lines during the 1830s combined the equivalent of three road coach bodies on a single underframe, providing about eighteen seats, all inside. And, in marked contrast with road passenger transport, steam locomotive haulage made it possible for a single passenger train to consist of many such carriages – something that is readily apparent from the prints that were published in the 1830s to illustrate the new railways.

Although the Newcastle & Carlisle Railway appears initially to have followed stagecoach practice by also offering cheap 'outside' seats on its carriages, most other companies provided separate accommodation for lower-class passengers in unglazed and frequently unroofed vehicles which owed more to goods wagon design than stage coach precedent. Such rolling stock gave even more passenger capacity than the coach-built first-class carriage: the L&M second-class vehicle provided 24 seats. Early railway passengers weighing the choice between higher and lower fare accommodation could reflect that the discomfort of a seat (or, at worst, a place to stand) in an open or partially-enclosed railway carriage would have to be endured for a much shorter time than would be required for the equivalent 'outside' road journey by stagecoach or by carrier's wagon.

This increase in the total supply of passenger transport affected travel behaviour just as profoundly as did the shorter journey times which railways offered. Around 5.4 million passenger journeys were made by rail in Great Britain in 1838; in the 12 months ending in June 1844 the total had grown almost five-fold to 25.2 million, and by 1860 had reached 153.5 million. The proportionate growth in the number of journeys substantially exceeded the rates which both the total population and railway route mileage were expanding, reflecting the increasing pervasiveness of rail travel among most classes of society. By 1855 more journeys were being made at third-class fares than by first- and second-class passengers combined; by the early 1860s third-class passengers were generating more revenue than either of the other classes, despite the substantially lower fares (and generally shorter journeys) associated with third-class travel.

The tendency to travel more seems to have applied to most categories of journey, with the Royal Family setting an early example. Business travel was clearly important from the outset: the secretary of the Liverpool & Manchester was quick to describe the advantages to the 'man of business in Manchester', who 'will breakfast at home – proceed to Liverpool by Railway, transact his business, and return to Manchester before dinner'. More strenuously, an engineer quoted by Kellett claimed in parliamentary evidence in 1866 to travel 25,000 to 28,000 miles annually by railway, 'and to have done so for the last 25 years'. His profession may have influenced the extent of his need to travel, but a weekly average of around 500 miles, unthinkable in a pre-railway age, would certainly have been demanding by early Victorian train. Doubtless, however, there were many such as Trollope who soon came to value the opportunity that railway journeys provided to write or otherwise catch up on work. For those who simply preferred to pass the time on their journey by relaxing with a book or periodical, the station bookstall was already a feature at many places by the end of the 1840s.

Railways also quickly attracted passengers whose sole purpose in travelling was for leisure – the Liverpool & Manchester has already been mentioned in connection with seaside trips, and by the mid-1840s railway travel was reinforcing the role of places such as Blackpool as recreational destinations for industrial workers, besides adding to the numbers visiting more fashionable inland or coastal resorts. Race meetings and other sporting events also generated crowds of passengers from an early stage. Thomas Cook famously organised his first temperance excursion in 1841, a trip for almost 600 passengers by special train from Leicester to Loughborough, and sightseeing by rail soon became routine both for organised parties and for independent travellers. The Great Exhibition provides the most spectacular early demonstration of the railways' role in catering for excursionists: between May and October 1851 around six million people visited the Crystal Palace, from all

YE FRESMONNE HIS ARRIVAL AT & BY YE RAILWAY STATION

**The end of an early cross-country journey: Edward Bradley's sketch of his arrival at Durham Gilesgate station in the mid-1840s, part of his cartoon set 'Ye Freshmonne his adventures at Univ. Coll. Durham'.**

over Britain as well as from further afield. A national exhibition on this scale could not have been mounted so successfully without the longer distance and local access that the railways provided, and railway artefacts found a natural place in Prince Albert's Great Exhibition of Works of all Nations.

Other journeys were made from necessity, in search of betterment through work, education or a new beginning. Edward Bradley, who later published his humorous writings and drawings under the pseudonym 'Cuthbert Bede', sketched his arrival as a freshman at the recently-founded University of Durham in 1845. The set of cartoons includes his alighting from the train at the city's then branch terminus (presumably at the conclusion of a long cross-country journey from his family home in Worcestershire), and the rough transfer by omnibus to his hotel. When Bradley relocated his fictional student alter ego Verdant Green to Oxford on the advice of his publisher, he took the opportunity to send him by the Birmingham–Oxford stagecoach, which ceased to run in May 1852 when the railway between the two cities opened.

Not all passengers were as fortunate in being able to find humour in the circumstances of their journeys. Michael Freeman, in his *Railways and the Victorian imagination,* remarks on the travelling that must have been undertaken by young women entering into domestic service, the largest single category of paid female employment at the 1851 census, and just one example of the factors making up the widespread internal economic migration that reshaped nineteenth century society. The railways' business from such domestic relocation was supplemented both by British emigrants travelling to

51

the ports, and by foreign nationals in transit: there was a significant traffic in European migrants arriving by sea at Hull and other east coast ports who travelled onwards by rail to Liverpool to re-embark for America.

There was however one type of passenger travel from which the early railways failed to gain significant business – the daily journey to work. Although the suburbanisation of London and the other great cities was beginning as early as the 1830s, this was largely a middle-class phenomenon, fostered primarily by the growth of horse-drawn omnibus services. Most working-class wages were too low to cover daily fares on top of other living costs, so the majority of the population continued to live within walking distance of their employment – or of the casual labour markets that still prevailed in some occupations. A few early railways, such as the Newcastle & North Shields, the London & Greenwich, the London & Blackwall, and the Glasgow, Paisley & Greenock, were short-distance lines, built for local traffic. However, the majority of companies concentrated on more rewarding longer-distance business, and there seems to have been no interest in cultivating daily travel to and from work by train. The geography and economy of London probably ensured that some such traffic was generated by default from wealthier commuters living in established towns such as Croydon or even Brighton, but Kellett's outside estimate was that in the mid-1850s no more than 27,000 commuters travelled into London by train each day, compared with 244,000 on foot or by horse omnibus. He concurred with the view of the official historians of London Transport that 7,000–10,000 was the more likely range. So the railways' initial role in suburbanisation was minimal, and even where companies were formed to exploit local commuter traffic, such as the Liverpool, Crosby & Southport, opened in 1848, they did so to take advantage of markets that had been initially developed by other modes of short-distance transport, horse omnibuses, and in this particular case the Mersey steamers.

Within 30 years of the opening of the Liverpool & Manchester line, railways were part of the experience of the great majority of people in Britain. Whether for the frequent business traveller or the perhaps once-yearly excursionist, the railways offered a common mode of transport that was shared more widely across the population than any other form of travel except walking, even if there was still a great gap between the levels of amenity that different passengers enjoyed. In most parts of England, if less so in Scotland or Wales, even those who travelled only rarely were still likely to be aware of the dramatic changes that railway building had made to the natural and built environment,

**The chalk cutting at Brighton: the opening of the Shoreham Branch of the London & Brighton Railway on 12 May 1840.**
Lithograph by H.G. Hine, published by W.H. Mason

whether from the embankments, cuttings, viaducts and tunnels by which the new lines strode through the countryside, or from the radical alterations to townscapes as diverse as those of Manchester and Berwick. Perspectives would have differed: a slum dweller in the no-man's land between the railway approaches to Euston and Kings Cross had less reason to welcome the impact of the railway on his city than, say, the middle-class resident of Newcastle, who saw how well John Dobson's Central Station complemented the same architect's collaboration with Richard Grainger in the redevelopment of the city centre, and how effectively Robert Stephenson's High Level Bridge now linked the two banks of the Tyne for foot and road travellers as well as railway passengers, avoiding the need to descend the steep hill to the ancient river crossing at the quayside.

And while some shared Ruskin's and Wordsworth's condemnation of the railways' 'rash assault' on unspoiled tracts of countryside, others saw beauty in design and in the juxtaposition of well-executed modernity with an apparently ageless landscape – although the latter was a concept which might be questioned by those of a more inquiring bent who instead enthused at the way

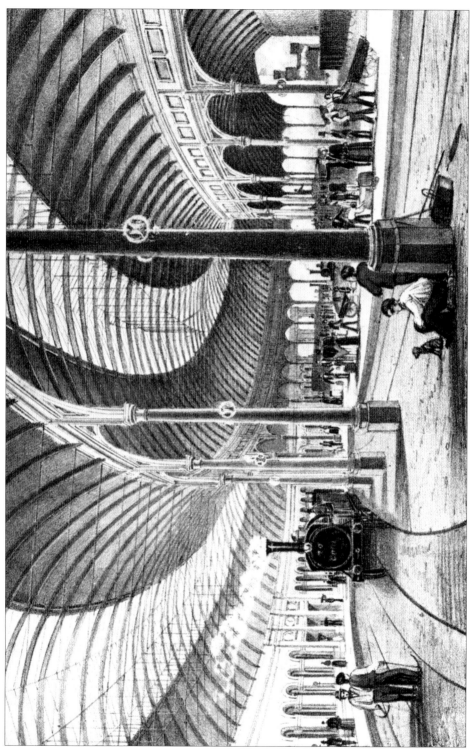

Central station, Newcastle upon Tyne.

that deep railway cuttings exposed the strata and fossil beds that had been hidden for aeons but were beginning to inform the scientific reasoning of contemporary geologists .

Even if far from the immediate sight or sound of a railway, the children in their varieties of parish, charitable and private schools would probably be familiar with images of railways in the printed texts, alphabet books and multiplication tables that they used. If they were from a more comfortable level of society they might also be lucky enough to have at home a railway board game or perhaps even a toy train. The skilled workman seeking self-improvement from periodicals, texts, and lectures in his Mechanics' Institute would have no shortage of information about the latest advances in railway engineering, and a wealthier member of society who had come through the Railway Mania with some sound railway shares or debentures would keep abreast of company performance through his daily newspaper and perhaps the specialist railway financial press.

Depictions of railway scenes were even beginning to find their way into the art galleries, and railway themes could also be encountered in the novels of the day, besides featuring more specifically in reference works. Those who did not purchase such books could still catch up with current publications if they belonged to a subscription library or had access to one of the new municipal libraries established under the Public Libraries Act of 1850. The reading room there perhaps held the *Illustrated London News*, founded in 1842, the pages of which still provide a valuable archive of railway development during this period.

In common with the London and regional daily papers, the *Illustrated London News* depended for its growing circulation on the rapid distribution service provided by trains, in the same way that the ubiquity and speed of the nationwide postal service was built around the railways – the Liverpool & Manchester was entrusted with the mails between its termini within two months of its opening, and the introduction of the Penny Post in 1840 stimulated an immediate expansion in the volume of mail and therefore in the importance of railway postal traffic. The emergence of another form of communication was also aided by the railways: the concept of electrically-powered telegraphy had been identified as early as the eighteenth century, and by the 1830s a number of systems had been tested successfully in Britain and elsewhere. But it was the railways which provided a practical application for the technology, initially to support the safe movement of trains, and also offered the long linear routes which enabled commercial telegraph companies to provide an effective network for near-instantaneous communication between distant points. So in addition to their direct role in moving people, goods, and written communications, the railways helped to underpin another mid-century innovation which bound Victorian Britain together.

Both the railways and the electric telegraph assisted in the propagation of another unifying change: the use of Greenwich time throughout Britain (but not Ireland). In an age when longer journeys were measured in days rather than hours, the local variation of time from east to west in accordance with the passage of the sun had not been an issue. However, the speed and nature of railway transport changed this – it quickly became appreciated that, where there were significant variations in local time within a single route, timetables needed to be expressed and understood on a consistent basis, for safety reasons as well as for the convenience of the travelling public.

The first long east–west railway, the Newcastle & Carlisle, adopted Newcastle time across its entire line when end-to-end running began in 1838, and in 1840 both the Great Western and the London & South Western applied Greenwich time throughout their systems. The Greenwich standard was adopted by several other companies over the next few years, and in 1847 the Railway Clearing House recommended all its members to do the same. This example was followed, if gradually and in some cases reluctantly, by local and ecclesiastical authorities, but it was not until 1880 that Greenwich Mean Time became the British legal standard. In the interim, the description 'railway time' came into currency as an alternative to 'London time' to distinguish Greenwich from locally-determined time.

Within a remarkably short period of time for so profound a change, the railways came to permeate the society and economy of mid-nineteenth century Britain at almost every level: to adapt the words of Michael Freeman, they became part of the Victorian imagination. However, although important aspects of the changes that the Victorians experienced could be directly traced to the effects of railway building and railway transport, it is evident that the new system developed at a time when profound industrial, social, and political change was already well under way. The railways were therefore part of a wider set of processes which, by the time of Queen Victoria's accession in 1837, were altering the face, structure, and psyche of Britain in unprecedented ways. Some of these processes clearly overlapped and directly fed on each other, such as the adoption of steam power across a wide range of economic sectors, with consequent effects on productivity, on coal and iron output, and on transport demand.

While it is not necessarily fanciful to invoke 'the spirit of the age' as an underlying theme, not all aspects of contemporary change displayed such tangible examples of linkage. Apart from the immediate political consequences of the melancholy events at Parkside and Eccles on 15 September 1830, and the inconvenient interruption of the parliamentary progress of some railway Bills during the constitutional turmoil of the time, there was no direct connection between the early railways and the passage of the Reform Bill: the very effective nationwide campaign for reform was successfully orchestrated, in the main from Birmingham and Newcastle upon Tyne, without the assistance of the easier inter-regional links that the railways were soon to make available. But leading participants in that campaign (for example, Thomas Attwood) can also be found among the subscribers and committee-men of early railway schemes, while the fact that the Prime Minister of the day and other leading figures had found it important to attend the opening of the Liverpool & Manchester Railway tells us much about the significance of that event within the national – and indeed international – consciousness of the time. Within a few years some of the leading engineers and railway magnates who had helped to forge the early railways had themselves become part of the post-Reform Act political establishment as MPs – Robert Stephenson, George Hudson, Joseph Locke, and Daniel Gooch among them.

The railway companies themselves also quickly became a power in the land, especially the large amalgamated undertakings that were formed in the 1840s and 1850s. These were giants in the contemporary commercial world, representing accumulations of capital well in excess of those needed for other forms of enterprise, and necessitating new approaches to corporate governance and to business management which, if not an immediate template for most other sectors of industry, at least represented the development of new sets of transferable skills which were available to a growing domestic economy and which could be directly exported through the medium of British-funded overseas railway undertakings.

In summary therefore, while railways alone cannot account for the economic and other changes which fundamentally altered the nature of Britain and of British life over the years between 1830 and 1860, they were so bound up with so many of those changes as to make them the aptest single symbol of the age, acknowledged as such by those who lived through these years. The historians who have subsequently attempted to quantify the role of railways in Britain's nineteenth-century development and have in consequence qualified previous assumptions about their direct economic impact are nonetheless also generally agreed that, in Professor Gourvish's words: 'railways had a greater influence than any other single innovation before the age of oil and electricity.' The Victorians' ready identification of railways with the progress that was so much a theme of their time was not therefore misguided: their railways were indeed a key aspect of Britain's transition to modernity.

# Further reading

Most statistical references in this chapter are taken from B.R. Mitchell and Phyllis Deane, *Abstract of British historical statistics,* Cambridge 1962.
They have been supplemented in some cases with information from the annual *Railway Returns* or with material relating to individual railway companies which has been drawn from the standard histories or in some instances company records.

**For the general political and economic history of the period, see especially the following works:**

Asa Briggs, *England in the age of improvement,* London 1959 [or subsequent editions]

W.L. Burn, *The age of equipoise,* London 1964

Sir John Clapham, *An economic history of modern Britain: Vol.1, the early railway age 1820–1850,* 2nd edition reprinted, Cambridge 1939

W.H.B. Court, *A concise economic history of Britain from 1750 to recent times,* Cambridge 1962

C.R. Fay, *Huskisson and his age,* London 1951 [A more recent treatment can be found in Simon Garfield, *The last journey of William Huskisson,* London 2002]

Roderick Floud and Donald McCloskey (eds), *The economic history of Britain since 1700: Vol.1 1700–1860,* 2nd edition, Cambridge 1994 [The more extensive treatment of transport in chapter 12 of the 1st (1981) edition remains relevant]

Peter Mathias, *The first industrial nation,* London 1969

**For discussion of the economic impact of railways, see especially:**

Michael J. Freeman and Derek H. Aldcroft (eds), *Transport in Victorian Britain,* Manchester 1988

T.R. Gourvish, *Railways and the British economy 1830–1914,* Basingstoke 1980

G.R. Hawke, *Railways and economic growth in England and Wales 1840–1870,* Oxford 1970

B.R. Mitchell, 'The coming of the railway and United Kingdom economic growth', *Journal of Economic History,* XXIV, 1964 [Quoted extensively by Hawke, above.]

Patrick O'Brien, *The new economic history of the railways,* London 1977

Patrick O'Brien (ed), *Railways and the economic development of western Europe 1830–1914,* London 1983

**Thematic surveys of the contemporary effects of railways can be found in:**

Michael J. Freeman, *Railways and the Victorian imagination,* New Haven 1999

John R. Kellett, *The impact of railways on Victorian cities,* London 1969

Harold Perkin, *The age of the railway,* Newton Abbot 1971

Jack Simmons, *The Victorian railway,* London 1991

**The most comprehensive survey of transport in Britain in the pre-railway age remains:**

W.T. Jackman, *The development of transportation in modern England,* 2nd edition, London 1962

**For an introduction to many of the topics and companies discussed in this chapter, including references to relevant standard railway company histories, see:**

Jack Simmons and Gordon Biddle (eds), *The Oxford companion to British railway history,* Oxford 1997

# CHAPTER 3

# The Finance of Railways

## and how they came to account for half the total value of companies on the London Stock Exchange

### *Andrew Jones*

I N 1830, when the Liverpool & Manchester Railway had its grand opening, railways accounted for barely 3½ per cent of the value of the London Stock Exchange, with canals being the biggest component at 41 per cent. By 1844 and the height of railway mania railway stocks accounted for 52 per cent of the market, canals only 12 per cent. Railways, both domestic and foreign, would continue to hold this pre-eminent position on the London Exchange until the late 1930s. How is it that a single new industry could come to dominate the stock market so quickly, and for so long?

## Background

THE London Stock Exchange, as a properly constituted and regulated entity, only came into existence a few decades prior to the opening of the first modern railway. Both the Stock Exchange and the railways had precursors exhibiting some of the elements necessary for the development of the later structures, and both were very much products of the early nineteenth century each owing much of its early success to the other.

## Joint Stock Companies, Stock Exchanges and Economics

BEFORE going further let's briefly consider the background of the Stock Exchange, the companies on it and the basic economics underlying its operation.

Whilst the terms stock market and stock exchange are often used inter-changeably they have quite distinct meanings: A stock *market* is simply the meeting together of buyers and sellers of stocks and shares, wherever, whenever and however that might take place. It is unregulated and may or may not have a physical presence; the phrase is also used to describe the buying and selling of stocks and shares in total, both on and off the Stock Exchange. A stock *exchange*, on the other hand, is something quite specific. It is a market where specialised intermediaries buy and sell securities (e.g. government issued bonds or shares in joint stock companies) under a common set of rules and regulations through a closed system dedicated to that purpose.

In a joint-stock company, as the name suggests, a number of individuals jointly own the stock (in the earliest examples simply a stock of goods for sale) and as a result have the right to share in the proceeds from the sale of that stock, or to share in the profits from the trading of the company as it continues to buy and sell. Once such an enterprise was underway, there was the possibility, certainly in the case of more formal companies, for the share in it to be sold to others if so desired. If the prospect of profits was thought favourable the share might be sold at a profit – a premium. If things were not looking so good it may be sold at a loss – a discount.

Formal public companies had been created in England as early as the sixteenth century granting the proprietors the right to a share in the year's earnings as a dividend. To begin with there were only a few companies, dominated by the large overseas trading concerns such as the East India Company, Hudson's Bay Company, and the Royal African Company. The shares could be sold and bought and once there are regularly both sellers and buyers of an item a market for them will soon emerge.

From the earliest days shares would be traded simply where and when those wishing to sell could find buyers prepared to buy; sometimes the sale would be carried out by public auction in the same way as goods and livestock; sometimes sales were agreed after advertisements seeking buyers or sellers for particular shares had appeared in the press; occasionally sales would take place after buyer and seller met, or were introduced, in some social setting; and in many towns and cities there were places, such as coffee houses and inns, where buyers and sellers were known to congregate on certain days and times, introductions might be made, and deals struck more readily – the stock market in London certainly grew up from the business transacted in and around a coffee house in the City, eventually leading to the founding of the Stock Exchange proper.

By the early 1700s the number of companies had expanded dramatically, as had the number of individuals owning shares; expansion in the trading of stocks and shares followed suit with numerous men of business setting themselves up to trade in them either on behalf of others or on their own account. Even so it wasn't until 1801 that the London Stock Exchange, with its rules and regulations, was formally established.

As a result of the South Sea Bubble of the early eighteenth century (when the number of joint-stock companies virtually doubled, the price of shares rose enormously as would-be investors clamoured for a chance to share in the promised great profits, before falling dramatically on the realisation that not all could make the massive profits they were predicting) the Bubble Act of 1720 was passed prohibiting the formation of joint-stock companies in England except when authorised by Act of Parliament. For the next century-and-a-half this would effectively limit the creation of companies to those undertakings of public utility requiring a large capital outlay that would warrant the cost of approaching Parliament, and that could satisfy the requirements of both the legislators and investors as to their worthiness. During the latter part of the eighteenth century the majority of such companies were those of the canals – hence their predominance on the Stock Exchange in the early days.

Any free market for the sale and purchase of goods or services (or shares) will naturally operate under certain basic economic principles. Economic theorists have attempted to explain the operation of economic systems by means of various observed 'laws'. In the context of the market for stocks and shares the principal driver is the law of supply and demand.

At its simplest level if the supply of something is restricted its price will tend to rise, all else being equal, as there will be more people able and willing to purchase than are able and willing to sell; eager purchasers will offer more money to ensure that they get what they want or need and sellers will naturally seek the best price for their wares. Conversely if there is an abundance and few willing or able to purchase then the price will fall; purchasers can shop around for the best deal and sellers will have to accept lower prices if they are to make a sale at all. A similar, converse, scenario exists with regard to demand when all else is equal; more people able or willing to purchase and the price goes up; less, the price goes down.

Extrapolating from this, it can be seen that new supplies of stocks and shares (i.e. new companies) will affect prices, either pushing them down or preventing them from rising as they otherwise might have done, and an influx of new prospective shareholders with cash to invest will cause prices to rise as they all chase the same available shares. For existing companies good news, such as increased profits and dividends, will increase demand for their stock and therefore the share price; bad news such as falling profits and dividends will depress demand and thereby the share price. An established and well-regulated stock exchange is one of the best markets in which to see the effects of this operate as prices quickly adjust to balance out the levels of supply and demand so that trade continues.

The effect of supply and demand is fundamental to the operation of the London Stock Exchange and in explaining how railways came to dominate and maintain their position for so long. The basic fact is that, for a large part of the nineteenth century at least, the volume of railway company shares available simply far outweighed the total of all the other types available on the Stock Exchange. But even this simple statement belies the underlying truth that, without there being the necessary demand, companies issuing shares and thereby the supply of shares, and in turn the financing and construction of the physical railways, just could not and would not have come about.

## What Caused Railways To Dominate?

### a) Government

PROBABLY the UK Government's greatest contribution to the development of the railways and their financial dominance on the Stock Exchange came from its doing nothing. Unlike in France, for example, there was no attempt by government to plan the railway network centrally, lines were built as individual companies were formed and raised sufficient capital to do so, always in the belief that the free market and competition would ensure the best results. Ultimately supply and demand would be allowed to determine the development of the railway network in Britain. As a result of this *laissez faire* attitude many more lines were proposed than could ever be economically built, some were put forward in direct competition to others in an attempt to divert away some of the profits, some were mere pipe dreams of unrealistic magnitude, whilst others had merit but still had to prove their worth and fight those who resisted them for whatever reason.

Government, like everybody involved in promoting investment in the first railways, anticipated that they would be profitable, too profitable and almost monopolistic. Most enabling Acts therefore carried a stipulation that the company could not pay a dividend in excess of 10 per cent, or at least not without first cutting fares. This attitude, and the very inclusion of the clause in the Acts, no doubt unintentionally stimulated a great deal of demand for railway investment; the government appeared to be saying that returns in excess of 10 per cent were achievable, a fact which more than one company seized upon and made great play of in their promotion.

In the first dozen years of railway construction there was an unprecedented demand to build lines, a veritable railway mania, and in 1845 the bubble burst and railway share prices crashed from an unsustainable level. The collapse was not dissimilar to that of the South Sea Bubble of 1720, the Internet frenzy a century-and-a-half later, or others both before and since. Everyone who had the funds wanted to invest in the belief that profits and prices would only ever go up; the law of supply and demand dictated that as demand went up so did prices seeming to prove the point and fuelling the mania. New supplies in the form of new, often dubious, companies would appear offering shares to join in the frenzy. The roots soon proved inadequate to support the weight of growth and the crash came causing financial ruin and misery for many.

As a direct consequence Parliament, in its usual way of reacting to events rather than pre-empting them, set up an Advisory Committee under Lord Dalhousie to examine all railway Bills before they came to Parliament in an effort to weed out the unsuitable, unscrupulous and impossible, reduce the amount of time expended by Parliament debating such Bills and, indirectly, restore some confidence in the process of new railway construction. Although earnest in its efforts the committee was overwhelmed with proposals and the arrangement lasted less than a year against the impossible head of steam built up in the world of railway construction. Even the ruin of so many could not dent belief in the benefits of railways and railway investment for long, the demand was just too strong.

In an effort to restrict the demand for railway Acts and lessen some of the pressures on its own operations, Parliament maintained a requirement that more than half the necessary capital be raised before an application for an Act came before them in an attempt to stem the flow of unsuitable and un-financeable schemes. This, and the general manner in which such business was handled in the Palace of Westminster, had its effect on the expansion of the railways with the result that the costs of getting a Bill through Parliament against all the obstacles thrown in its path, for even the most worthy of cases, rose from an already expensive base.

While in the committee stage railway Bills would be challenged on the slightest detail, and by anyone who had the slightest interest, with the lawyers representing the various parties often being the only winners. For example, an Ipswich QC, Charles Austin, recorded that he had earned more working on railway matters in the four years to 1847 than he had in the previous seventeen. For some lines the legal and administrative costs in getting parliamentary approval to proceed would exceed the initial costs of building the line and for others the process exhausted all their funds without ever getting approval, to the ultimate loss of the initial investors. For those who were successful these costs ultimately appeared as part of the capital costs of the company and would thereafter be contained in their stock market valuation, indirectly adding to the cumulative total of railway investment on the Stock Exchange.

The continuing expectation of profitability and apparent near monopoly over long-distance transport enjoyed by the railways led to Parliament considering the nationalisation of railway companies as early as 1844, although the suggestion was that it would only happen after the private investors had had the chance to receive a reasonable return on their investment (say after ten years) – a proposal that was actually supported by a surprising number of railway company directors. Despite the possibility that the state could conceivably take ownership of a railway being public knowledge the demand for shares was never heavily reduced, no doubt the belief that it would either never happen, or that government would have to adequately recompense existing owners if it did, maintained confidence in railway investment.

Notwithstanding this level of government non-interference/interference in the finance and operation of the railways, Parliament's tendency to react strongly to events, and the alarming fluctuation and failures in share prices, railways continued to retain their position as an investment of choice. Indeed pamphlets and publications appeared in the later nineteenth century extolling the virtues of railway investments over government bonds, on the grounds that railways were less risky than governments (for example *Facts And Arguments To Shew That Guaranteed Railway Stock Offers a Better Investment Than Do Government Securities*, John Whitehead, London 1849), and demand continued virtually unabated.

## b) Society

As the railways expanded in the nineteenth century the amount of capital they needed to raise grew dramatically as the scope of work increased, understanding of what was involved improved, and legal and parliamentary costs were factored in. The supply of available investment capital in the country, let alone the immediate geographic area of any proposed line, would soon be exhausted if as in the days of the canals and earliest railways only large industrialists and business magnates were the ones with funds to invest.

The Industrial Revolution over the previous century had brought a new prosperity to many. There was new money in different hands from just the landed aristocracy of earlier times. This new wealth needed a home – there were limited ways in which it could be readily invested outside of the industry or business in which it was first found, but the supply of investment opportunities was limited. Government stocks or depositing with a bank were the usual recipients of this unused capital but these provided limited returns and, in the case of banks, carried the risk that they may fail. Those

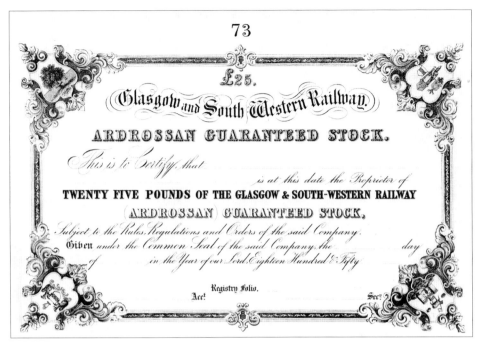

73

£25.

## Glasgow and South Western Railway.

### ARDROSSAN GUARANTEED STOCK.

This is to Certify, that

is at this date the Proprietor of

**TWENTY FIVE POUNDS OF THE GLASGOW & SOUTH-WESTERN RAILWAY**

ARDROSSAN GUARANTEED STOCK,

Subject to the Rules, Regulations and Orders of the said Company.
Given under the Common Seal of the said Company, the     day
of     in the Year of our Lord Eighteen Hundred & Fifty

Registry Folio.
Acc.ᵗ          Sec.ʸ

**Stock certificate**

with money to invest were on the lookout for new ways to put it to use and a whole new industry, one that supported existing businesses in many ways and was, once built, secured on a physical asset, was going to be a prime candidate to receive it.

This new middle class had money they were keen to invest but had limited opportunity to do so. A single share in an existing canal company, the biggest non-government component of the Stock Exchange until railways came to dominate, could change hands for over £1,000 (in excess of £40,000 today) pricing existing investments far out of reach of these new investors. A new railway share could be as little as £25 (£1,000 today) but with perhaps only £1 being paid initially and the rest called up in instalments of £5 or £10 over a number of years. Many railway prospectuses promised minimum periods between each call to reassure prospective investors that they would not have to find the money too quickly.

These new shares in railways were much more attractive to the would-be small investor. In due course the promised dividends would provide an income at rates far above that on offer from government stock or bank deposits. If an investor was unable, or unwilling, to meet the cost of an instalment all was not lost as the share might be sold in its part paid form, possibly at a premium (a profit) in the case of sought-after stocks.

This did lead to speculation on the stock markets, those buying shares with no intention of holding them for long, or even paying the later instalments, but merely in the belief that the price would rise and they could sell them quickly at a profit. During the height of railway mania 'shares' were being sold and bought almost immediately the intention to form a company had been publicised regardless of whether the company being promoted could, or would, ever materialise or had even issued any shares.

So a whole new section of society became shareholders, including widows, spinsters, clergymen, army officers, tradesmen and gentlemen. A new supply of investors and investment money had been found. The railway companies would now have to deal with the sensibilities of a whole new class of less hard-nosed investors. For example, for the first five years of its existence the Liverpool & Manchester Railway's accounts included an entry specifically stating what portion of the profit per share was attributable to Sunday operations, no doubt so that those who had qualms about trade on the Sabbath could make arrangements to dispose of this part of their income as they saw fit.

Not only did the middle classes have money but they were also becoming more confident in the country. The 1832 Reform Act had widened the parliamentary vote to a greater proportion of the populace, including many more of the middle classes, and did away with at least some of the worst abuses of the parliamentary system. By the same measure the manufacturing towns and cities were at last represented in Parliament and so, therefore, were manufacturing – and railway – interests. The ending of the Napoleonic Wars in 1815 meant that the country was once again prospering from international trade and not having to fund the conflict through high taxation. This all contributed to the right environment for railways, and investment, to boom.

Both actions by, and changes in, government and society in the early nineteenth century resulted in railway companies dominating the London Stock Exchange, but the driver was the inter-operation of these with the laws of supply and demand. Throughout the nineteenth century the demand for new lines to be built encouraged the supply of money to invest in them; the supply of profitable railways encouraged demands for more shares to invest in; the demand for funds to invest in railway schemes encouraged the supply of new financial practices – both good and bad. Supply and demand was the line on which the increasing prosperity of railway companies ran.

# How railways were financed

PROMOTION of any new railway company followed a similar pattern to that of the canal companies and other enterprises, either before or after. First merchants, industrialists and other interested parties would identify that a need for improved communication existed between locations and that a railway could be constructed to meet that need. They might join together and, amongst themselves, pay for a survey to establish a suitable route, or they may call a public meeting to seek support and obtain subscriptions towards the cost of such a survey. In due course a definite route and plan would be decided upon, further meetings would be held to sell scrip (a temporary document representing a share in the company to be formed – until the company gets its Act passed by Parliament and is formally incorporated, shares proper cannot be issued).

A committee would be formed for the promotion of the company, and further activity undertaken to sell scrip and take in deposit money. Those subscribing would sign the subscription contract, which Parliament would require before an application could be made for the relevant Act of incorporation. All being well an Act would be obtained authorising the company to go ahead, raise the necessary capital, construct and operate the line. If an Act wasn't obtained, if it was rejected by Parliament or the promoters failed to get an Act before their money ran out, the money deposited by investors and used in surveying, legal and parliamentary expenses would be lost. Despite the risks involved it is amazing how much demand there was for these investments, though the still limited supply of available capital remained a major headache for every company.

The willingness of individuals to invest in a proposed company would be driven by: their desire to see the railway in operation, possibly to the benefit of their existing business interests; their belief that the railway would actually be built, succeed, be profitable and return the promised dividend; the anticipation that there would be a ready market should they need, or want, to sell their shares in the future – the Stock Exchange was therefore pivotal to the success of railway finances.

In establishing a new company of any sort, it is first necessary to bring together those like-minded individuals who can and will contribute either expertise or funds, or both. The gathering together of such disparate groups of people and enticing them to invest hard capital in a new and untried venture requires men of some standing and influence. The early companies regularly relied on the charismatic efforts of company secretaries and chairmen in persuading sufficient quantities of investors to participate in their schemes –

indeed chairmen or secretaries would be appointed as much for their abilities to charm would-be investors as for their business acumen or other characteristics.

In the early days of the railways, especially when their entire concept, design, construction and operation was effectively virgin territory, investors willing to be involved were largely drawn from those men of money who could see a personal business benefit from the promised improved communication link, or had intimate knowledge of the technologies involved, or those with the foresight to understand the possibilities and profits that such works could bring.

Consequently many of the early investors were those with business or personal interests in the immediate vicinity of the proposed line, but they alone could not raise sufficient funds and others had to be recruited. With the early lines being built in the north of England and the capital market (the Stock Exchange) in London it initially fell to those with strong business networks, such as Quaker businessmen, to mobilise the necessary additional capital. Quakers were often to be found involving themselves with the finance and operations of the railways – excluded from the universities, Parliament, the church, and most professions until the latter part of the nineteenth century they actively sought other ways to use their talents and were particularly prominent in industry and innovation.

Known to be men of repute due to their beliefs Quakers could often call on networks of like-minded individuals across the country, many possessed of business wealth, which was invaluable in the days before established finance markets were available to assist in raising money for such large capital projects. Once the first lines were successfully operating interest in investing could be sought further afield, by newspaper advertisement for example; those who had successfully invested in one line were often eager to invest in others as they came along often borrowing against their existing shareholdings in order to do so. But until the first few lines were demonstrating the possibilities it fell to these tireless men to find supplies of finance, generate demand for the investment and champion the cause.

## Financing the first railways

THE Stockton & Darlington Railway was effectively the first modern railway to be financed and constructed – it was the first to provide a level of truly public service using steam locomotives. It had an initial authorised capital of £113,000 (over £6million today) but required more than that before it was fully completed. Unlike earlier track and tramways the S&DR couldn't raise sufficient funds solely from the owners of the collieries and other businesses it would serve; it would require more than they had available or could possibly borrow, and would serve a greater clientele. Similarly the railway was in the north of England and the money markets, such as they were, in London. In order to raise the necessary capital the company required to entice investors from across the country and it fell to the likes of Edward Pease to help pull it all together. Pease was a Quaker banker and businessman who personally put up a sizeable chunk of the funds required to get the necessary Act of Parliament as well as canvassing support from the Quaker community across the country. As a result of this wider involvement in investment whilst the S&DR had many shareholders from its immediate vicinity it also had many from the Quaker heartlands as far away as Westmorland and East Anglia.

The Liverpool & Manchester Railway, the second major railway of the modern age, and the first true inter-city one, had an original authorised capital of £510,000 (equal to over £25million today) and required powers to borrow a further £127,500 before it was completed. A railway between the two cities had been proposed as early as the 1820s as an alternative to the slow and expensive waterways link. One of the first promoters of the line, William James, spent some £150,000 of his own money in trying to get the scheme started but was unsuccessful and ended up imprisoned for bankruptcy. It wasn't until the Mayor of Liverpool, Charles Lawrence, took the reins that this progressed sufficiently for the company to get its necessary Acts of Parliament. It eventually required four separate Acts because of changes in the proposed route and the need to raise additional funds.

After the earlier success of the S&DR raising the necessary capital for a new railway was perhaps a little easier as the concept of a railway was now more demonstrable. Nevertheless it still took the efforts of Quakers such as Joseph Sandes to mobilise the necessary funds from across the country, and even, unusually at this time, a loan from government to complete the work. Once the L&MR was complete and operating as a success further railway enterprises could draw on the established knowledge, both engineering and financial, in promoting their new venture. For some years both Liverpool and Manchester would remain important centres for the raising of new railway capital and railway prospectuses would make a point of stipulating the level of involvement from Mancunian and Liverpudlian investors to show that demand was there and encourage others to participate.

## Railway manias

MENTION has already been made of the stock market bubble caused by railway mania. This was greatly felt in the mid 1840s during which time Parliament authorised Acts for the construction of some 9,000 miles of railway at an expected capital cost of over £500million (half-a-billion, equal to over £22 billion today). Not all these railways would or could be built; there was simply insufficient money available in the country to fund them. This did not stop demand for shares from driving the prices up unsustainably until the inevitable happened: bad harvests and rising food prices resulted in investors selling their shares, demand evaporated and the supply of shares being offered for sale continued to increase dramatically, share prices crashed, the bubble burst, and many were financially ruined.

It was not just the prospect of new companies that drove the mania, the apparent profitability of those already constructed was also driving demand for railway shares, and hence their prices, up to improbable levels. There were many causes for this but the actions of the railway companies' promoters, chairmen and directors, and one in particular, are often held to blame.

George Hudson hailed from Yorkshire, born of farming stock, from humble beginnings rose to be a man of consequence first as a tradesman in York and then, after receiving an inheritance from a distant relative, became a successful investor in railways as well as a local politician and then MP. Using business and accounting practices that were often at best questionable if not outright illegal he was instrumental in the operating success of numerous railway enterprises radiating out from his native York. The formation of the Midland Railway is almost entirely down to his efforts and his involvement was influential in the founding and early success of the Railway Clearing House (enabling the individual railway companies to work together to provide services that crossed between more than one company).

At the height of his success he was hailed as the 'railway king' and his society much sought after. In 1849 when MP for Sunderland and after a bid to defeat the parliamentary Bill for a new line competing with his own companies' interests, Hudson stepped down as chairman of the Eastern Counties Railway. After a subsequent enquiry within the ECR it was discovered that Hudson had been paying dividends not supported by profits but out of the capital itself. Enquiries in the other companies with which Hudson was involved produced a whole catalogue of such goings on though not without difficulty. In most cases there were no accounts to speak of as Hudson had kept all such details in his head employing no auditors saying that 'every shareholder is his own auditor'.

During his reign as 'railway king' demand for shares in any line with which Hudson was involved was on an unprecedented scale, especially with his promises of large 'guaranteed' dividends. Shares in those lines often changed hands at a substantial premium. It was subsequently shown that Hudson was not alone in these dubious accounting and business practices but, when the truth came to light, railway share prices inevitably fell, effectively marking the end of that period of railway mania.

# Banks

IN the nineteenth century, banks were not the large financial institutions that they are today. Earlier bank failures had prompted government to pass legislation restricting their size, if they wanted to issue banknotes, by limiting them to six partners all personally liable for their bank's financial stability and for its losses in case of default. The only joint stock banks permitted until 1826 were those incorporated by either Act of Parliament or Royal Charter such as the Bank of England, Bank of Scotland and Royal Bank of Scotland. After 1826 joint stock banks were permitted but only if they had no office within 65 miles of London.

As a consequence banks' involvement in the finance of the railways was limited but nevertheless the banks and their directors were involved. In many cases company promoters were also bank directors, for example Edward Pease and the S&DR previously mentioned.

Those promoting a railway company would by necessity have to use the services of one or more banks. Due to the fact that the banks' branch networks were not well developed at this time, a different bank would have to be appointed in each of the main centres in which it was hoped to raise capital. Deposits from those subscribing for scrip would be placed with these banks and, from this basis, it was not unknown for a banking relationship to be established resulting in loans being advanced during construction either against the personal guarantee of directors or against security granted by the company against its assets or future receipts. This was easier to arrange when both the bank and the company shared many of the same directors.

Bank successes with railways primarily came when there was some charismatic individual involved in the management of both the bank and the railway. Today we would see this as a conflict of interest but in the nineteenth century such an arrangement was almost essential, and these men frequently acted in a way that served both railway and bank to good effect. One such was George Carr Glyn a partner in the banking house of Glyn, Halifax, Mills & Co. Glyn was a promoter of, involved in raising finance for, and ultimately a director of the London & Birmingham Railway and later became chairman of the LNWR after it had absorbed the L&BR.

Glyn's determination that the railways should be a success resulted in him being heavily influential in the formation of the Railway Clearing House. (The RCH was based on the clearinghouse operated by the banks for cheque payments and in the railway case enabled passengers and goods to travel over the lines operated by different companies for the payment of a single fare, which would be equitably split between the various operators by the RCH). And he was so successful in his work with the bank that it became known in some circles as the 'railway bank', remaining as banker to many railway enterprises through its subsequent guises of Williams & Glyns and then The Royal Bank of Scotland almost to the present day.

The banks by way of loans to railway contractors also indirectly financed railway construction. The contractors would not be paid until such time as the work was completed to the satisfaction of the railway company's engineer but yet still had to pay for materials and labour. This method of operation assisted the railway companies to balance the books when they still had to call in further payments from their shareholders but placed a heavy strain on the contractors, many of whom would be placed in very precarious positions and even go bankrupt unless they had access to bank loans.

Once the railways were up and running, banks would often be asked for, and sometimes grant, loans against the security of shares in existing established companies. These loans were often for the purpose of investing, or speculating, in later share issues. The various reverses of railways share prices over the years demonstrated that this was a risky venture and the more prudent banks became reluctant to enter into this sort of business for fear that they were just financing gambling on railway shares. They recognised that their actions were fuelling the boom and bust of the stock exchanges and causing problems that would rebound by way of later bad debts.

With the reluctance of the normal banks to lend against railway shares new bank-like companies with an appetite for greater risk were formed, in Scotland at least. Called exchange companies, with names such as West of Scotland Exchange Investment Company, Northern Investment Company, and North British Exchange Reversionary and Guarantee Company, these specialised in providing finance against the security of existing shareholdings. However these ventures were relatively short-lived and either succumbed to the fate of the unwary advancing funds against uncertain security and went bankrupt, or were absorbed into the existing joint-stock banks.

The effects of stock market crashes inevitably took their toll on banks that over extended themselves in the new shares. One of the most notable was Overend, Gurney and Company which had grown out of one of the greatest Quaker banking dynasties and had made a name for itself successfully discounting bills of exchange. Its success was such that for a time it was known as the 'bankers bank', even helping to bail out other banks during the crash of the 1840s when the Bank of England was unable to do so. The lure of profits from railway business proved too much, the bank massively over-extended itself and eventually collapsed owing millions in 1866. The effect of the crash was felt throughout the economy with many businesses and other banks also failing as a result.

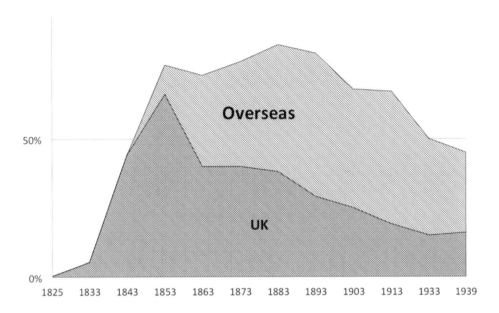

**Railway stocks on the London Stock Exchange**
**UK and overseas company value as a percentage of total exchange**
**(cumulative)**

Demand for funds to reinvest in railway shares led to new supply routes being found but the general operation of supply and demand meant that over-supply of unfounded money inevitably led to disaster when external factors dented demand and prices fell.

## Foreign railways

As well as exporting the expertise in railway construction, and locomotives and other hardware, Britain also exported the knowledge of how to finance railways. British engineers and businessmen often supplied this foreign demand for railways and financing expertise; their knowledge and experience was much sought after. It's therefore unsurprising that the London Stock Exchange soon became a place to trade in overseas railway shares and for these foreign railway companies to raise money for their construction and expansion.

Railways as far apart as Europe, India (where the routes were dictated by government although financed by private means), America and much of the British Empire all sought capital by way of the London Exchange. This is so much the case that, although railway stocks continued to account for over half the value of the London Stock Exchange until the late 1930s, from the 1880s onwards overseas railways accounted for more than half of the value of railway stocks quoted on the Exchange *(see figure above)*.

This involvement in international railways, coupled with links to Empire and comparative political stability in the country would all lead to the London Stock Exchange becoming predominant as an international finance centre.

## Lasting effects

IN the same way that railways drove innovation and change in industrial processes, mechanical and civil engineering, the need to finance them and service the growing ranks of the shareholding public resulted in innovation and change in the realm of finance and the operations of the stock exchanges.

To begin with the London Stock Exchange was of limited value to those investors in the north of England, the merchants of Liverpool and Manchester for example, wanting to effect a trade in the shares they held. To sell or buy shares in the Exchange required the personal presence of both buyer and seller, or the presence of a trusted and authorised agent. In the best tradition of supply and demand the need for a means to trade in shares without the bother and expense of going to London resulted in numerous regional stock exchanges being established in places such as Liverpool, Manchester, Newcastle, Edinburgh, Glasgow and Aberdeen. Principally they would trade in shares of local companies. With the plethora of railway companies springing up around the country it was often the desire to trade in their shares that drove the formation of these exchanges.

As the railways physically connected up the country they were also involved in improving other communications, either by helping to speed up the postal service or their early involvement in the introduction of the electric telegraph. Now information about share prices and the business operation of the railway companies could be conveyed around the country quickly and efficiently, thereby smoothing the operation of the exchanges. In due course these innovations would result in the demise of the regional stock exchanges as transactions migrated to the London market where better deals could be done, all serving to keep railway shares as a major component.

Newspapers and other publishers also took up the cause of the railway shareholder, no doubt realising the numbers of those involved who would buy their publications. George Bradshaw, publisher of the first consolidated railway timetable for Britain's trains, as well as guides for what could be seen from the railways, also published, annually from 1848, a 'shareholders' guide'. This detailed all domestic railway companies, along with a selection of overseas ones favoured by UK investors, with information about their boards and finances. The guide continued to be published each year until 1923, and the formation of the 'Big Four' railway companies, at which point such a compendious work no doubt ceased to be useful.

Such media attention served to enhance the public appetite for railway investments, and as an unintended consequence amplify the effects of railway manias. Such an interest in the workings of the stock exchanges ensured its success as well as marking the beginning of the financial press we know today.

The effects of railway mania, like that of the South Sea Bubble over a century before, resulted in increased regulation of the railways' investment activities and the market for shares. Many of the rules and regulations of the London Stock Exchange began in this period. Similarly the actions of unscrupulous men, such as George Hudson, directly resulted in changes to company law and accounting practices.

The professional accountancy bodies in the UK all started life in the nineteenth century, the earliest immediately after the revelations about Hudson's dubious accounting arrangements. Similarly the early railway companies struggled to know how to calculate and present certain aspects of financial information to their shareholders, such as how to calculate and explain the necessity to keep back funds from profit to pay for repairs and replacement of the capital infrastructure (what we would call depreciation today), leading to the development and codifying of accounting standards adopted by all.

Like much else in the country the Stock Exchange developed and expanded as a result, whether direct or indirect, of the development and expansion of the railways. Reciprocally the railways, both domestic and overseas, were able to develop and expand as a result of advances and changes in the operation of the London Stock Exchange. Ultimately railways came to account for over half the total value of companies on the London Stock Exchange because railway investment effectively built the Exchange; and equally the work of the Stock Exchange enabled the railways to expand across Britain and much of the world.

# Further reading

Hamilton Ellis, *British Railway History 1830–1876*, George Allen and Unwin Ltd 1954

Henry Grote Lewin, *The Railway Mania and its Aftermath*, David & Charles (revised edition) 1968

Ranald Michie, *The London Stock Exchange – A History*, Oxford University Press 1999

Adrian Vaughan, *Railwaymen Politics & Money – The Great Age of Railways in Britain*, John Murray 1997

# CAMPING HOLIDAYS

CAMPING COACHES · YOUTH HOSTELS · SITES FOR CAMPS

LONDON AND NORTH EASTERN RAILWAY

No. 17 (1938 ISSUE)

# CHAPTER 4

# Railways and the Leisure Revolution

*Philip Scowcroft*

T HE coming of the railways in this country brought about an expansion in leisure opportunities, patterns and activity and further, this was for the generality of the population. Previously only royalty and the monied classes could afford the money and the time to go away on holidays, or even on shorter excursions, and even they had to put up with the delays attendant then on their travel by road, though admittedly by the end of the Napoleonic Wars (1815) this was beginning to improve substantially with more sophisticated vehicles, stronger and better bred coach horses and above all better roads, both in a technical sense and administratively (in 1815 turnpike trusts were at their zenith). Surely it cannot be a coincidence that Bath, having then been a place of resort for the leisured classes for more than a century, saw the first mail coaches? Despite being expensive even by coach standards, and a byword in horsed road transport in several respects, these appeared on the Bath road.

To a degree excursions did take place after 1800 on canals and other inland waterways. It was railways, carrying greater numbers and at less cost and greater speed than road or water transport, which took only a little time in general terms to develop as an aid to leisure activities. This was due to their relative cheapness quite as much as, if not more than, the readiness of access that they brought. This applied particularly to shorter term leisure opportunities, day trips and the like, not least visits to horse-racing and other sporting events, older ones, like cricket and, however much frowned on, prize-fighting, and more recent ones, like football and golf (especially as an English, as against Scottish, sport). We shall look at these in more detail later.

While railways were still a novelty, their own official openings and other railway events, whether of national or more local significance, presented excursion opportunities. Possibly the earliest piece of railway music celebrated an early, maybe the first, railway excursion; this dated from 1831 and was a ballad entitled *Johnny Green's Trip Fro 'Owdam* [Oldham] *To See The Manchester Railway*, the railway of course being the Liverpool & Manchester opened the year before. The trail-blazing excursionists were apparently a party of 150 Manchester area school children.

From that beginning, if 'beginning' it was, the railway excursion took shape as an institution and fairly quickly. One excursion in particular has caught the eye of railway historians, the temperance venture from Leicester to Loughborough in 1841 patronised by 570 teetotallers who paid a shilling (5p), not because it was the first (it was not, by a long chalk) but doubtless because it was organised by Thomas Cook, an iconic name in leisure travel and, not least, leisure rail travel; nor was it the biggest (even before 1841 there were bigger ones). Not only did Cook's 1841 venture have many railway predecessors, which will be exemplified in a moment, but other forms of transport had had their excursions, pre-advertised and at reduced fares, notably the early steamships. Particulars of a number of them have been found on the river Humber in the 1830s and these were doubtless not isolated instances.

As early as 13 April 1840 the Bodmin & Wadebridge Railway, isolated in the far west and a tiny undertaking, organised a macabre excursion to a public execution in Bodmin. For another quite early railway excursion and on a much larger scale, we have to look north of the Border. In 1840 two railway companies joined forces to carry between them 24,000 passengers from Glasgow to Paisley and back, apparently for a race-meeting. Not always were excursions purely for pleasure. The Victorians rarely missed an opportunity to 'improve' themselves and not a few excursions were arranged by mechanics institutions.

In that same year, 1840, Leeds Mechanics Institute organised an outing to Hull, 1,250 passengers cramming into a forty carriage train. It was quite common for such early excursions to be carried in 'monster' trains. Another Leeds–Hull excursion, in 1844, took 6,600 passengers in 240 carriages, hauled by nine locomotives, though the rolling stock in that case was probably split between several trains. Around the same period the London & Brighton Railway carried (i.e. from London to Brighton) 1,710 excursionists in forty-six carriages one August Sunday (nevertheless space could not be found for 300 disappointed would-be customers). Gradually, though, excursion trains decreased in size while increasing in frequency.

The *Railway Chronicle* noted in 1844 that railway excursions were 'becoming our chief national amusement'. Observers asked questions about their expediency, not least their social desirability and their perceived power to persuade the poorer classes to waste their money; one wonders also whether the upper- and middle-class inhabitants of Brighton regarded the influx of the 1,710 excursionists mentioned above with much approval.

Such arguments were maybe disingenuous as excursions included provision for first- and second-class passengers as well as those in third and 'fourth' class, the latter travelling in wagons open to the elements; the less poor passengers, quite as much as those of the middle class, going to excursion destinations like Brighton, may not have viewed with pleasure being cheek-by-jowl with those less fortunate.

Others, company shareholders among them, questioned whether excursion trains were profitable, though the companies themselves were to find that question answered in the affirmative; admittedly precise computation of profitability is or was difficult for historians (or observers at the time) as excursion receipts rarely appeared separately in company accounts.

Still others raised safety issues. Substandard, often time-expired, stock was for a long time used for excursion trains, some vehicles having not only no top covers but no buffers either. Yet to generalise on this issue, there were, as we shall see, relatively few serious accidents which overtook excursion trains: Burnley (1852) and Round Oak (1857), notable ones in the early days; Armagh in Northern Ireland (1890), Radstock (1876), on the Somerset & Dorset line (though the S&DR had been a byword for inefficiency and not just in their excursions, before 1876); Welshampton (1897, Cambrian Railways); and Hexthorpe (Doncaster) (1887), where a race special came to grief.

It is a fact that some railways, notably the lordly London & North Western, the self-styled 'Premier Line', did not particularly care for excursions, though they had to bow to the pressure of events and to run a large number of such trains. Speaking generally, the United Kingdom did more for the excursion train than other European countries. This was possibly explained by the higher wages of the working classes and their lower working hours in this country, though there is more than an element of guesswork here. But we can assert with confidence that the excursion train was a peculiarly British institution and was certainly to be boosted by the Bank Holidays Act 1871.

To list excursions in detail from, say 1840, and from every major railway centre, however instructive such an exercise might be, is clearly impossible here for reasons of space and also because the primary sources do not exist in the required volume. The writer has attempted elsewhere to do so for his home town of Doncaster, a growing industrial centre from 1850 onwards.

Doncaster's first railway (GNR) northwards to Askern (Lancashire & York-shire Railway) was opened as late as 1848. The earliest Doncaster excursion

I have so far traced was on 28 June 1850 to Rowsley (for Chatsworth House, Haddon Hall and Bakewell), a joint venture between the Midland and South Yorkshire Railways for which, interestingly and unusually, no third-class fare was quoted. Despite unfavourable weather there were 450 takers, but only a small number of them from Doncaster itself. Later in 1850, advantage was taken of the fact that the Great Northern Railway's route from London via Peterborough, Boston, Lincoln and Retford had just opened to Doncaster and points northwards when a 'grand excursion trip to the metropolis' was advertised by the GNR, allowing four or eight days in London. This started, unusually, from George Hudson's outpost, Whitby (York & North Midland Railway), at 6am and proceeded via York (depart 11.15am) and Doncaster (1pm) to London, reached apparently, at 7.40pm, not bad timing for 1850. Some 640 passengers went (though only forty booked from Doncaster), packed into twenty-four carriages – not quite a 'monster' train like some we have instanced, but quite a long one.

By 1850, railway excursions were well established but their number was soon to be dwarfed by those the following year to view the Great Exhibition in Hyde Park, which opened on 1 May 1851. Every railway became involved during the period of the Exhibition and again the experience of Doncaster is quoted as a sample. In 1851 it was a town of just under 13,000 inhabitants and not then industrial in character. The decision to build the GNR's Plant Works was taken in the same year but it was not established until 1852/53. The direct 'towns route' via Peterborough, Grantham and Newark did not open until 1852 and in 1851 the GNR was still working to London via Lincoln and Boston. It was nevertheless the primary excursion operator, although ready rail access from Doncaster via the South Yorkshire Railway to Swinton (Midland Railway) since 10 November 1849 meant that Doncaster passengers could travel to Euston rather than 'King's Cross' (strictly, Maiden Lane) if they so wished. The first excursion stated by its publicity as affording access to the Exhibition left Wakefield, Pontefract, Knottingley and Doncaster on 30 April, with options to stay in London for four, five, six or eleven days (return could be made on ordinary trains on the appropriate day). Fares quoted were 35*s* (£1.75) first class, 25*s* (£1.25) second class and 16*s* (80p) third class. These were soon reduced drastically as competition hotted up and the frequency of excursion trains increased (not until 2 June 1851 did these depart on every weekday). During June fares came down to 32*s* 6*d* (£1.63) first class, 21*s* (£1.05) second class and 15*s* 6*d* (78p) third class for both GNR and Midland, but these continued to plummet; by the end of July they were 18*s* (90p), 10*s* (50p) and 5*s* (25p), the latter being considered as barely economic as reports from the worried companies pointed out.

By September though, excursion trains were reported to have 'fallen off very considerably' though as the closing date for the Exhibition (on 11 October) approached there was a final upsurge. On 6 October, a Leeds–Maiden Lane GNR excursion had thirty-five carriages 'filled to overflowing'. Also on 6 October two trains from York, thirty-five and eighteen carriages respectively (3,000 passengers in all, 250 of which booked from Doncaster), provided a climax.

The Great Exhibition was an enormous fillip countrywide to rail travel generally and to excursion travel in particular.

For railway excursion opportunities after 1851 and well into the twentieth century Doncaster is again taken as a hopefully representative example. With so many major pre-grouping companies working into and out of Doncaster after mid-century most of them became involved in the excursion business, though the GNR seems to have been the lead player in that respect. Not the only player, though; the Midland had organised excursions which were open to Doncaster folk even before Doncaster itself had a railway station – they had to travel to Swinton by coach or aquabus along the Don Navigation after Swinton station opened in 1840. Many Midland excursions around mid-century and for decades afterwards were organised by Thomas Cook, no less, and these ranged more widely as time went on. Other railways organising excursions from Doncaster included the North Eastern Railway (formed in 1854 by amalgamation), the South Yorkshire Railway, the Manchester Sheffield & Lincolnshire (which absorbed the SYR in 1864 and was restyled Great Central in 1897) and the Lancashire & Yorkshire Railway.

After the junketings of 1851, London remained popular as an excursion venue both generally and ostensibly for specific occasions like the International Exhibition of 1862, in scale almost a repeat of 1851 with third-class ('covered carriages') excursion fares to London again coming down to five shillings. Between 1 May and 31 October 1862 the GNR booked 280,943 extra passengers on its system, compared with 1861. Some single day excursions to London appeared in the portfolios from the 1860s although these set off at the deadly hour of 2.30am and returned late. Seaside excursions soon diversified: to Cleethorpes, in conjunction with the MSLR; to Skegness and, after 1877, Mablethorpe, both by the GNR and both having some preference for Doncaster customers – both places were effectively exclusively GNR resorts and both were a comfortable distance for a day's outing. For the more venturesome there were sundry East Anglian resorts, or Newcastle, Edinburgh and Glasgow.

When the Great Northern/Great Eastern Joint Line opened in 1882, from March to Lincoln and Doncaster, it organised its own Doncaster excursions separately from the GNR. The GNR's Hull and Grimsby excursions, often jointly promoted with the MSLR, had an extension option of steamer trips up the

Yorkshire coast. The whole of the country, plus Scotland, the Isle of Man and Dublin, even the Continent, afforded opportunities.

In 1879 the GNR appointed an excursion agent, O.H. Caygill, late of Thomas Cook's agency, but he was dismissed soon after 'defaulting on his financial obligations' and was replaced by Swan & Leach, a London firm. The appointment of an agent in itself confirms that excursions were now big business for the GNR.

Cultural, sporting and other events frequently presented opportunities for generally shorter range excursions, for example to brass band contests at Boston, Lincoln and elsewhere, especially around 1860 when Doncaster's own Plant Works Band excelled in competition, to festivals such as the Handel Festivals at the Crystal Palace and to other later festivals including that at Morecambe devoted to choirs and to pantomimes at Sheffield, Leeds and Manchester. We shall return to these and also sporting occasions including horse-racing which, in discussing the St Leger excursions, we shall be looking mainly at excursions *to* (rather than *from*) Doncaster, cricket, football (especially after it had become professionalised) and from the 1890s onwards, rugby league.

Not all the town's railway excursions were organised by its half dozen or so railway companies. Other institutions got in on the act: the YMCA, working mens' clubs (which often took their members to Scarborough), Doncaster Cooperative Society, for many years, and a host of smaller organisations, church choirs and the like; many of these would not require a complete train but had their customers travelling at excursion rates on ordinary trains.

The GNR itself annually arranged excursions for its own employees especially at certain holiday times. By no means all excursions traversed long distances. A regular outing to Conisbrough (MSLR) on every Good Friday for nonconformists' gatherings and always well-patronised ran for most of the period from 1860 to 1900. Askern Spa, a scarcely longer 'hop', mileage-wise, (5 miles), was first visited by Doncaster Plant Works schoolchildren in 1855 who were marched to the station, accompanied by the Plant Works Band; on arrival at Askern's Swan Hotel, boys and girls were segregated and then regaled with buns and coffee.

As the end of the nineteenth century approached and the railways themselves expanded, so did both the number and diversity of excursions. But we have no comprehensive figures for those, whether for Doncaster or across the country. For the latter an army of researchers would be needed. Excursion handbills are essentially ephemeral and we can scarcely deduce reliable patterns from those that do survive; and even the local press, which has provided the bulk of the material for the writer's Doncaster excursion writings, did not advertise by any means all the excursions which did take place.

To take 1900 as an example of this, the Doncaster newspapers contain no advertisements of LYR excursions that year (and there were surely some) and practically no GCR ones (and there had been a lot of these back to the days of the SYR in the 1850s). In contrast there are particulars of 255 GNR excursions, exclusive of twenty four from the GN/GE Joint Line. Newspapers do come up with interesting curiosities. One GNR venture from 1898 utilised the metals of the new Lancashire Derbyshire & East Coast Railway for a trip round the Dukeries including a (horsed) coach drive. At this time the Dukeries was a not infrequent and publicly advertised road excursion from Doncaster, first by horse power and later, from 1908, by horse charabanc.

The death of Queen Victoria in January 1901 brought the cancellation of all excursions scheduled for 2 February 1901 but subsequently excursions continued apace and followed a similar pattern as they had done before 1900, until the middle of the new century. The Queen's reign had seen the emergence of the excursion from an occasional feature to an almost everyday occurrence in Doncaster and surely thoughout her realm. Excursions were big business for all British railways, although the GNR did not introduce Sunday excursions until 1904.

The Grouping made little or no difference as such to excursion traffic, whether in Doncaster or generally. Certainly all the railways and perhaps particularly the ever-enterprising LNER continued a full excursion programme after 1922 *(see plate 5)*. But there were other factors coming into play, which affected all railway traffic and not just excursions. The motor coach and private cars (though relatively few yet had them) were more flexible. But as will be seen, excursions to football matches and race-meetings held up well and imaginative new excursion ideas were developed. One or two of the grouped companies invented 'land cruises' in which customers lived and slept on the trains, alighting for excursions (excursions within excursions?) along the route. The GWR was still noted for the variety and inventiveness in the excursion field in the 1930s. In 1932, 56 per cent of its passenger journeys were excursions, etc, 52 per cent in 1937.

In 1938 the LNER ran excursion trains from King's Cross to Cambridge and back, in commemoration of the Railway Races to Scotland in 1895, the trains being made up of stock, like a Stirling 'eight footer' and a rake of six-wheeled carriages, all dating back to that earlier period. Excursions continued into the nationalisation era, though management was less enthusiastic about them, being anxious to reduce the amount of stock kept primarily for excursions and holiday periods in a period of ever-growing competition from motor vehicles. Occasionally interest in excursions flickered up afresh as for example with British Rail's 'Merrymakers' venture in 1971. And continuing enthusiasm for railways as such has meant that enthusiasts' groups often organised their own rail outings and continue to do so to this day.

We pass – for a moment – from railway excursions to the obviously related topic of how the railways affected longer holidays. The two topics shade into one another; as we have seen, not a few excursions, even as early as 1851, and not least to London, allowed a ticket holder to return up to almost a fortnight after the 'start' date. Before 1830 and indeed after, holidays at the seaside and elsewhere were for the well-to-do and, quite as important, for those with time to spare. Seaside holiday resorts in around 1830 included Brighton, beloved of King George IV, Weymouth, ditto of George III, and small ones like Lyme Regis, celebrated in the pages of Jane Austen's *Persuasion*. These were mainly on the South Coast – the East and North-East Coasts being then considerably more remote. There was, of course, Scarborough but it was then a spa town rather than a seaside resort as such. Whitby, primarily a seaport, was later to become an elegant seaside resort with the development of its West Cliff, but before 1836 when the railway reached Whitby, access to and from the town was largely by sea, road contact being at best difficult.

The advent of steamships on the river Thames during the 1820s, written up in the pages of Charles Dickens, boosted Margate, Ramsgate *(see plate 7)* and, to an extent, Southend; in due course, however, the railway brought many more holidaymakers to these resorts than ever before. Often, as in the case of Brighton, the new visitors were often of socially different classes than previously. As regards Weymouth and Lyme Regis, it took decades for them to acquire rail connections, Weymouth in 1857, Lyme Regis even later. However the railways created, directly or indirectly, new resorts in profusion, in some cases from almost nothing. A few were eagerly encouraged by the companies themselves. This was beginning to gather momentum by the 1840s which may be seen as a pivotal period in this respect.

Major examples were Bournemouth, whose Royal Bath Hotel dated from 1838 (though visitor numbers only really took off when improved rail facilities were in place during the 1880s), Eastbourne and, further away from London, Torquay and Blackpool. Specifically 'railway' seaside resorts included several along the East and North-East coasts, previously almost barren as holiday destinations, among them Cleethorpes, virtually a MSLR resort, Skegness *(see plate 9)*, cherished by the GNR, and Saltburn, an enterprise of the pioneer Stockton & Darlington Railway, later absorbed into the NER. East Anglian resorts, possibly leaving out Southend, which for decades was served by river craft along the Thames, similarly emerged during the 1840s with the coming of the railways. Great Yarmouth's first station, Vauxhall, opened in 1844; in 1846, over 80,000 visitors thronged the resort. Others admittedly came later, like Felixstowe, which needed a branch line as so many seaside resorts did, in 1877; Cromer and Sheringham appeared before that but still after the 1840s 'watershed'.

This watershed affected other parts of the country which have not yet been looked at in detail. It was in 1840 that the Preston & Wyre Railway opened a route to Fleetwood which was then viewed partly as a port, partly as a sea bathing resort. The following year Weston-super-Mare became the earliest established resort to which a branch was built off a main line. In 1845 a new line from York to Scarborough brought a re-birth of the latter, previously a relatively little frequented but bracing spa resort, as an equally bracing seaside resort *(see plate 8)*; unfortunately it was too late for Anne Brontë to derive benefit from this in 1849. It was in the years 1846–49 that Blackpool, Southport, Eastbourne and Torquay acquired rail connection.

Of the resorts established by the railways themselves, Silloth, in Cumbria, failed, but – later in the century – Barry (South Wales) flourished, first as a port, then as a resort for the Barry Railway's own employees. Saltburn, the creation of the SDR in 1861, was arguably the most successful, albeit still small, of the directly-created railway resorts, the company building a hotel, assembly rooms, pier and pleasure grounds. Hunstanton (GER, but originally established by the Lynn & Hunstanton Railway) was similarly prosperous if again on a small scale. Other resorts, if not specifically railway creations, developed, among them Whitley Bay (NER), Westgate-on-Sea (SER) and Penarth (Taff Vale Railway), all assisted by ready railway access.

By 1914 almost 200 coastal towns and villages were served by the railway and can be reckoned, to a greater or lesser degree, to be resorts. Brighton was the largest of them, population-wise, especially if we count Hove in with it, dwarfing Bournemouth, Southsea and Blackpool, major resorts though those were.

Combining therapy with amusement, inland spas like Buxton, Malvern, Leamington, Droitwich, Tunbridge Wells and the oldest of them all, Bath, had easy rail connections with Manchester (Buxton), Birmingham (Leamington, Droitwich and Malvern), and London (Bath and Tunbridge Wells). The less wealthy were particularly assisted by railways for short holidays or day outings. Examples are Epping Forest, even though it was not fully opened up by rail as a 'lung' for Londoners until the 1880s. But on Easter Monday 1863, 200,000 were estimated to have visited, even if its rail access was at best indirect and peripheral.

The dales and moors of the north, Derbyshire, Yorkshire and Scotland, were not ignored. Scotland had been early in the field of the railway holiday especially through its short-range holiday and excursion manifestations.

As early as the 1830s resorts along the Clyde were encouraged by the railways. In 1829 the Kilmarnock & Troon Railway was credited with 'making Troon a fashionable sea-bathing town'. A few years later Greenock followed suit. The Highlands had to wait longer.

Before Epping Forest was fully opened up, Londoners were catered for by other short-range holidays and excursions. The London & Greenwich Railway was a pioneer, followed by the London & Southampton (LSWR) and the London & Brighton (LBSCR) Railways. The Newcastle & North Shields Railway (NER) mirrored the experience of the capital's earlier railways in the north-east.

Railways also assisted activity which we can describe as pastimes rather than sport as such, which latter we have still to cover in detail. Walking for pleasure, later called 'rambling' (the Southern Railway published a book *Southern Rambles* in 1930) or 'hiking' started to be catered for in the 1930s; the GWR ran special hikers' trains from Paddington to stations in the Vale of the White Horse, west of Swindon. Cycling dated back to the 1870s; eventually the railways were to help cyclists by conveying the cycles and their owners into the country. In summer 1898, 60,000 cycles were dealt with at Liverpool Street station. In Scotland the Caledonian Railway provided cycle racks in some of its latest rolling stock to preserve the cycles from damage.

Camping coaches – railway carriages converted into living accommodation and parked in sidings or in rural station yards – were holiday opportunities which most railways imaginatively came up with and which appear to have reached their peak in the inter-war years. Few equalled the scenic backdrop of one parked on the Kyle Line in the Scottish Highlands.

Whether for excursions or longer-term holidays, railway companies had to provide facilities for the vastly increased numbers of trains. Llandudno, Blackpool and Weston-super-Mare built dedicated excursion platforms, Scarborough had its Londesborough Road excursion station close to the main station and to the town centre. Brighton had no room (or perhaps no desire?) to provide such facilities but instead lengthened the platforms of its station.

The railways' share of the holiday/excursion/leisure market tended to decline to a degree after 1918, while still remaining very important until after the 1950s, with summer Saturdays then being busy days with services to holiday resorts especially in the South-West, notably Torbay and the 'Cornish Riviera'. But motor transport, public and private, and better roads hastened this decline especially after petrol restrictions had been eased by 1960. Holiday destinations changed too, with the expansion of air transport at reasonable prices. Among other activities within the general excursion topic that remain to claim our attention are sport and culture.

Great Britain has long been reckoned a great sporting country and from the 1830s onwards railways gave a big impetus to various different sporting events. Sport was largely a creation of the nineteenth century, with a few older exceptions like horse-racing, cricket (but only to a limited extent then), prize-fighting and, north of the Border, golf. Even as late as the first third of the nineteenth century, horse-racing was very much an affair for the monied classes because of the cost of transport by road vehicles, whether stage-coaches or privately-owned carriages and the time it took to travel. This was certainly the case with historic courses like Doncaster, Newmarket and Epsom. An important consideration was transporting the competing horses themselves, and this governed the number of appearances each horse could fulfil in the course of a season.

Before looking at horse-racing in the Railway Age, what about the railways' effect on other sports, several of these newly invented or at least (as with football) properly codified? In a few cases some sports, with a degree of professionalism, came along after the railways' first appearance; one thinks of lawn tennis, athletics, rugby, and even the then professionalised Rugby League code. Apart from horse-racing, prize-fighting was the first spectator sport to be helped by the railway's activities. Admittedly by the Railway Age the latter sport was in decline and the subject of moral disapproval despite its aristocratic patronage. The crowds which gathered to see the spectacle were reckoned a potential and sometimes an actual threat to public order. Railway companies ran specials to prize-fights mainly in the South-East and particularly during the 1840s and 1850s until Parliament in 1868 forbade companies to arrange such excursions.

One can sometimes be surprised by the railways' encouragement for lesser, non-professional sports which were not, properly speaking, spectator sports at all. As early as the 1850s there were excursions for anglers to Thorne and other nearby places laid on by the SYR both before and after this company was taken over by the MSLR. Special anglers' tickets were on sale on the Cambrian Railways and by 1900 all important lines were catering for anglers.

Cricket was well-established, albeit on a local level, but it was the railways which caused the game to spread widely beyond the area of its birth in the south-eastern counties during the early to mid-eighteenth century. The great touring XIs, All England, United All England and others which were their offshoots, made their appearance from the late 1840s onwards and which flourished until supplanted by county cricket some 20 years later, were assisted in their countrywide pilgrimages by railways as of course was county cricket in its turn.

Excursions were arranged to important county matches. Even less-important club games were touched by the railway; in 'railway towns' like

Doncaster, club cricket was stimulated by it. The good offices of the Doncaster stationmaster enabled the Doncaster Town XI to travel to Newark, presumably free of charge or at least at a much reduced fee, as this was by goods train, in June 1861. Some railway stations were built to serve major cricket grounds – examples are St John's Wood (Metropolitan Railway) for Lord's, The Oval for the eponymous Surrey club ground (maybe the first station to be called after a major sporting venue) and others serving Old Trafford in Manchester and Trent Bridge in Nottingham.

Even more than cricket, golf was a game for the upper classes, and which until the nineteenth century was largely confined to Scotland where (and when) railway hotels serving golf courses were built, of which Gleneagles *(see plate 6)* was (and is) surely the most celebrated. These later had their counterparts south of the Border, though generally golf, of all the important spectator sports, was least dependant on railways. A number of English courses were served by specially opened stations or halts but generally these were to appear in the later pre-grouping period and were soon closed because travel by road had become so much more convenient after 1920. An example was Bessacarr (Doncaster) Golf Halt on the Doncaster–Lincoln GN/GE line; others included Rickmansworth, Denham and Carpenter's Park.

Rugby, Union and League, and tennis were slower to develop as spectator sports in a big way though Rugby Union offered one great exception to that rule, in the shape of the Five Nations matches (now Six Nations) begun in the 1870s, for which Twickenham (England) and Cardiff Arms Park (Wales, now called the Millennium Stadium) were both excellently served by railways. The All England Club's annual tennis championships, founded in 1877, did not expand vastly as a spectator event until the 1930s. Speedway and greyhound racing emerged as popular, basically working-class sports between the wars.

Compared with football on the one hand and horse-racing on the other, their clienteles were mainly localised and both sports created relatively little business for the railways except maybe for a few major venues mainly in London. But other sports which were hardly spectator events were still touched by the railways like angling, already mentioned, and fox-hunting, which was given a new lease of life by the railways making many hunts more accessible to more people, particularly enthusiasts living in London.

The Olympic Games in 1948 afforded opportunities and challenges for the underground railways in particular as did those of 2012, when special services like 'javelin trains' were devised.

Football, by which its Association code is meant, became formalised from its ultimately medieval origins in the mid-nineteenth century and professionalised by 1880. Once again the railways were vital not only for the clubs themselves to fulfil fixtures often far afield but, and especially so, for spectators which followed and supported those clubs in large numbers. We hear of crowds of 10,000 regularly arriving at White Hart Lane station in London to watch Tottenham Hotspur as early as the 1880s. That station was fitted with specially wide doors to ease the crush and this practice was followed at many stations adjacent to grounds up and down the country. Football supporters were catered for by both ordinary trains and by excursions which were to be an important part of the football scene for maybe a century. Big challenges soon appeared for the railways.

The FA Challenge Cup was first competed for in 1872 and was at first a small affair. Soon, though, professional clubs came to dominate this competition. Furthermore and for a long time, even up to 1940, most of the competing teams in the Finals came from the Midlands and even more so, from further north, rather than from London where the Final was invariably played, and at various venues. A crowd of 110,000 was recorded at the Crystal Palace in 1901 to watch Tottenham Hotspur play Sheffield United, surely the biggest football crowd then assembled in Britain. It did not hold the record, if record it was, for very long. Good rail communications were necessary to handle crowds of such size. While the Cup Final was at Crystal Palace, it was useful to have two stations on hand to serve it (LBSCR and South Eastern & Chatham Railway).

Wembley Stadium was opened, initially for the British Empire Exhibitions of 1923 and 1924 and then for FA Challenge Cup finals and for other sporting occasions like the Rugby League Challenge Cup from 1929, greyhound racing, speedway and, in 1948, some Olympic Games events though the Games had several venues. Wembley's two existing stations were joined by another, Wembley Stadium, for the new venue. The first Wembley FA Cup Final (1923) was attended by maybe 225,000 (although around 100,000 did not go through the turnstiles but entered the ground by irregular means) and this takes no account of many thousands transported thereto by train but, not being able to gain admittance, went back home more or less straightaway.

The logistical achievement of the railways, including Underground ones, on that day was astonishing. Even though numbers allowed in to later finals was by ticket and limited to 100,000, more recently 90,000, Cup Final day was long to be busy for the railways; maybe it is still.

Railway access to the grounds of major League clubs was very important for perhaps a century from 1880 and this brought about one or two interesting sidelights. The GWR leased a stadium to Queen's Park Rangers in 1907 from surplus land. Arsenal moved to a new ground at Highbury in 1913 and its 1930s manager compelled – rather arrogantly, some may think – a change of

## No. 168
# Lancashire and Yorkshire Railway.

# DONCASTER HUNT STEEPLECHASES.

## On TUESDAY and WEDNESDAY, March 1st and 2nd, 1898,
### CHEAP TICKETS (IN CONNECTION WITH FAST EXCURSION)
WILL BE ISSUED TO

# DONCASTER

(BY THE NEW ROUTE VIA HARE PARK), AS UNDER:—

| FROM | Times of Starting EACH DAY. | Fares for the Double Journey, the same day only | |
|---|---|---|---|
| | a.m. | 1st Class | 3rd Class |
| Hollinwood | 9 57 | | |
| Failsworth | 10 0 | | |
| Dean Lane (Newton H'th) | 10 3 | | |
| Miles Platting | 10 6 | | |
| Radcliffe | 9 45 | 6/0 | 3/0 |
| Whitefield | 9 52 | | |
| Prestwich | 9 55 | | |
| Heaton Park | 9 59 | | |
| Crumpsall | 10 2 | | |
| Doncaster ......... arrive | noon 12 0 | | |

*Passengers join Special Train at Victoria Station, Manchester.*

## RETURNING each day from DONCASTER at 5-35 p.m.

IF THE RACES ARE POSTPONED THE EXCURSION TICKETS WILL NOT BE ISSUED.

**Children, above 3 and under 12 years of age, Half-fares. Tickets not transferable, and only available by Trains named.**

### NO LUGGAGE ALLOWED.

Day Excursion Tickets cannot be extended, nor can any allowance be made on return portions not used.

TICKETS, Bills, and all particulars may be obtained at the Stations.

For information as to Excursion Trains apply to Mr. CHAS. J. NICHOLSON, Passenger Superintendent, Victoria Station, Manchester.

Telephone No. 2746. Telegraphic Address: "TRAINS, Manchester."

Manchester, February, 1898. [35471] J. H. STAFFORD, General Manager.

[150-2000] Henry Blacklock & Co. Ltd., Albert Square, Manchester.

name of the Underground station serving the ground from Gillespie Road to 'Arsenal'. West Bromwich Albion's ground (The Hawthorns) was served by its own so-called 'halt' between 1931 and 1968. Wadsley Bridge station, on the Sheffield Victoria to Manchester line (MSLR/GCR/LNER) remained open for the benefit of Sheffield Wednesday's nearby Hillsborough stadium long after this wayside station had been closed for other traffic.

The football excursion became a social institution for almost a century until private car ownership became the norm. Unhappily its last years in the late twentieth century were disfigured by hooliganism and vandalism. The Hull & Barnsley Railway's excursion business, largely based on football, whether Association or Rugby League, was profitable while its 'ordinary' passenger business was not. Football was a sport particularly well suited to the railway, helped by the fact that so many of the grounds were within easy walking distance from a centrally-located railway station.

Horse-racing, maybe this country's oldest sport, dates from the seventeenth century, if not earlier. Until the nineteenth century, going to the races was, for spectators and particularly those coming from a distance, a matter for the richer classes, as we have argued. In any case there were many fewer meetings then because of the difficulties of transporting the horses themselves around the country, often on their own four feet. After the 1830s more courses were established to add to the older ones like Newmarket, Aintree (stager of the Grand National), Epsom (home of the Derby), and Doncaster, whose St Leger is the oldest of the five classic horse races (it dates from 1776 and adopted the St Leger name two years later). Epsom was to have three railway stations primarily dedicated to its race traffic.

Newmarket was racing's headquarters and home of the Jockey Club, which incidentally discouraged race excursionists when these were transported to nearby locations before Newmarket acquired its own railway station in 1848; it was by no means the earliest racecourse to acquire rail connection. That distinction may well have been claimed by Chester in 1840, which, from the start, laid on special facilities for race goers and their railway specials. Apart from Epsom, several other courses acquired their own stations or at least specially assigned platforms. These included Newbury (GWR, rather late in the field, after 1900), Aintree, Cheltenham, Stratford-upon-Avon, Wetherby and York; but not Doncaster, although one was proposed, on the South Yorkshire Joint Railway in 1904 and 1905. Its line skirted, and still skirts, the course on its side away from the town centre, but the GNR, despite being a partner in the SYJR, primarily a coal-carrying line, stamped on the proposal, saying it would reduce its income (and would reflect on its own arrangements in dealing with the race traffic at Doncaster [Central] station). The idea was dropped in April

1907 and perhaps it was as well because substantial infrastructure works and other facilities would have been necessary.

Doncaster is in many ways the most fascinating of all these racecourses in dealing with race traffic. Until 1848 it had no railway station nearer than Swinton – opened in 1840 on the North Midland Railway – and the ranks of the spectators at Doncaster then came for basically just one meeting, the St Leger, in September. For a few years around 1851 a spring meeting emerged, and excursions also ran to that. This and other meetings were permanently added to the calendar and had been swelled by people arriving at Swinton for 8 years from September 1840 and proceeding to Doncaster by coach or by aquabus along the Navigation.

In September race week in 1840 the NMR took over £1,000 more compared with the previous and subsequent weeks, a trend sustained until 1848, when there was at last a Doncaster railway station, opened in fact just in time for the St Leger meeting if only for traffic coming from the north. Even so, six race specials brought 8,000 people in 243 carriages.

More options were available in 1849 as rails to London and stations thereto (via Retford, Lincoln and Boston) were now in place. One special on Leger Day left London (Bishopsgate) at 5.45am, arriving at Doncaster at 12 noon (return was at 5.30pm, scheduled back in London at 11.30pm). Other specials came from Manchester, Liverpool, Leeds, Wakefield, Bradford, Halifax, Huddersfield, Hull, York and Newcastle. In 1850 the GNR ran race specials (to and from London and other places) on every race day of the week (then, Tuesday to Friday) and the LNWR, Midland, LYR, and soon the SYR, chimed in. The *Doncaster Gazette* opined that 'the railways have opened Doncaster races to the masses'.

Crowds grew steadily and urgent arrangements had to be made to cater for them and their trains. A two-platform station, as Doncaster then was, was clearly inadequate both for dealing with the crowds and stabling the excursion stock until it was needed for the return journey. Sidings all round the station, not least the Plant Works sidings (the Works' employees were on holiday, conveniently or indeed deliberately, during the week) were pressed into service. Extra staff were drafted in profusely: policemen, porters, signalmen and so on, not forgetting catering staff to keep the 'extras' fed and watered.

Station alterations in the 1870s were primarily geared to the September influx, as were later ones including those in the 1940s (started in the 1930s and interrupted by the Second World War). Horse specials and special trains for aristocratic parties, like those from Elsecar – a goods station usually but here serving Wentworth Woodhouse for Lord Fitzwilliam's passengers – increased the traffic, though by the first decade of the twentieth century some of the aristocrats were making their way to the races by car. Occasionally there were glitches, or worse, most notably the Hexthorpe disaster on the race Friday in September 1887 when a scheduled MSLR express ran into a stationary Midland race special at Hexthorpe ticket platform killing twenty-five, mainly from the race special, and injuring many more. Perhaps the most amazing fact about this accident was that it took place at 12.15pm but the lines were apparently cleared by 4.30pm the same day for the returning specials.

There is not the space here to outline all developments, but the 1,149 trains – special and scheduled – in 1888 appears to have been a peak in quantity of trains; this may not represent the peak numbers of passengers as trains were in general now becoming longer. In any case the vintage period for race trains lasted at least until 1913.

Refinements, even novelties, were gradually introduced into the arrangements which were a feat of organisation for the GNR: refreshment facilities on some special trains; hugely increased horse traffic by rail handled conveniently and appropriately at Marshgate Cattle Dock; a longer turntable to deal with newer and larger locos; and interchangeability of tickets. From the 1920s alternative means of travelling to the St Leger meeting were developing – private cars, charabancs, even, for the few, aeroplanes – though the railway traffic was still very large. In 1932, some 170 excursions ran in the four race days plus seventy to eighty horse specials; even in the late 1950s the writer remembers being surprised at the numbers of people issuing from the station on race days. The run-up to the St Leger was a busy time for the GNR and later for the LNER and British Railways. As the Plant Works took its annual holiday at that time, deliberately so, excursion trains also ran from Doncaster and almost at the same time. This meant of course that the Plant Works sidings were available for stabling the incoming specials and for them to be supplied with water, even coal, and possibly for some rudimentary cleaning to be carried out to the carriages. Doncaster's wealth of sidings, and not just the Plant ones, meant that Doncaster never had to build a special race station.

Other occasions besides race meetings ensured Doncaster was an excursion focus as well as a jumping-off point. Another sporting event, the town's Air Display, was Britain's first, in October 1909 *(see plate 4)*. This beat Blackpool's event two days later, much to the chagrin, rather gracelessly expressed, of the Lancashire resort and especially of the (Royal) Aero Club which had identified itself with the Blackpool Display. It is interesting to note that both Doncaster and Blackpool had long had plenty of experience in dealing with leisure visitors by rail on a large scale.

It was partly the weather's fault that ensured that the number of visitors at both venues were on a much lesser scale than anticipated and than either was used to. Most Doncaster railway excursion visitors in October 1909, catered for by at least half a dozen different companies, came by ordinary trains; probably only one special train (GNR) was run for the Display. The GNR made elaborate preparations nevertheless; it gave a cup for completion by the aviators and even laid on foreign language speaking at the station; as it turned out all the prizes awarded at the Doncaster meeting were won by French airmen. Another Air Display took place in Doncaster in 1910, not as big but still providing business for Doncaster's railways.

So much for railways and sport. But the related subject of railways and culture is a topic worth mention. 'Culture' here refers to the performing arts rather than the visual arts – in railway terms the latter can point to examples from Turner's *Rain, Steam and Speed* and the lithographs of Bourne, Ackermann and others immortalising the railways of the heroic age and onwards up to the present – and literature, poetry and prose. With railways musical, and especially theatrical, performers and their equipment could get around the country so much more readily than before and their audiences were similarly catered for as they also could now travel from a distance.

A few examples, musical ones, must suffice to illustrate this. The celebrated late nineteenth-century singer Sims Reeves gave a 'farewell concert' (one of many!) in Doncaster and excursions were run from Thorne and Mexborough and other places little more distant and returned when the concert was over. Excursions were run ostensibly to the Handel Commemorations at the Crystal Palace, to brass band competitions and to other musical events. Orchestras and bands became part of the scene at seaside and inland spa resorts – not a few of which were created or encouraged by railways – Bournemouth, Scarborough, Buxton, Hastings and Brighton among them.

As a young man the composer Edward Elgar went to hear orchestral concerts at the Crystal Palace in the 1890s even after he was again living in Malvern. He rose at 6am on Saturday and walked to the station for a 7am train which arrived at Paddington at 11am. An Underground train to Crystal Palace via Victoria allowed him to hear the last part of the rehearsal and then the concert in the afternoon. Returning to Paddington the same way, his train to Malvern enabled him to return home by midnight.

Doncaster Musical Society's conductor between 1900 and 1912, Thomas Brameld, lived in Rawmarsh where he worked for the Parkgate Iron and Steel Company. His rehearsals with the DMS often overran a little but when they did, the Doncaster stationmaster would hold up the departure of the last train to Rawmarsh until he was assured that Brameld was on board! In 1926 the LNER ran a special train for all its (male voice) choirs to give a concert at the Usher Hall in Edinburgh. This started from Liverpool Street and picked up singers *en route* to Waverley.

Railway excursions dating from 1830 were arranged by the Liverpool & Manchester Railway, no less. Other railways and other bodies like mechanics' institutions were quick to follow suit. Excursion destinations had astonishing variety: London most of all, and not only for major events like the Great Exhibition in 1851. Excursion traffic effectively created the seaside holiday, especially for the middle and lower classes, and other types of holiday as well, rambling and cycling ones among them.

The inventiveness of railways in feeding the leisure industry in things like camping coaches and themed excursions was indeed remarkable. Thomas Cook played an important part but others did also. We must not attribute too much to him purely on account of his name. Railways provided leisure opportunities for their own workers at Swindon, Doncaster and other railway towns, and for the workers of other industries (an example is Bass, at Burton-on-Trent, on the Midland Railway but there were many others).

Railways encouraged sport, older ones like horse-racing and many newer ones like football. Many of these newer sports would not have existed without them or at least would have had barely a fraction of their impact. We may debate cause and effect as between railway enterprise and the Bank Holiday Act of 1871; surely the interaction was continuous over a period of half a century, maybe longer.

For a majority of the population excursions were passports to freedom and all the major rail companies did well out of them. They had to work hard to achieve this result as many questioned their social desirability, their viability (because of their cheapness and, particularly later on, the retention of stock specially for the excursion traffic) and their safety. Accidents to excursions and names like Radstock, Hexthorpe and, most of all Armagh, struck an ominous ring for long after they happened but, generally speaking, the initial safety fears proved to be exaggerated. Excursions benefited the lower classes most of all but all areas of society were touched by the railways, even the upper classes not least for its cultural aspects, the encouragement of spa resorts and, to a degree, horse-racing. Railway posters, as old as railways themselves, developed as tools for leisure excursions, even if attractive pictorial posters did not appear on the scene until almost 1900 and even if many latter-day posters promoted aspects of the railways other than excursions. Hardly any aspect of the leisure industry was not influenced by the railway. It is not too much to say that leisure, as a major industry, was created by the railways whose contribution thereto may fairly be described as having brought about a leisure revolution.

*The writer is greatly obliged to Graham Wild for typing services and other assistance in preparing this for publication.*

# Further reading

Relevant articles by the writer, including several with particular reference to excursions to and from Doncaster, have been published in the *Journal of the Railway & Canal Historical Society*:

'Early Railway Excursions from Doncaster', Vol.XXVII (1981), pp.25–30

'Railways and the St Leger', Vol.XXVII (1983), pp.266–276

'Nineteenth Century Rail Excursions from Doncaster', Vol.XXVIII (July 1985), pp.187–196

'Aspects of the LNER Musical Society', No.210 (March 2011), pp.47–49

See also Vol.XXXI (November 1993), pp.185–187, for details of Doncaster's 1909 Air Display and its relation to the railways.

Apart from these sources the following can be mentioned:

Bill Crosbie-Hill, 'Great Western Railway Excursions in the 1930s', in *Journal of the R&CHS*, No.214, July 2012, pp.7–15

Lorna Frost, *Railway Posters*, 2012

T. Mason, *Association Football and English Society 1863–1915*, 1981

J.A.R. Pimlott, *The Englishman's Holiday*, 1947

Philip L. Scowcroft, *Cricket in Doncaster and District: An Outline Survey*, 1985

Philip L. Scowcroft, *Lines to Doncaster*, 1986

Philip L. Scowcroft, *Packet Boats from Thorne 1809–1860*, Thorne Local History Occasional Paper No.19, 1995

Jack Simmons, *The Victorian Railway*, 1991. Especially chapters 12 and 13

David St John Thomas, *Railway Season*, 2011. Especially pp.79–91, 'Excursion'; pp.104–115 'Summer Saturdays' and pp.116–123 'Railway Occasions'

J.K. Walton, *The Blackpool Landlady*, 1978

J.K. Walton, *The English Seaside Resort 1750–1914*, 1983

For more information on Bessacarr Golf Halt see the writer's article in the *Bessacarr and Cantley Times*, Issue 18, pp.24–28

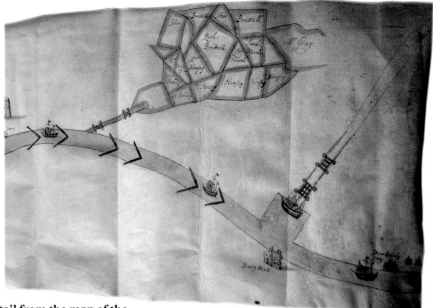

Plate 1: Detail from the map of the Stour Navigation (of 1660s and 1670s). This shows two railways (called 'footrayles') near Stourbridge, running from collieries on Pensnett Chase and at Brettell down to the river Stour at Amblecote. The map was probably drawn by Andrew Yarranton, but is highly diagrammatic, with the odd perspective that the wheels on both sides can be seen at once.
Staffordshire Record Office, Aqualate Collection, D(W) 1788/P37/B8, map

Plates 2 and 3: Close-up and general view of archaeological remains of a waggonway at Bersham Furnace near Wrexham. Wrexham Heritage Service

**Plates 4–9:
Railway posters.**
Doncaster Council (top
left) and National
Railway Museum
collection

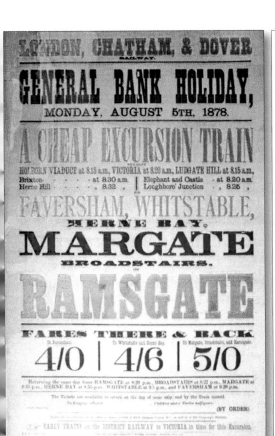

Cheap Week-end, Ten-day and Tourist Tickets
issued to Scarborough (North Eastern Railway) from the
principal stations.

## SKEGNESS IS SO BRACING
### IT'S QUICKER BY RAIL
FREE ILLUSTRATED GUIDE FROM ANY L·N·E·R OFFICE OR AGENCY, OR DEPT. E. TOWN HALL, SKEGNESS

**Plate 10: Private Investment 1**
**The new departure hall at London Kings Cross**
**on Saturday 21 September 2013.**

**Plate 11: Private Investment 2**
**The London Transport station at Harrow-on-the-Hill as a new Metropolitan line S8 unit**
**arrives on a service to Aldgate. Private funding is modernising the Tube.**

**Plate 12:**
Modernisation saw new diesels replace steam traction with undue haste. English Electric Type 3 (Class 37) D6700 in the yard at the NRM in York 2 November 2012 in green 1960s livery.

**Plate 13: A new age of signaling**
Leeds station frames a Northern Rail 'Pacer' Class 142 DMU and modern colour light signal with route indicator.

Plate 14: Competition – Watkin's folly
These days Marylebone does a steady trade as Chiltern Railways
has earned a reputation for being innovative and reliable.

Plates 15-17: Colours & Brands
— First Transpennine unit 185.130 stands at York on its way to Manchester Airport on Saturday 21 September 2013.
— Public owned but still distinctive. East Coast branding applied to Mark IV carriage at Leeds 7 September 2013.
— Guard on Northern Rail. Her uniform matches the colourful interior of this Class 321 EMU. Privatisation has certainly added colour to the railway.

102

Plate 18: Crimple Viaduct,
now an integral part of the north Yorkshire landscape,
near Harrogate, 1984.

Plate 19: Gisburn Tunnel,
built to hide the railway from the drive to Lord Ribblesdale's house
at Gisburne [sic] Park in north Lancashire, 1983.

**Plate 20:**
The station house at County School station, Norfolk, 2010.

**Plate 21: A typically ornate *cottage ornée* design of 1867 at Cemmes Road in North Wales, the station for Cemmaes ¾ miles away. The Cambrian Railway used the Anglicised spelling, in contrast to the little Mawddwy Railway's station close to the village, 1965.**

# CHAPTER 5

# Railways and Towns

## *Tony Kirby*

IN the early Spring of 1887, William Morris visited Peterborough:

> You travel by railway, get to your dull hotel by night, get up in
> the morning and breakfast in company with one or two men of the
> usual middle-class types, who even as they drink their tea and eat
> their eggs … are obviously doing their business to come … You
> go out into the street and wander up it: all about the station,
> and stretching away to the left, is a wilderness of small, dull
> houses built of a sickly-coloured yellow brick pretending to look
> like stone, and not even able to blush a faint brown blush at the
> imposture, and roofed with thin, cold, purple-coloured slates.
> They cry out at you at the first glance, workmen's houses; and a
> kind of instinct of information whispers to you: railway workmen
> and engineers. Bright as the Spring morning is, a kind of sick
> feeling of hopeless disgust comes over you, and you go on further
> … The street betters a little as you go on; shabbyish shops indeed,
> and mean houses of the bourgeoisie of a dull market town,
> exhibiting in their shop fronts a show of goods a trifle below the
> London standard … and above them dull houses, greyish and
> reddish, recalling some associations of the stage-coach days and
> Mr Pickwick and Mr Jingle [and] a greengrocer's shop whose
> country produce probably comes mostly from Covent Garden.

But then, at the end of the street, is:

> a mass of grey stone traceried and carved and moulded into a
> great triple portico beset with pinnacles and spires … that even

without any thought of its history or meaning fills your whole soul with satisfaction.

He is in front of the cathedral. Separated by 'an ancient gate' from the commercial world outside, its only connection with that world seems to be:

the wind from the north-west driving the smoke from the railway-works round the long roof and besmirching it somewhat.

This, he reflects, is what was once Medehamstead, the 'Golden Borough', but now known 'chiefly as a depot of the Great Northern Railway'.

In 1851, the journalist Samuel Sidney (1813–83) in *Rides on the Railways* had been even less complimentary about:

a city without population, without manufactures, without trade, without a good inn or even a copy of *The Times* except at the railway station … and which, by the accident of situation, has had railway greatness thrust upon it in a most extraordinary manner … There is, therefore the best of consolation on being landed in this dull inhospitable city, that it is the easiest possible thing to leave it.

Sidney was a perceptive observer: it was indeed Peterborough's 'accident of situation' that had made it a railway centre, as a natural interchange point between East Anglia and the Midlands and also, following the collapse of earlier schemes for a London–York main line through Cambridge and Lincoln, offering the Great Northern Railway a much easier route to the north than through nearby Stamford, which until then had overshadowed it in commercial importance. In seven years the landscape to the west and south of the city had been transformed. The London & Birmingham was first on the scene with its branch from Blisworth via Northampton in 1845, closely followed by an isolated stretch of the Midland Railway from Stamford in October 1846, and the Eastern Counties Railway from Ely in early 1847. 1848 saw the Stamford line joined to its parent system at Syston, north of Leicester and more significantly the opening of the first section of the Great Northern, the 'Loop Line' from Peterborough to Lincoln via Boston. The GNR's line from London followed in 1850, and with the opening of the 'Towns Line' (today's East Coast mainline through Grantham and Newark) in 1852, the city's basic railway geography was complete, other than for the opening of the Peterborough, Wisbech & Sutton Bridge in 1866 and the LNWR's Wansford–Seaton 'cut-off', shortening the distance to Rugby by 15 miles by avoiding a detour round through Stamford, in 1879. Not surprisingly, it

Peterborough (GN) viewed from the south in 1912, with construction of the new Crescent road bridge to replace the infamous level crossing in progress. Apart from the motive power, the scene is little changed from when William Morris visited the city 25 years earlier, the miserable collection of buildings constituting the passenger station rather overshadowed by the bulk of the Great Northern Hotel. An up coal train headed by an Ivatt 'Long Tom' 0-8-0 starts its journey to London whilst a passenger train – which must be making a lengthy station call – behind a 'Single' stands in Platform 2. The operational inconvenience of the station is evident: the coal train will already have crossed the main line at the north end of the station, on exiting New England yards. Vivacity – Peterborough Museum and Art Gallery

was claimed by the *Peterborough Advertiser* in 1893 that 'if the mass of railway signals, railway engines, railway carriages, railway workshops and railway workers were suddenly removed the city would collapse'.

Peterborough typifies the contrast between 'ancient' and 'modern' that characterised Victorian Britain, a society undergoing a dramatic transformation from rural to urban. What is less typical, though, is the role of the railway in its development as the 'urban hierarchy' – the ranking of towns – had already been profoundly affected by the Industrial Revolution and the coming of the canals which had made the growth of places such as Manchester and Birmingham possible. Britain was already the most urbanised and industrialised country in the world: 20 per cent of the population were town-dwellers in 1801, 48 per cent in 1841. Towns were growing at a phenomenal rate: in the decade 1821–31 the population of Birmingham, Liverpool, Manchester and Leeds grew by 40 per cent, Bradford by 60 per cent. From this it would be possible to argue that the railways were a relatively minor factor in urban growth: but it must be asked (although the question is ultimately unanswerable) whether this rapid expansion could have continued without them. At the very least, there would have been intolerable overcrowding, an exacerbation of an already rapidly-deteriorating urban environment and most importantly a subsistence crisis: the towns could not have been fed.

## Railways and the urban landscape

For various reasons, railways were at best geographically peripheral to many towns. Early railway engineers sought direct routes, avoiding gradients, which meant that many important centres were by-passed. (Northampton and Sheffield are the best-known examples: although both acquired railways relatively early, Sheffield in 1838, Northampton in 1845, these were merely branch lines). Even if a town was on a railway, physical factors could dictate it was at some distance from the existing built-up area: the GWR's Exeter St David's station lay in the valley bottom, between the high ground to the east and the river Exe, as did Nottingham's first station (1839) at Carrington Street; the topography of Cornwall (deeply-incised river valleys) meant that Truro and Liskeard's stations were similarly distant from the town centres.

Other factors could also come into play. Many smaller towns were effectively incidental to the early railway promoters' main purpose, which was to connect major centres. If they were unlucky – the towns off Brunel's GWR mainline, for example, such as Abingdon, Farringdon and Wantage – they were by-passed completely, although in later years they would be equally unlucky not to get a branch line, albeit in many cases too late to prevent stagnation or decline. In Essex, Great Dunmow got its railway in 1869; but its population fell from 2,983 in 1871 to 2,704 in 1901. The damage to such towns' prosperity had already been done, as they had lost out as markets to earlier and better-connected rivals (Bishop's Stortford and Braintree, in Dunmow's case).

Not far away, at Thaxted in 1877 a contemporary noted: 'huge granaries and maltings falling into decay … To such a state of inactivity does 7 miles from a railway station reduce a once thriving borough'.

Once rail-connected, some small towns found a new role as educational centres, their rail connections enabling them to tap at least a regional and often a national market. Some former grammar schools changed their character (and their statutes) to cater for a new largely middle-class clientele, including two not far from Peterborough: Oundle (1556, re-founded by the Grocers' Company 1876) and Uppingham (1584, and transformed under the Rev.

Edward Thring, headmaster from 1853 to 1857). Others were new 'proprietary' schools, such as Marlborough (1843), specifically for the sons of Anglican clergymen, tellingly set up in the Castle Inn – closed as trade had deserted the Bath Road in favour of the GWR.

In larger towns the railway was rarely central, at least initially, either because of the expense of land acquisition or local opposition to the disruption of railway construction or to the very idea of the railway itself. So major cities found themselves ringed by termini. Birmingham had the L&BR at Curzon Street, the MR at Lawley Street, both east of the city centre. Leeds had four stations by mid-century: Marsh Lane to the east (1834), Hunslet to the south (1840), Wellington (1846) and the slightly-misnamed Central (1848) to the west. There were no rail connections between them, which is why small-scale maps of the early railway network are a little misleading: they don't show the gaps. The lack of facilities for interchange also explains why rail freight traffic was so slow to grow in the first 20 years or so of the Railway Age.

Some cities, such as Edinburgh Waverley (1846), did manage early 'central' stations. York even got a station inside the city walls with a well-mannered Tudoresque arch knocked through them by the architect George Townsend Andrews for the York & North Midland's terminus of 1841. It was perhaps a mark of York's relative economic decline in the eighteenth and early nineteenth centuries that space was available: all that had to be moved were a market garden and the city's House of Correction. In other cases, towns had to wait until the inconvenience of the early locations for both local people and – more importantly, perhaps – interchange of traffic between companies became evident and overcame the expense of the necessary property acquisition. Birmingham thus got New Street (MR/LNWR) in 1854, Leeds its New Station ('City' from 1938) (LNWR/NER) in 1869. That these extensions were usually driven through areas of urban decay – and thus gave middle-class passengers a grandstand view of the slums – may have been a significant stimulus to social reform from the 1870s onwards. The older stations, which now found themselves on the end of terminal spurs were rarely abandoned completely, although this could occasionally happen (as with Harrogate Brunswick, for example, in 1862). More usually they were converted to goods depots, as happened to Marsh Lane and Hunslet in Leeds, to Nine Elms in London (1838) when the LSWR extended to Waterloo in 1846, and Manchester's Liverpool Road (1830) replaced by Victoria in 1844. York's original station became a curiously tucked-away group of carriage sidings.

In smaller towns, a similar process can be seen, especially where they lay at the end of a branch line that was subsequently extended to become a through line and the existing built-up area or other obstacles necessitated a deviation. This happened at Sudbury in 1865 and Newmarket in 1851, although here the deviation (caused by the need to tunnel under the racehorse training ground of Warren Hill) was minimal and the original station – with a new low-level island platform added on the through line in 1879 – continued in use until 1902. At Ipswich – and a mark of the poverty of the Eastern Counties Railway – the original terminus of 1846 continued in use until 1860, all trains for the Norwich direction having to reverse out before continuing their journey.

The actual number of stations in a town often reflected company rivalries and relationships: where there was no competition for traffic, companies could happily co-exist, as at Shrewsbury and Aberdeen (another late 'central' scheme where the Joint Station of 1867 replaced Guild Street (1854) and Waterloo Quay (1856), which were 1½ miles apart. Where there was competition, separate stations were almost inevitable, although Cambridge and Carlisle are exceptions to this general rule. In Cambridge, the efforts of the GNR to acquire a more central location were thwarted by opposition from the University, and it had to be content with what was effectively a separate part of the GER station (today's Platform 3).

At Peterborough, both geography and railway politics (the mutual mistrust of the GNR and the other companies serving the city) made a single station impossible. The ECR/GER, MR and LNWR were usually friendly and shared the GER's Peterborough East station, which had an imposing Jacobethan frontage but throughout its existence only two through platforms (unusually separated by only a single line) and a bay. The GNR provided a station of quite staggering architectural insignificance at Peterborough North, again with only two through platforms until a third was added in 1866. A curious feature here was that the Midland ran past the station on the west side and had its own short-lived station, 'Crescent', from 1858 to 1866, whereafter the new third platform was used. In spite of this some Midland trains continued to sail serenely past without stopping until 1966. Connections from the north to east and west were accidental rather than otherwise and for generations of Cambridge students travelling from Yorkshire and beyond a luggage-laden trudge from North to East was a beginning and end-of-term ritual (other than for the handful who enjoyed – or endured – an unhurried progress up or down the 'Joint Line' via Lincoln).

Passengers rarely get the best view of a British town from the train, although there are exceptions, such as from the viaducts at Truro and Durham, approaching Bath from Paddington, or across the Medway from Strood towards Rochester cathedral and castle. Immediately outside the station is rarely much better (Morris's 'shabbyish shops' were only too typical), although again there are exceptions: emerging into Princes Street from Edinburgh Waverley, or the panorama of the city walls at York. In contrast to the Continent, stations rarely provided a new urban focus. There are exceptions, however: Huddersfield had a grand façade and was an integral part of the redevelopment of the town; Liverpool Corporation gave £24,000 to the LNWR for the façade of Lime Street station as part of the St George's Square development, and in the Potteries the NSR built its new central station at Stoke-on-Trent (one of the less important 'Six Towns'), not only an imposing building in itself (it contained the Company's offices) but with a square, housing and a hotel outside, the best bit of planning in a squalid conurbation, and this led to 'Stoke' eventually becoming the official name of the new borough created in 1910.

The layout of towns was already changing before the railways, in response to the growth of road traffic. The building of stations introduced a further variable as they would usually require new access roads, sometimes from the very start: the 'green-field' location of Cambridge meant that Station Road was laid out in 1845. In other cases, they were developed later when existing means of access proved inconvenient: Prince of Wales Road in Norwich, for example, in 1862. Ipswich got two such roads to its new station of 1860: Princess Street from the town centre, and Portman Road from the developing west end of the town. When Newmarket eventually got a new station in 1902, Rous Road was laid out to connect it to the town centre.

The very presence of the railway could alter the character of the townscape, especially with viaducts, as at Durham, Berwick, Truro and Stockport for example, although some major structures could oddly have little impact, as at Wakefield where the 'Ninety-nine Arches' carrying the West Riding & Grimsby over the Calder valley barely impinged. And railways were no respecters of the urban scene or urban archaeology: the earthworks of Huntingdon castle were destroyed, the great hall of Berwick-on-Tweed castle (or what remained of it: the locals had been using it as a quarry of building materials for 100 years) disappeared under the station, as did the medieval Sexton tithe barn at Peterborough. Later in the century, however, the rise of a conservationist lobby was able to protect some important sites, such as Roman Leicester from the Great Central in the 1890s.

The railways could act as a physical barrier, dictating the direction of town growth, as at Peterborough. Before the railway, as in many other medium-sized late-Georgian towns, it had been starting to expand from its medieval core along Cowgate and Thorpe Road, the main approach from the west (expansion to the east was precluded by the impossibility of building on the Fens), with a handful of substantial detached houses and a Regency 'Crescent'. The coming

of the railways cut off western Peterborough from the city proper, access to and fro only being possible by a level crossing (replaced by a bridge in 1913, as a prelude to a remodelling of the track layout that eventually was carried out 60 years later) and thus there was no alternative to expansion north and south, producing the long thin city that is obvious on maps down to the 1970s.

A 'railway quarter' almost invariably developed, even in quite small towns, with housing for workers and pubs and hotels catering especially for commercial travellers. These were not always successful: the Victoria Hotel, Colchester, opened next to the station in 1843, was converted to a hospital for mentally-handicapped children as early as 1850. But usually they became the town's leading hotel, even in Peterborough where the 'Great Northern' (1853) had a uniformly bad press in its early years: the American writer Nathaniel Hawthorne stayed there in May 1857 and wrote (*Passages from English Notebooks*):

> We left Peterborough this afternoon and … were glad to get away
> from the hotel: for although outwardly pretentious, it is a
> wretched and uncomfortable place, with scanty table, poor
> attendance and enormous charges.

Things improved when the GNR took over direct management in the 1860s: Morris merely found it 'dull'. Other visitors may have been disconcerted to find it an integral part of Peterborough's first locomotive shed and workshops.

Railway workers' housing was often – but not always – nearby. The railways offered a substantial new field of employment (for 28,000 people in 1851), much of the workforce being drawn from rural areas, where under-employment had been endemic since the early 1800s as a result of the post-1750 'demographic revolution'. Consequently, towns large and small, faced an influx of workers who had to live within a reasonable distance of the railway. This could mean a considerable change in their social composition, as can be seen in the case of Malton (NR YORKS). Here, railwaymen formed a sizeable

**The tight-knit nature of the medieval city and the physical dominance of the cathedral are apparent, as is the way that growth to the south and west was inhibited by the railways. 'Bright Street', towards the top of the map, is at the southern end of the Peterborough Land Company's development, which parallels the railway northwards towards Millfield and New England. This 1:10 560 OS map dates from the 1930s, but was reproduced for the information of members of BR's Eastern Area Board visiting Peterborough in November 1955, hence the arrows pointing to (from north to south) the switch and crossing works, Peterborough North station and the goods depot.** Crown Copyright new group in the population, especially after the original York–Scarborough line of 1845 was joined by branches to Thirsk and Driffield in 1853 and it became quite an important railway centre. Malton itself – almost entirely controlled by the Fitzwilliam Estate – offered little available housing or building land, and so the railway workers settled in the suburb of Norton, on the East Riding side of the Derwent, which was also where the station was located. Norton was already growing, with both lower middle-class and working-class housing, and its population in 1851 was 2,315, against Malton's 5,346. The railwaymen were an important contributor to further growth, to 3,842 in 1901 (by when Malton had declined to 4,758) and by the 1920s it was bigger than its parent community. The 1881 census records seventy three railway households: interestingly, relatively few railwaymen (seventeen of the seventy three) had been born in the town itself, the majority coming from the surrounding rural area (within a radius of 10 miles or so) and most of the 'locals' were in relatively unskilled jobs (platelayers, labourers and porters), the more skilled workers such as signalmen and engine drivers coming from further afield, especially (and unsurprisingly, on the NER) Northumberland and Durham.

At Peterborough, the GNR went in for housing development on a large scale on the east side of the main line at New England, two miles north of the city, where 'The Barracks', eventually totalling 226 houses were built over a 20-year period from 1853. This reflected the rural location of the yards and locomotive sheds, and the consequent difficulty of recruiting and retaining labour, as Sturrock, the railway's Locomotive Superintendent, pointed out to his Board in early 1853: 'the men employed at the new locomotive shed at Peterborough New England are leaving me in consequence of there not being any cottages near the works for their accommodation'.

In spite of their rather forbidding nickname, these were substantial terraced properties, with gas and water laid on (albeit only one tap for every two houses for the latter, with water probably drawn from the river Nene, which may explain a typhoid outbreak in 1875), and a strict socio-occupational segregation: the higher you were in the company's hierarchy, the further you lived from the yards. A school, largely financed by the GNR, was opened in 1856, a Wesleyan chapel in 1866 and an Anglican church (St Paul's), again largely financed by the company against the wishes of a vociferous body of Nonconformist shareholders in 1869. 'Rational recreation' was encouraged, with a recreation ground being provided in 1892 and substantial areas given over to allotments.

This was unusual: other than in isolated rural areas it was more common for railway companies to rely on private landlords to provide urban housing, and this in fact happened in Peterborough where the GER built only a handful of houses on London Road and the other companies none. Into the breach stepped the Peterborough Land Company, which from the 1860s developed the area between the Lincoln Road and the GNR main line with the 'sickly-coloured yellow brick' terraces that had so appalled William Morris. Liberal in politics, the names it gave the streets are a pantheon of Victorian radical heroes: Bright, Cobden, Cromwell, Russell, Garibaldi and Gladstone.

In Cambridge, similarly, private landlords created a completely new suburb, Romsey Town, after 1850. Literally on 'the wrong side of the tracks', it was isolated from the rest of the town in terms of distance and by a level crossing which reinforced its 'otherness'. 648 railway workers were recorded as living in this area in the 1901 census, and it remained an isolated and self-contained community, with its own shops, schools, church and chapels and culture ('Red Romsey') even after the level crossing was replaced by a bridge in 1889, as until the 1930s the road through it led nowhere other than to fields, a cement works and perhaps significantly the town's isolation hospital. Although 'gentrified' by the late-twentieth century, a mark of the house price inflation that resulted from the 'Cambridge Phenomenon' (the bio-tech revolution) of the period, it retains a sense of fierce local pride and identity even today.

Cattle markets were also often found near the station: although in some towns they had already moved from central locations by the 1840s as a result of public health concerns, and were not prepared to move again. More often they did, as at Leicester, York, Cambridge in 1885 and St Ives (Hunts) the following year. Peterborough, short-sightedly, moved its market to a location just north of the city centre in 1861. This was implemented by a private company, and proved unsuccessful; the Corporation took it over in 1891, but its financial troubles continued. Ironically, vast numbers of cattle (65,000 a year in 1900) actually passed through the city by rail, en route from Holyhead and Birkenhead for fattening on the lush East Norfolk pastures.

## Industrial location

INDUSTRIAL Britain pre-dated the railway, and the industries of the Industrial Revolution had sought canal or riverside locations for either power or transport purposes. For many of these, moving to a rail-side location offered few benefits, especially for industries such as cotton and wool: the usual practice was the railway companies to provide large central warehouses for these.

Where heavy goods were being produced, or bulky raw materials were required, these could still be brought in by water from the nearest railhead (particularly common in the West Midlands). Because railways tended to follow valley routes, some fortunate industrialists might well find that they were adjacent to the railway anyway, and it did not escape the notice of others that there was much to be said for being able to site a new factory convenient for both forms of transport: Sir Titus Salt's giant new alpaca mill at Saltaire (1851) was well-served by the MR on one side and the Leeds & Liverpool Canal on the other, and the Cadburys' Bournville was similarly sited. Others moved: the Fosters, Cambridge millers, transferred their operations from the head of navigation of the river Cam down to the station in the 30 years after 1854, after it became clear that a branch line to this area would not be acceptable to the University, as it 'would result in the destruction, beauty, comfort and benefit of the college walks near the river'. Not surprisingly, it was accused by the Borough Council of: 'wishing to reduce the town to a collection of a few shopkeepers'.

Colmans of Norwich made a similar move from Stoke Holy Cross to Carrow (where they had extensive sidings) in 1856. Rowntrees of York did the same, from Lendal Bridge to Haxby Road, in 1895 and like Colmans had an 'extensive internal rail system.'

New industries – those created after the railways had arrived – tended to rail-side locations from the start, as can be seen in Chelmsford where Hoffmann's ball bearings in 1898 and Marconi in 1912 established themselves on sites bordering the 'Lower Yard'. In Lincolnshire, rail communications were crucial to the location and development of major agricultural engineering concerns: in Lincoln the Stamp End works of Clayton & Shuttleworth were sited between the navigable Witham and the MSLR; in Gainsborough Marshalls, established in 1848, moved to a site near the railway in 1856: by 1904 the works covered 28 acres and employed 3,600 men, transforming the town into essentially a factory community.

The railways also enabled industrial diversification, either because of the facilities for distribution they offered or by providing a reservoir of trained engineering workers. At Peterborough, cycle manufacture and agricultural implement making were established by the 1870s, and in the early-twentieth century it was railways and a supply of skilled workers, plus cheap land, that led two major engineering firms, Baker Perkins and Peter Brotherhood to move here from London in 1904 and 1906 respectively. The real industrial-isation of Peterborough was however due to its location: the growth of the brick industry, geared largely to the London market, following the discovery of the 'Fletton process' c.1880. It expanded very rapidly in the 1890s as metropolitan house-building and public works accelerated; thirty-one yards were in production by 1900, with a capacity of 400 million bricks a year, nearly all located along the GNR main line south of Peterborough (with eastern outliers on the GER at Whittlesey and the M&GN at Dogsthorpe and Eye). 1,000 wagons a day were leaving the various works by the 1920s, and to handle this traffic the LNER provided the two powerful Gresley 'P1' 2-8-2s, 2393/94 in 1925. Allocated to New England throughout their 20-year life, they never perhaps achieved their full potential, as the trains they were capable of hauling were too long for the loops and refuge sidings between Peterborough and Hitchin.

For light industry, employers realised the advantage of the large number of potential women workers available, the wives and daughters of railwaymen. This helped, for example Rowntrees, where by the 1950s wage levels were such that York footplatemen were able to refuse 'lodging turns' as they did not need the extra money: consequently York played surprisingly little part in working East Coast mainline traffic.

## Suburbanisation

SEPARATION of home and workplace was a process that had started in the late eighteenth century, well before the railways, as the middle classes started to desert congested, disorderly and unhealthy town centres for newly-developed residential areas; 'living over the shop', at least for professional men such as bankers and lawyers, had become increasingly rare by the 1840s. The physical distance involved could often be very small, a matter of a few hundred yards: this can be seen in Malton for example, with the development of The Mount and York Road areas in the 1840s with substantial detached or semi-detached houses. From here it was possible to walk to work, which even in larger towns remained the norm for many people: in the 1850s 200,000 people reportedly did so to the City of London. 40 years later, in the Grossmiths' *Diary of a Nobody* (1892) Mr Pooter, although he lives in Holloway ('The Laurels', Brickfield Terrace), next to the GNR main line out of King's Cross, walks or takes the omnibus to his place of work in the City.

However, three of the earliest railways in the London area (the London & Greenwich, the London & Blackwall and London & Croydon) were built specifically for suburban traffic and season tickets were offered by some companies from the earliest days, the first by the Canterbury & Whitstable in 1834 (although one cannot imagine a heavy demand). Most major companies were offering them by the mid-1850s.

There was no automatic correlation between the existence of a railway and suburban development. Many factors came into play, most notably the willing-ness (or otherwise) of landowners to release land for building, the desirability of the location and the attitude of the railway companies. The MR and GWR were notoriously reluctant to provide suburban services and so the suburbs on

117

the main lines out of St Pancras and Paddington were relatively slow to develop. In 1910, Paddington saw only thirteen departures that could be considered 'suburban' between 5pm and 7pm (plus a further four from the Bishop's Road platforms, which had come through from Aldgate): a mark of the up-market Thames Valley clientele is that of those running beyond Southall, two were for Maidenhead, two for Windsor (plus a further slip coach dropped at Slough) and two for Henley. St Pancras had only nine departures in the same period (plus seven from Moorgate) of which only four ran beyond St Albans, and then only to Luton.

The GNR is an interesting case: at first sight it would seem most likely to adopt the same attitude as the MR and GWR, and continued references to the 'suburban incubus' (a phrase first coined by a shareholder in the 1870s) would seem to support this. Certainly in the early days suburban traffic was not envisaged, as there were only seven intermediate stations in the 31¼ miles out to Hitchin. All this changed after the opening of the Northern Heights and Enfield branches in the 1860s, plus a direct link to the City via the 'Widened Lines'. Finchley, for example, got its railway in 1867; in 1871 its population was 7,146 and this grew to 39,419 in 1911. On the main line itself, suburban growth was slower until the inter-war years, when the suburban area extended out to places such as Potter's Bar and Cuffley. After 1950, commuting from Hitchin and Baldock was common and following electrification (in stages from 1979 to 1992) the travel-to-work area now extends as far north as Peterborough and King's Lynn.

By and large, only the larger cities, notably Birmingham, Newcastle, Manchester, Liverpool and Glasgow, could hope to see much in the way of rail-based inner-suburban development, and then sometimes only temporarily until alternative (cheaper and more convenient) forms of transport (electric trams and motor buses, later the private car) came into play, although some smaller towns and cities had a surprisingly comprehensive service: in Aberdeen, for example, two million passengers a year were being carried on the 'subbies' by 1900. The GWR developed suburban services around Plymouth after 1900, using steam rail-motors, with lowered fares and new stations at St Budeaux, Keyham, Ford and Dockyard. Much of this succumbed to road competition in the 1920s, but a frequent service ran to Saltash until the opening of the Tamar road bridge in 1961 made it largely redundant. Equally surprising was Brighton, where the short Kemp Town branch (1869) had a remarkably intensive service of thirty-five trains each way on weekdays (and twenty-five on Sundays) in 1910. Again a victim of bus competition, it closed to passengers on the last day of 1932 (although remaining open for freight until 1971).

London, of course, is exceptional in the scale and variety of its suburbs, from the working-class areas of northeast London, where growth was stimulated by the GER's obligation (under its 1864 Act) to provide cheap workmen's fares as a quid pro quo for the destruction of property caused by its extension to the new Liverpool Street in 1874 (all companies had to offer these under the 1883 Cheap Trains Act), to the middle class areas largely (but not exclusively) south of the Thames, where the railway companies – the LBSCR, LCDR and SER – lacking much in the way of long-distance passenger and heavy freight traffic, were – like the GER – desperate for all the traffic they could get.

A new development of the Railway Age was longer-distance commuting (20–30 miles or more each way) – 'residential traffic' – often from coastal or inland resorts – for the favoured few (mainly wealthy businessmen) who could afford the money and time involved. Examples include Bradford woollen merchants travelling from Morecambe each morning (mirrored by Leeds businessmen commuting from Scarborough); the growth, again within the Leeds/Bradford orbit, of Harrogate, Knaresborough and Ilkley (whose population grew from 1,043 in 1861 to 4,736 in 1881, following the arrival of the MR in 1865) and Hull's mercantile elite settling in Hornsea, Withernsea and Bridlington, all of which by 1912 had fast morning trains to the city and return workings in the evening.

The same trend can be seen south of London in Surrey, Sussex and Kent. Redhill (Surrey) before the railways was little more than a hamlet where the new Brighton road (laid out in 1818 to avoid the previous detour via Reigate) crossed that from Dorking to Sevenoaks, with a scatter of agricultural workers' and squatters' cottages around Redhill Common. The London & Brighton Railway arrived in 1841, the SER's line to Ashford followed in 1842 and the Reading, Guildford & Reigate in 1849. The area round the station grew rapidly with housing for railway workers and the relatively frequent train service and easy availability of building land led to a considerable spread of housing for middle class commuters from the 1860s onwards: in 1876 it was described in James Thorne's *Handbook to the Environs of London* as:

> a populous railway town of hideous brick shops and habitations, and around it a belt of ostentatious villas, comfortable-looking mansions, and tasteful and ornate dwellings of many varieties, with a super-abundance of builders' detached and semi-detached malformations.

By 1891 Redhill had a population of 13,800 and was larger than its older neighbour Reigate, although here also there was substantial – and very select – development after the coming of the railway (names such as Alma Road and Raglan Road give a clue to date).

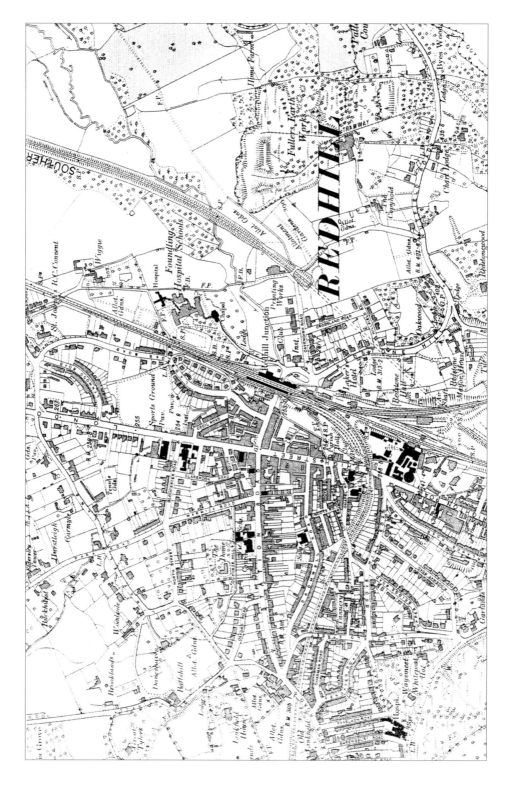

Above all there was 'Metroland', unusual in that it was actually the creation of the Metropolitan Railway which unlike other railway companies found a way of developing its 'surplus lands' without falling foul of the law. The process started with Willesden Green (1880) which had 1,000 tenants by 1885 and a rent-roll of £80,000 a year, Pinner (1900) and Wembley Park (1906); in 1919 Metropolitan Railway Country Estates Ltd was founded to carry the programme forward and had built a further ten estates by 1933. The Metropolitan was joined in its efforts by private landowners, such as Gonville & Caius College, Cambridge, the fortunate possessor of substantial holdings in Rickmansworth, development of which rescued the College's finances from the collapse of agricultural rents in Norfolk, which had been its main source of income, during the post-1875 agricultural depression.

However, railway facilities in themselves would not necessarily lead to suburbanisation if other factors were missing: the GER was spectacularly unlucky here with its Churchbury Loop (Lower Edmonton to Cheshunt), opened in 1891 in the expectation of substantial middle-class housing development which failed to materialise. The few potential passengers which there were evidently preferred the trams and the line was closed in 1909. It was not much more successful with the Fairlop Loop (Ilford to Woodford) of 1903: Hainault station on this was closed due to lack of patronage in 1908, Barkingside in 1917.

The inter-war period was the apogee of rail-based suburban development in the London area, with the construction of the vast LCC estates at St Helier (served by a new SR branch from Wimbledon to Sutton, opened in 1930) and Becontree (1921–34), which was initially badly rail-served, the existing stations on the Tilbury line, particularly Barking, being overwhelmed by traffic until the extension of the District line by London Transport in 1932, with new stations at Upney, Becontree, Heathway and Upminster Bridge.

**Ninety years after the coming of the railway, Redhill has grown into a substantial town. The station ('Redhill Junction') is prominent: it opened in 1844, the Brighton and SER companies originally having separate establishments on their respective lines just off the southern edge of the map. The area around the central crossroads was largely developed by 1860; that in the angle between the Reading line and the Brighton Road, where houses are obviously larger and set in more spacious surroundings, was the work of the National Freehold Land Society from the 1870s. Moving further out, the large detached houses of prosperous commuters are very evident, although Redhill never quite achieved the social cachet of its western neighbour Reigate. To the east runs the LBSCR's 1900 'Quarry Line' (Coulsdon to Earlswood), built to avoid that section of the main line controlled by the rival SER.**

'Southern Electric' also led to the rapid expansion of 'semi-detached London', in Alan Jackson's phrase: 'places such as Purley, Epsom, Leatherhead and Caterham saw very substantial building activity in the inter-war years, aided by the availability of cheap mortgages'. This was curtailed by green-belt legislation (1938), which led to construction of the SR's new Motspur Park – Epsom branch being abandoned south of Chessington. Consequently, post-war development was further out from London, beyond the green-belt limit and towns such as Reigate, Redhill and Horley received a new stimulus to their growth, which continued into the early 21st century: in Redhill large areas of former industrial, quarrying and institutional land on either side of the 'Quarry Line' (avoiding Redhill station) were covered in high-density housing after 1990.

# Ports

PETERBOROUGH, in common with most towns of any size, stood on a navigable river – the Nene. Barges brought in coal, building materials and a variety of other goods and took away local products (mainly agricultural) towards Wisbech and the sea, or upstream to Northampton. Most of this traffic transferred to rail, although this was not an overnight process and in the 1850s and 1860s there was still a considerable amount of rail/water transhipment of coal and fertilisers out to the Fens with agricultural produce in return. The GNR even built a basin near its Nene viaduct, and the LNWR and GER also had wharves at Woodston and outside Peterborough East station respectively, but trade fell away over the years, not least due to the physical deterioration of the Nene and in particular a gravel shoal at Northey, some three miles downstream, which meant there was sometimes only a water depth of six inches at Peterborough. Elsewhere in the Fens, however, barge traffic con-tinued for many years: the GER built docks at Chatteris, Ely and Littleport to enable it to tap areas only easily-accessible by water, and these continued to be of some importance until the improvement of Fenland roads in the Second World War.

Ports proper – those on the coast – had very varying fortunes. Those depending on the coasting trade, such as the string of tiny harbours along the North Norfolk coast, quietly sank into obscurity as their trade disappeared. This possibility was not appreciated by some early railway promoters, who projected lines inland from ports to act effectively as 'mechanised rivers'.

This happened at Ipswich, where the new Wet Dock of 1837–43 was followed by the Ipswich & Bury Railway (1846), an attempt to capture the trade of west Suffolk which had hitherto been channelled through King's Lynn. Lynn itself, at the mouth of the Great Ouse, had been the fulcrum of the mid-Anglian economy for several centuries, with a hinterland stretching to Cambridge, Bedford and beyond. In the Railway Mania local interests promoted lines to Dereham, Bedford (never completed in its entirety) and Wisbech (a similar attempt to Ipswich's to capture the trade of a rival) on the assumption trade would continue in its old channels. It did not: coal imports fell from 242,000 tons in 1848 to 159,000 in 1855, and the population declined from 20,540 in 1851 to 16,700 10 years later. Lynn's salvation was the opening of what eventually became the Eastern & Midlands Railway in 1863–5, the Alexandra Dock in 1869, and a second dock, the Bentinck, in 1883. The E&M gave the MR and GNR (which formally assumed control of the company as the M&GN Joint in 1893) access to an east coast port (particularly important for the former) and so Lynn acquired a new hinterland, exporting manufactured goods and coal from the Midlands. Wisbech, also on the M&GN, failed to develop docks, in spite of several proposals from the 1850s onwards, but even it benefited to some extent, exporting salt from Droitwich for example.

Others were luckier, especially the 'packet ports' where railway companies were prepared to invest heavily: the SER at Folkestone (the Harbour was bought by the railway in 1844), the LBSCR at Newhaven where – under the guise of the Newhaven Harbour Company – financed new deep-water quays in 1878, the GER at Harwich from 1854 (although the physical limitations of the harbour led to the company developing the new port of Parkeston Quay in the 1880s), the GWR at Millbay (Plymouth) and above all the LSWR at Southampton (which it bought outright in 1892).

In the late-eighteenth century the Duke of Bridgewater had famously observed that to be successful a canal had to have 'coal at the heels of it' and the same could be said of ports, the most spectacular successes being those geared to exporting coal. This particularly applied to South Wales, where the railways brought coal from the valleys down to Cardiff initially and later to other ports such as Barry and Newport, and thus contributed to a major shift of the centre of the economic gravity of the region to the coastal plain. In the north-east, West Hartlepool and Blyth were similar. Further south, Hull had been an early pioneer of docks (Queen's 1779, Humber 1809 and Prince's 1829) and more followed quickly after the opening of the Hull & Selby line in 1840: the Railway (1846), Victoria (1850), Albert (1869) and St Andrews (1883). It handled a variety of traffic from the Trent and Ouse basins but its main trade was coal from the West Riding pits.

Perceived unfair treatment by the NER (which allegedly favoured Hartle-pool) led to Hull interests promoting their own line to tap the coalfields, the Hull & Barnsley (authorised 1880, opened 1885). Expensively engineered through the Yorkshire Wolds (the NER already had the best route along the northern shore of the Humber) and serving no major centre of population other than Hull itself, it was a financial failure, not least because it spurred the NER into action, taking over the Hull Dock Company in 1893 and investing heavily in the port's rail facilities, for example quadrupling the main approach from the west (Staddlethorpe–Hessle) in 1903. A rapprochement between the two companies led to their joint involvement in constructing the downstream King George Dock in 1914 and investment continued after the First World War, especially the new mechanised Inwards Yard of 1935.

On the other bank of the Humber was the Great Central's Immingham, authorised in 1904 and opened in 1912, very largely to handle coal exports. The dock itself covered 45 acres, and there were no less than 170 miles of sidings. As it was built in a green-field area, with little local housing, the labour force was drawn from Grimsby, the GCR providing the Grimsby District Electric Railway to ferry them in, a role it continued to fulfil until 1961.

With coal, the railways were simply taking over – and handling more efficiently and in greater volumes – a function that could be performed equally well by inland waterways. But a new type of trade depended completely on the speed of distribution the railways offered: wet fish. Although fish (alive, in tanks) were occasionally transported by road in the early-nineteenth century, most people would only ever eat smoked or dried fish.

Only the railway could carry fresh fish any distance inland, and another form of steam technology, in the shape of trawlers, enabled the rapid expansion of the industry. Most ports had some sort of fish trade, even where there was no direct rail access to the harbour (Scarborough, for example: there were three train paths to York during the herring season in the NER working timetable in 1891), but the trade was dominated by a handful of major centres where the railway was a key player. At Grimsby, the MSLR financed the first fish dock opened in 1856 and revived the fortunes of the port (it had invested £1 million in port facilities by 1870) to the extent that it alone handled 25 per cent of all rail-borne fish in the late-nineteenth century and its population had grown from 8,860 in 1851 to 75,000 by 1901. The LYR similarly invested heavily in Fleetwood, building two docks in 1878 and 1909, and the ECR bought Lowestoft in 1848. It also provided rail access by a street tramway along the quays to the fish market at Great Yarmouth but in a reflection of the hostility of Hull towards Hartlepool, Yarmouth interests always felt that they were being unfairly treated, the ECR (and its successor the Great Eastern) unduly favouring its own port.

The later twentieth century saw the link between ports and railways much weakened, as road transport increasingly took over the railway's role other than for bulk cargoes. The decline in rail traffic was graphically illustrated at Hull: in 1927 the port saw 120 freight train arrivals on a typical weekday; by 1979 there were only seven and by 1992 three. There was some revival of rail traffic from the late 1990s, however, due to coal (and later biomas) imports. Here the Hull & Barnsley Railway eventually came into its own, rail access to the docks being by its high-level line round the north side of the city rather than former NER lines. Immingham handles massive imports of coal and iron ore, and the line from the port to Scunthorpe probably carries the heaviest freight traffic on Network Rail. However, the great success story was the post-1970 container revolution, and nowhere more so than at Felixstowe, Suffolk. A speculative port, seaside resort and branch line venture by a local landowner in the 1880s, it enjoyed a quiet existence until it was able to capitalise on its proximity to Europe, ability to handle large vessels and lack of restrictive labour practices, to become the country's busiest container port by 1990, with about one-third of all containers shipped inland by rail. In 2012 there were twenty nine daily train departures from the port (taxing the single line to the limit of its capacity) and substantial sums were being invested to upgrade the direct rail link to the Midlands via Ely, including raising clearances, a new east to north curve at Ipswich (opened in March 2014), doubling of the Ely–Soham line and a flyover at Nuneaton.

## Railway Towns

RAILWAY towns fall into several categories. Most obvious and best-known are, of course, the engineering centres the railways created to meet their needs for locomotives and rolling stock. The ideal location was the centre of a company's system, although this was not always met in practice, but is exemplified by Swindon (1843) and Crewe (1838), both significantly on green-field sites, although even then the Great Western found it necessary to have major repair shops elsewhere on its system, for example at Wolverhampton (which also built locomotives down to 1908) and Newton Abbot, and the LNWR's Wolverton works (which met the criterion of centrality for its original promoters, the London & Birmingham) retained responsibility for carriage and wagon construction and repair under successive owners down to the present day.

Peterborough could have joined the list: it was the preferred location of Sturrock for the GNR's works (superseding a temporary facility at Boston) and 28 acres of land were bought for the purpose in 1846, but he was over-ruled by dominant Yorkshire interests on the company's board, and Doncaster was chosen instead. Even so, the GNR developed a range of engineering activities at Peterborough, starting with a switch-and-crossing works in 1860 and then, in 1865–66, boiler, turning and coppersmiths' shops at New England, and later

125

in the century, rope and tarpaulin works and sheet stores. The Midland opened locomotive workshops in 1871 and enlarged these in the 1880s to include a foundry and (separate) carriage works at Spital (which survived as a wagon works into the early twenty-first century). There were also, by 1914, nine private wagon repair depots here.

At Doncaster, a new industrial sector was grafted onto a town which until the 1850s was a market and fashionable social centre for the surrounding area, with a degree of architectural elegance that can still be discerned in some parts, but 'The Plant' became the town's major employer, with 4,500 employees by 1900 and covering 200 acres. The same happened at Derby, geographically-central for the Midland Railway, although in this case it was already an important industrial town. In both cases the railway community remained socially, geographically and culturally rather distinct from the life of the established population.

London-based companies tended to have their works in the capital, taking advantage of the reservoir of engineering skills already available: the ECR at Stratford, the LSWR at Nine Elms and the LCDR at Longhedge (Battersea) for example. Lack of space meant that Nine Elms was replaced by a green-field site at Eastleigh after 1891; Longhedge was run down in favour of Ashford (originally developed by the SER in place of its first New Cross works in 1845) following the working union of the LCDR and the SER in 1899, but Stratford remained a major centre until the late-twentieth century.

Mid-nineteenth century amalgamations meant that some companies had several works: the NER for example had York, Gateshead and Darlington by the 1860s, and eventually concentrated construction and major overhauls on the latter, reflecting both its central location and the availability of ample land for expansion. This process of consolidation was carried on after the 1923 Grouping, which saw the down-grading of several smaller companies' works by their new owners, for example the Cambrian's Oswestry, although some – such as Inverurie – survived thanks to their remote geographical position.

The second type of railway town was the operational centre: usually, but not invariably, places where several companies met and traffic exchanged. The earliest example was Normanton, the 'Crewe of the Coalfields', where the North Midland met the Manchester & Leeds and York & North Midland, all opened in 1840. An imposing station (later rebuilt) was provided, adjoined by a station hotel (for many years the 'dining stop' for the Midland's Anglo-Scottish expresses: five courses in half-an-hour!) but Normanton's real importance was for freight traffic and extensive yards were developed by the 1850s and the population grew from 495 in 1851 to 12,352 in 1901. Normanton lost some of its importance after the 1923 Grouping and was badly-hit by the inter-war depression in the mining industry but remained a busy centre until its functions were largely taken over by the new Healey Mills yard on the Calder Valley main line west of Wakefield in 1963. Today all that remains at Normanton is a simple double-track railway and an unstaffed halt.

Peterborough was a classic case, with interchange of east-west traffic between the LNWR, the MR and the GER, and the sorting of north-south coal traffic on the GNR (and some interchange with the other companies): most coal was carried in private-owner wagons, which were the property of either the collieries themselves or individual coal merchants, and thus had to be sorted (both loaded and empty) for their eventual destinations. The logical point to do this was Peterborough, where the land bought for the abortive works proposal developed instead as the Westwood and New England marshalling yards; the other companies interchanged traffic in the extensive yards that grew up at Peterborough East and later at Stanground, in open countryside east of the city on the GE line to March. By 1900, three million tons of coal was passing through Peterborough on the GN from Derbyshire alone and New England had a daily throughput of about 1,500 wagons; a further 1,000 were handed over by the MR to the GER. The GNR had 200 locomotives allocated here, the GER 75, the MR 50 and the LNWR 15.

Other examples include March, after the opening of the GE & GN Joint Line in 1881, where the sprawling Whitemoor complex, extensively remodelled by the LNER, had become the biggest marshalling yard in Western Europe by the 1930s. Other marshalling centres were to be on the outskirts of large cities, due to the availability of land: Leeds was ringed by yards at Neville Hill (NER), Stourton (MR), Ardsley (GNR) and Farnley Junction (LNWR), but here the consequences for urban growth were more limited, the railway community either merging into the broader suburban scene or development being of a village rather than a town character.

The third type of railway town was the industrial. There were relatively few of these, all associated with the iron and steel industry, where the railways played a vital role. The earliest was Consett, County Durham and others include Barrow-in-Furness, the creation of the Furness Railway in the 1850s, and Scunthorpe which grew rapidly from the 1860s. The most spectacular was Middlesbrough, which originated as a port after the Stockton & Darlington Railway realised that Stockton was not the ideal location from which to ship West Durham coal and extended its line to a barren spot further down the Tees in 1830 and built (as the Company of the Proprietors of the Middlesbrough Estate) a small town to go with it.

Unimaginatively laid-out on a simple grid pattern, only a few feet above river level and with a graveyard in the centre it was far cry from the model

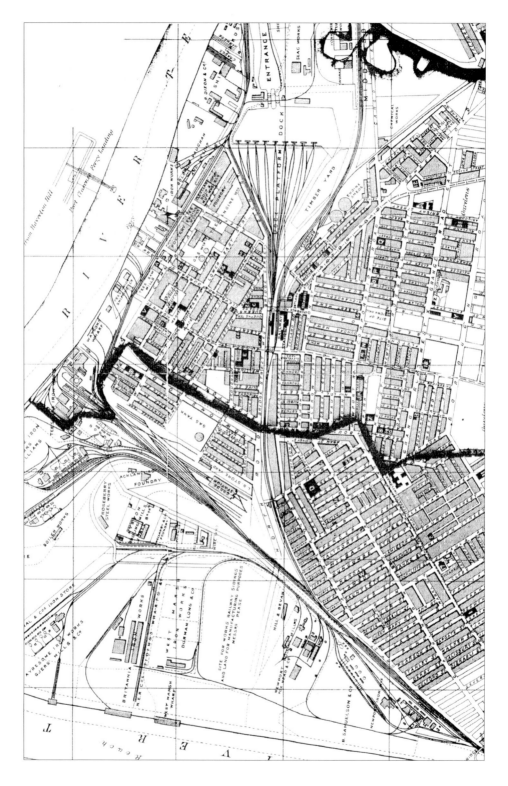

communities being developed by enlightened industrialists elsewhere: the only concession to better living standards was a prohibition on residents killing pigs in the street. It was transformed into 'Ironopolis' by the discovery of workable quantities of ironstone in the nearby Cleveland Hills, which led to the growth of iron (and later steel) works east and west of the town, intimately dependent on the railways to bring in iron ore, coal and limestone. The quantities of coal in particular were immense and led to the NER's electrification of the line from Shildon to Newport in 1915 (de-electrified in 1935).

In the twentieth century few if any new industrial towns were rail-influenced to such an extent, with the exception of Corby (1933): Stewart & Lloyd's new steelworks were built alongside the LMS (and depended on a complex network of industrial lines to bring iron ore to the works), although pre-war Corby was really an industrial village, rather than a new town.

## The eclipse of the railway?

TWENTIETH-CENTURY new towns were dependent on light industry, electrically rather than coal powered and producing consumer goods that were not likely to provide much in the way of rail traffic, although the pioneer – Letchworth Garden City of 1902 – showed what might have been, with a street layout focussed on the station (where the GNR, for about the only time in its existence, came up architectural trumps with a delightful Arts-and-Crafts building) and an industrial area east of the town centre served by a branch from the Hitchin–Cambridge line. The second Garden City, Welwyn (developed after 1919) also had its industrial area firmly set along the East Coast main line, with eleven private sidings (the most important being that of the Shredded Wheat Company) by 1956.

Towards the end of the Second World War, Sir Patrick Abercrombie's *Greater London Plan* (1944) proposed the re-housing of 515,000 people from

In 1830, there was only a solitary farmhouse in the area covered by this map. The S&DR's line to 'Port Darlington' (1830) runs arrow straight from the SW to the banks of the Tees where coal staithes were built. The new town of the Middlesbrough Owners with its strictly-geometrical layout is evident to the south of where these had been. Difficulties with the tidal river led to construction of the Dock in 1842, and the line to these was extended to Redcar in 1846. Subsequent urban development was to the south of the new railway; to the north-west the 'Ironmasters' District' with its complex network of sidings developed in the loop of the Tees from the 1860s onwards. Victorian Middlesbrough famously lacked a middle class (those who could afford it lived further away, at Redcar, Saltburn and Guisborough), and this is reflected in the serried ranks of terrace housing. From 'Middlesbrough's History in Maps' published by the Cleveland & Teesside Local History Society, 1980, and reproduced with their kind permission the metropolis to new towns lying beyond the 1938 Green Belt. This was enthusiastically adopted by the Attlee government, and the first eight were designated under the 1946 New Towns Act. Railway facilities were seemingly not taken greatly into consideration and the New Towns largely turned their backs on the railway, with the possible exception of Harlow where the original industrial areas were placed alongside the railway (although only one of the new firms, United Glass, had a private siding) and a large goods yard laid out; significantly, however, this location was chosen largely because it lay close to the proposed London–Norwich motorway and the town's layout was road-orientated with the new passenger station of Harlow Town (1960) badly sited in relation to both the town centre and the residential areas.

BR seemed curiously reluctant to recognise the existence of the new towns. The very first post-war new town, Stevenage, exemplified this, with its station far from the shopping, residential and industrial areas (although it achieved a brief moment of fame in January 1947, when opponents of the expansion scheme re-named it 'Silkingrad' – a reference to the then Minister for Housing & Local Government – as a publicity stunt), and it was not until 1973 that it was relocated to a more convenient location. Basildon (designated 1949) fared as badly, not getting a station until 1974.

Many of the other new towns and 'overspill' schemes that followed, mainly under the 1952 Town Development Act and subsequent legislation were even worse-served, having no rail passenger facilities at all or losing them at an early date: Haverhill (Essex) at the precise moment it started to grow lost all its rail services in 1967 and Sudbury (Suffolk) – where, as at Haverhill, the new industrial areas were far from the railway – only just managed to retain a passenger service on what was in effect a long dead-end siding from Mark's Tey. Thetford, which saw perhaps the greatest transformation as a result of overspill, remains a busy station, but once again even those factories placed near the railway never acquired direct rail connections.

In all towns, the role of the railway in the early twenty-first century was very different to that of 50 years earlier. Many smaller centres, such as Wisbech and Dereham, and some larger ones such as Hawick and Mansfield, were victims of the Beeching Axe of the 1960s.

Railway workshops have been reduced to a handful, as have marshalling yards, and everywhere the minimal requirements of the modern railway have led to substantial redevelopment of former railway land as shopping centres (Nottingham Victoria) and retail parks (the Riverside shopping centre on the site of Norwich Thorpe goods depot), residential areas (CB1 in Cambridge) or simply car parks. Occasionally former railway lines have been used for new relief or ring roads (as at North Walsham and East Grinstead), although the relatively narrow right of way of even a double track railway has meant this is less common in urban areas than in the countryside.

Peterborough today is very different to the city that Morris saw 125 years ago. Designated as a New Town in 1967, its population has grown from 62,340 (1961) to 183,600 (2011). However, the Great Northern Hotel still stands opposite the rebuilt station, and a walk into the city centre now takes the visitor through the Queensgate shopping centre, where one suspects Morris would have felt even more of a feeling of sick disgust than he did for Gladstone Street and Cromwell Road.

And still the cathedral suddenly reveals itself (although travellers on the main line are more likely to notice the two mosques). It is many years since soots from the railway fell on to the cathedral roof but the city still has a steam presence in the shape of the Nene Valley Railway. And it remains a major rail centre: a new island platform was added in 2014 and although the New England and Westwood yards have largely disappeared the procession of Class 91s and electric and diesel multiple units is still regularly punctuated by the passage of freight trains, although today's flows are of aggregates and containers, not the coal and bricks that were once the lifeblood of the city's railways.

# Further reading

### General works

A. Alexander, *Britain's New Towns: Garden Cities to Sustainable Communities,* London: Routledge, 2009

H. Carter and C.R. Lewis, *An Urban Geography of England and Wales in the Nineteenth Century,* Edward Arnold, London 1990

H.J. Dyos and M. Wolff (eds), *The Victorian City: Image and Realities, Vol. 2,* Routledge, London 1978

M. Girouard, *The English Town,* Yale University Press, London 1990

J.R. Kellett, *The Impact of the Railway on Victorian Cities,* Routledge, London 1969

J. Simmons, *The Railway in Town and Country, 1830–1914,* David & Charles, Newton Abbot 1986

J. Simmons (ed), *Oxford Companion to British Railway History,* Oxford University Press, Oxford 1997

M. Quick, *Railway Passenger Stations in Great Britain: A Chronology,* Railway & Canal Historical Society, Oxford 4th ed. 2009

### Works on towns and areas mentioned in the text

T.M. Cunningham, 'Factors influencing the growth of Peterborough, 1850–1900', *Northamptonshire Past & Present,* Vol. 5, part 5, 1977 pp.427–436

R. Dane, *Railways of Peterborough,* Greater Peterborough Arts Council, Peterborough 1978

W. Fawcett, *A History of the York – Scarborough Railway,* Hutton Press, Beverley 1995 (for discussion of Malton as a railway centre)

W. Fawcett, *A History of* NER *Architecture, Vol. 3: Bell and Beyond,* North Eastern Railway Association, 2005 (for NER housing)

R. Griffiths and J. Hooper, *Great Northern Engine Sheds, Vol. 1: Southern Area,* Irwell Press, Pinner 1989 (detailed history of the New England complex)

A.A. Jackson, *London's Local Railways,* Capital Transport, Harrow Weald 1999

A.A. Jackson, *The Railway in Surrey,* Atlantic, Penryn 1999 (for Redhill)

P. Kay, *The London, Tilbury & Southend Railway: A History of the Company and Line, Vol. 3: 1912–1939,* The Author, Wivenhoe 2010 (construction and development of Becontree)

P.K. King and D.R. Hewins, *The Railways around Grimsby, Cleethorpes, Immingham and North-East Lincolnshire,* Foxline, Stockport 1988

W. Morris, 'Art and Industry in the Fourteenth Century: a lecture delivered to the Socialist League at Kelmscott House, Hammersmith, 15 May 1887' (for his visit to Peterborough earlier in the year)

M. Nicholson and W.B. Yeadon, *An Illustrated History of Hull's Railways,* Irwell Press, Oldham 1993

D. St John Thomas, *West Country Railway History,* David & Charles, Newton Abbot 1981 (for Plymouth suburban traffic)

N.R. Wright, *Lincolnshire Towns and Industry, 1700–1914 (A History of Lincolnshire, Vol. XI),* History of Lincolnshire Committee, Lincoln 1982 (for urban growth in general, and the development of agricultural engineering)

W.B. Yeadon, *More Illustrated History of Hull's Railways,* Challenger, Oldham 1995

J.N. Young, *Great Northern Suburban,* David & Charles, Newton Abbot 1977

Investigation of the impact of the railway on Victorian towns, and especially the smaller ones that have tended to escape the attention of railway historians, has been made immensely easier by Alan Godfrey's reprints of 25" Ordnance Survey maps from the 1870s to the 1930s. A catalogue is available from Alan Godfrey Maps, Prospect Business Park, Leadgate, Consett, Co. Durham DH8 7PW, or on-line at www.alangodfreymaps.co.uk

# CHAPTER 6

# Railway Regulation

## The changing relationship between Government and Railways

### *Andy Brown*

RAILWAYS were capital intensive enterprises, heralds of modern big business. Railways' commercial challenges were instrumental in the evolution of management methods, but also they brought forth new challenges which influenced the development of what might be called industrial policy. These challenges included network planning in the construction phase; the industry's tendency towards monopoly; safety in operation and the impact of railways on the wider commercial and social environment.

The role of the state has often been debated in these contexts and although economic theorists have suggested universal economic laws, it is the case that government policy responses to them have differed by geography. In Belgium railways were a state enterprise at their outset, while in France the state became engaged as quickly as it could afford to, whereas in America and Britain (less so Ireland) the state stood aloof far longer. American sociologist Frank Dobbin has suggested that the main reason for these differences is socio-cultural; the state solves similar problems in the same ways over time.

In Britain authority had tended to be allocated to elite individuals who were protected by Parliament from their neighbours, bureaucracy and the Crown. As the industrial revolution progressed the equivalent notions were achieved through *laissez-faire*, then through gradual progressive regulation culminating in nationalisation, albeit the public corporation model protected commercial interests from excessive state control, before almost turning full circle with privatisation. Railway policy has been influenced by these notions, and yet it might be argued that government often has managed to do the wrong thing at the wrong time.

# Early Days (1830–1870)

RAILWAY beginnings coincided with Britain's economic hegemony. *Laissez-faire's* ideological dominance was cemented by a commercial success predicated on small firms' entrepreneurship and endeavour. Government should not interfere. 'The market was an arena in which God spoke directly to many people and so played a constitutive part in what Peel called "the great scheme of human redemption".' *

It was not that the British government chose not to plan its railway network, planning was never considered. The socio-cultural norm of turnpikes and canals built by market forces continued, entrepreneurs who could convince investors of their scheme's viability might petition Parliament for consent. Parliament (not the state as it was the Private Bill procedure) should not unreasonably withhold support, but it needed to approve land appropriation and had to be satisfied as to financial propriety to bestow limited liability status on the project.

This was the procedure for railways. Indeed, Parliament wrongly assumed that railways, like canals and turnpikes, would charge tolls to private carriers to use their way: practical safety issues demonstrated otherwise. Early railway enabling Acts specified maximum tariffs for using the line, actually recognising the risk of monopoly, but ignored handling, storage and cartage. This and the proliferation of different terms in various enabling Acts sowed the seeds of discontent which would be a spur for government intervention.

The success of the Liverpool & Manchester Railway encouraged imitation. The early to mid 1830s saw a number of mainline schemes including the London & Birmingham, and the Great Western to Bristol, approved and built. In 1839 a Parliamentary Select Committee accepted that railway companies required a monopoly of train movement. The Committee's findings influenced the Railway Regulation Act (1840).

This required the Board of Trade to receive reports on accidents and collect traffic statistics. It established the principal of railway inspection pre-opening to ensure safety and adherence to the enabling Act but also after serious accidents. The Board's response was to create the Railway Department. The Railway Regulation Act (1842), introduced by Gladstone, then youthful

* Boyd Hilton, *A Mad, Bad & Dangerous People? England 1783–1846*, 2006, p.326

** Jack Simmons & Gordon Biddle (eds), *The Oxford Companion to British Railway History*, 1997, p.430

† 'Fifth Report from Select Committee on Railways', Parliamentary Papers (PP), 24 May 1844, p.i

Conservative Vice-President of the Board of Trade under Peel, empowered the Board to delay the opening of unsafe lines and obtain greater details following accidents. Railways and their inspectors learned by experience. Early railway safety relied upon time intervals and simple signalling operated by railway policemen and separate pointsmen. Brakes on trains were rudimentary. Traffic was light and speeds slow enough for these basic practices to work. Free-market safety policy was to inspect, publish and embarrass: informed passengers might avoid unsafe railways, while companies would improve safety to retain custom.

> The single greatest force in railway safety has been the Railway
> Inspectorate. Set up under an Act of 1840 ... the inspectorate
> was never given comprehensive powers and the legislative
> framework was patchy. Much of what was gained was
> accomplished by a combination of tact, diplomacy and
> persistence.★★

The economy improved mid-1840s re-igniting line-building into Railway Mania mid-decade. Parliamentary recognition of railway monopoly and the emergence of mergers, especially the creation of the Midland (1844), were beginning to cause concerns. Gladstone was appointed chairman of a Select Committee in 1844 tasked with identifying 'any arrangements advantageous to the public with regards to existing railway companies generally'.† Its recommendations formed the basis of the Regulation of Railways Act (1844), the most significant government measure in this period. The Act achieved two key measures: it introduced Parliamentary Trains and contained powers for the state in the future to assume ownership of railways. Procedural changes accompanying it also introduced a new concept, Equivalents, which was a short-lived but sophisticated counter to monopoly.

Parliamentary Trains set standards: fares at 1d per mile, speed, safety and comfort for third-class travel: companies were encouraged to adopt these in exchange for exemptions from Passenger Duty. Many railways had poor third-class provision, services were slow, inconvenient and their vehicles resembled goods wagons. Britain in the early 1830s was a troubled place: prolonged economic difficulties after the Napoleonic Wars (with the poor expected to return to their home parishes for assistance), the clamour for electoral reform (Chartism) in urban areas and Captain Swing disturbances in rural areas combined to dissuade elite groups from any notion of promoting mass mobility. Railway companies were chasing the carriage trade and stagecoach users, not the poor. Gladstone's measure changed this. His social policy was reinvigorated by the provision of workmen's services after the Cheap Trains

Act of 1883 exempted all '1*d* per mile' fares from the government's Passenger Duty. Railways after 1850 also saw potential in third-class excursion traffic.

In 1844 the examples of the Midland Counties and Birmingham & Derby Junction railways and a spate of legal cases involving carriers like Pickfords demonstrated the potential for monopoly. Gladstone, supported by the intellectually able Samuel Laing (then senior clerk at the Railway Department), developed two remarkable measures. Firstly, legislation enabling the state to purchase railway lines 21 years hence if they were making excessive profits: this when belief in free-markets and small government was all but universal. Secondly, came Equivalents, an administrative device designed to weaken the monopoly position of any incumbent company. It recognised the futility and wasted capital created by competing lines and allowed the incumbent to protect itself from this folly by agreeing new lower tariffs with the Board. The public might receive benefits permanently; equivalent to the effect of competition, rather than just benefiting from a fleeting price war.

The elegance of Gladstone's policy is often overlooked because railway interests neutralised it. Gladstone faced off to George Hudson when the Railway King had just taken his throne. Hudson and the companies weakened the state-purchase proposals by ensuring they applied only to lines built after 1844 and the compensation that might be due to shareholders under such arrangements was set both high enough and ambiguously enough to deter implementation.

Equivalents was not part of the 1844 Act and opposition was more subtle. Rumour played its part. It was alleged (without foundation) that staff at the Railway Department could use to their personal advantage knowledge of their recommendations prior to publication. More damaging were suggestions of non-constitutional behaviour. Wrongly it was suggested that the President of the Board of Trade might be out-voted by his own officials when approving new lines. What finally killed off Equivalents was the case of the Oxford, Worcester & Wolverhampton Railway. Here the recommendations of Dalhousie (appointed President after Gladstone) were embarrassingly opposed by Peel and other members of the government in committee. Dalhousie confronted the Prime Minister saying that if the government was to ignore its own advice then his department would cease providing it. Peel concurred and Equivalents was dead.

Railway Mania meanwhile flared; ironically concerns expressed about excessive profits in debating the 1844 Act probably, at the margin, added heat to the flames. Without Equivalents the government had an empty policy toolbox as schemes vied one with another for success in the Private Bill process. Eventually the real economy braked sharply extinguishing the Mania.

Approved schemes were abandoned, calls on part-paid shares were ignored; half-finished railways resorted to litigation to complete their works and avoid complete ruin. Railway construction was a counter-cyclical benefit to the depressed economy.

By 1850 the national railway network was discernible and while expansion continued, with another peak in the 1860s, the opportunity to create a network in some planned fashion was irrevocably lost. The only guardian against monopoly was competition between railways. This competition was not typified by aggressive pricing that might benefit railway users, instead it was channelled into territorial battles – the threat and counter-threat of building lines through a neighbour's patch. Even this was interrupted regularly by mergers.

Until the mid-1860s government action was effectively absent. The stance on mergers was ineffective and varied. Cardwell, when President of the Board of Trade, chaired a select committee investigation into railway practices (1852–3) and his committee found mergers to be against the public interest. Yet in 1854 the North Eastern Railway merger was permitted: in the 1860s some 187 railway Bills were approved allowing amalgamation.

Cardwell's Act of 1854 was the only other half-significant legislative measure; it required railways not to prefer the business of one customer over another. This was supposed to assist carriers like Pickfords, but in reality unfair preference could only be demonstrated through expensive litigation and railways had deeper pockets. Even when judgement went against a railway, the company complied technically then moved on to use some new device to carry on discriminating. Customer frustration was building throughout the 1850s and 1860s, but the economy was generally prosperous, and railways had capacity to sell, enough to keep dissatisfaction in check.

In autumn 1864, as his 1844 Act approached its twenty-first anniversary, Gladstone badgered Palmerston to appoint a Royal Commission to consider its state-purchase provisions. Evidence was heard by the Duke of Devonshire's Commission. Besides traders expressing their dissatisfaction at railways' discriminatory pricing policies there were some prominent figures arguing for state ownership.

Amongst them were Commission member Sir Rowland Hill (who authored a Minority Report drawing on evidence presented by his brother Frederick); the Poor Law reformer and bureaucrat Sir Edwin Chadwick; and William Galt (whose writings advocating nationalisation reinvigorated Gladstone's interest in the state purchase provision within his 1844 Act). Galt wrote:

> The *laissez faire* system which is pursued in this country to such
> an extent that it has become an axiom with the Government ...

has been pregnant with great loss and inconvenience to the
country in carrying forward the railway system.[*]

The majority of Commissioners were unmoved. The government's ability to
borrow more cheaply than railway companies, a key benefit predicated for
state purchase enabling lower railway borrowing costs to feed into lower rates,
was built on the government buying railways for an amount based on their
25 years average net profits. Most Commissioners reasoned that arbitration
would make purchase more expensive. Indeed the government may need to
borrow an amount large enough to worsen the terms of all government
borrowing. The Commission rejected state purchase concluding the benefit
case unproven in comparison to its substantial cost and complexity.

The committee also recognised that 2,300 miles of predominantly main-
line railway had been authorised prior to the 1844 Act. This mileage was not
covered by the Act's state purchase terms and the companies would have to
agree to sell and have freedom to determine the price. No separate accounts
existed to determine the value of lines authorised since 1844 so the calculation
of compensation that the government should pay would be extremely difficult.
Gladstone's state-purchase mechanism was left dormant.

## The Railway System reaches Maturity (1870–1914)

PUBLIC attitudes to railways changed after 1870, perceiving railways more as
a utility. The industry matured and capacity was at times choked off by growth
in traffic. Britain retained economic hegemony (in 1870) but other nations
were catching up, especially the United States and Germany, causing unease.
Railways lacked clear rate-fixing principles and extended their practice of
quoting exceptional rates, discounts targeting specific traffic. Traders were
more vociferous in their criticism taking for granted the benefits of railway
technology and highlighting instead the unfairness of different mileage rates
for similar traffic. They thought railways advantaged foreign producers. While
railways still had friends in Parliament, their critics were starting to win the
argument. Requests for government intervention were now vested less in terms
of state-ownership and more often as pleas for rate-regulation. Government
more consistently discouraged railway amalgamations.

Railway price discrimination aided larger traders' access to more distant
markets and as such could be beneficial. The Railway and Canal Traffic Act

---

[*] William Galt, *Railway Reform: Its Importance and Practicability*, 1865, p.xv cites G.R. Porter, *The Progress of the Nation in its Various Economic and Social Relations from the Beginning of the Nineteenth Century to the Present Time*, 1836

(1854) allowed this only when costs differed. Railway companies naturally preferred to set rates with the level of competition in mind. Traders sought government protection from monopoly and advocated charges based on equal mileage rates and cost of services regardless of the length of haul, practices the companies argued would tend to reduce traffic.

The traders in the Midlands, who lacked seaborne communications, felt particularly aggrieved. Traders' lobbying led to a complete review of rates. Parliament established a committee in 1880 but this was unable by 1881 to complete its work and it was reconstituted in 1882. Railways stood accused of discriminating against individual trades and districts by charging different prices for what was perceived to be the same service and of unfairly charging lower rates for imported agricultural goods at the expense of domestic farmers. Against the evidence given by its customers before Parliament the North Eastern Railway, for example, was successful in defending most criticism, except for its apparent favouring of foreign agricultural imports which they could not deny.

The report of the Select Committee on Railways (Rates and Fares) 1882 acquitted 'the railway companies of any grave dereliction of their duty to the public'; nonetheless they found the system of freight classification and charges haphazard and recommended a new statutory classification. This caused prolonged debate. Eventually the Railway & Canal Traffic Act (1888) enabled the Board of Trade to set a uniform merchandise classification. It ordered its implementation within six months of it being completed alongside a schedule of rate maxima.

When implemented in 1893, company greed and bureaucratic wrangling saw the companies comply by setting the maximum charges permitted. A frustrated government and Parliament enacted measures to return the companies to the 1892 pricing and established arbitration that would only allow rate increases based on cost grounds. By 1900 it was clear that railways were unable to increase their rates at all, despite prices generally rising. The impact was to reduce transport costs through the early Edwardian period, but also to cause financial difficulties for the railway companies. Trader opposition gradually declined.

Safety improvements also required government intervention. Many railway accident reports re-iterated the Railway Inspectorate's mantra of 'brake, block and interlock'; yet it was only after the terrible Armagh tragedy that this advice was made mandatory.

More traffic, greater speeds and heavier trains began to take their toll. Technology progressed: signals could be interlocked with points. Telegraphy and the absolute block system – one train on one line at any time was safer than the time-interval lottery. Continuous fail-safe vacuum-operated train brakes meant than expresses could stop more quickly as braking took place across the length of the train, although there were at least twenty different systems in use and none were totally satisfactory. If the train divided the brakes would automatically stop runaways. Inspectors began readily to criticise companies who failed to heed their advice. Yet companies continued their procrastination and even opposition. Lives were lost as a result: for example at Ayno (1852 associated with time interval operation) and Welwyn (1866 associated with permissive block working).

Tragedy at Armagh on the Great Northern Railway of Ireland in June 1889 transformed government thinking. The accident involved a Sunday school outing rolling backwards out of control into a preceding train. Eighty were killed and many were children. This resulted in the passing of the Regulation of Railways Act (1889). This was the Railway Inspectorate's single greatest achievement ... a slim document that made compulsory the adoption of inter-locking and the block system on passenger lines, and continuous brakes on passenger trains. These remain corner-stones of railway safety.

Regulation was policy, but state-ownership (and socialist nationalisation) was still considered and questions about the role of the state flared periodically. James Allport defended the railway companies in a debate on state ownership at the Statistical Society in 1873. The middle-class National Railway Association sought state-ownership and operation, and as advocates of direct management they often cited the Post Office as a case in point. Others like John Stewart Mill favoured state-purchase but without state-operation – private leases would avoid state patronage. Radicals were slow to adopt railway nationalisation. Chartists had distinguished what God made (common property) from what man made (private property). Railways were the latter, early radical thought focussed more on land reform. In 1872 the Amalgamated Society of Railway Servants (ASRS) was established. State-ownership of railways was not a consideration; their focus was on long working hours.

Not until their October 1894 Congress did the ASRS call for railway nationalisation. Despite new found radicalism amongst its rank and file, pay and conditions remained the focus of campaigning. The union invested its funds in railway shares and its Liberal leaders were therefore cautious about appropriation. The Social Democratic Federation's pamphlet entitled 'The Nationalisation of our Railways System' in the mid-1880s saw nationalisation as the means to improve working conditions. The Royal Commission on Labour in 1892 heard this message too from advocates of railway national-isation such as Sydney Webb. Now socialists increasingly saw railways as wider common property. The Chambers of Commerce favoured nationalisation in the 1890s. The Railways Users' Association (1893), the Railway Reform Association (c.1894) and the Railway Nationalisation League (1895) all campaigned for state-ownership.

The General Election (1906) and a threatened national railway strike (1907) made railway nationalisation 'practical politics'.★ The election returned Labour MPs to the Commons and Lloyd-George was a more sympathetic figure appointed to the Board of Trade. Union demands presented to all companies in November 1907 were backed by a strike vote of 80,000 railwaymen. Government intervention forced railway companies to accept Conciliation Boards.

Within weeks a Commons motion was tabled to nationalise the railways and although it was talked out Lloyd-George offered an inquiry. The Railway Nationalisation Society (RNS), formed in 1908, was a cross-party organisation with support from Labour MPs and commercial interests. The RNS ran effective nationalisation campaigns before the war drawing diverse support. The same year saw the TUC Parliamentary Committee write a Bill to achieve nationalised railway and canals while the ASRS elected nationaliser J.R. Bell as its Chairman. Opponents were also structuring their arguments. Edwin A. Pratt, industrial correspondent of *The Times*, wrote several articles explaining railway rates and arguing against state-ownership later published as a book.

Government resolved the 1911 rail strike by allowing companies to raise rates to fund railwaymen's demands. The fall-out led to a Royal Commission, appointed in October 1913, to investigate relations between the state and railway companies. Nationalisation was imminent or so it seemed; *The Times* was reminding its readers of the purchase terms of Gladstone's Act encouraging railway companies to maximise dividends. The RNS drafted a Bill proposing purchase of the railways for 20 years profits to be funded by new 3½ per cent Railway Stock redeemed from a sinking fund after 63 years.

Traders' interests now no longer aligned to socialist agendas, fewer favoured railway nationalisation based on the evidence presented to Royal Commission, perhaps as motorised transport was beginning to compete with railways. Before the war public opinion seemed prepared to accept nationalisation and the Labour movement was committed to it. The Liberal government remained unconvinced, railway companies began to consider the advantages for themselves, but wider commerce was losing interest.

---

★ E.E. Barry, *Nationalisation in British Politics*, 1965), p.99

# Railways in Ireland (1830–1922)

IRELAND has a different narrative. The Irish economy remained un-modernised, agriculture dominant. Poverty and famine cast their shadow; their combined impact led to significant mortality and emigration. Many left behind were functionally illiterate, especially in the west where the economy was weakest. In Ireland the government became more inclined to intervene than on the mainland. By the time Arthur 'Bloody' Balfour was Chief Secretary for Ireland government policy began to address regional differentials offering additional support to the 'Congested Districts', the poorer counties nearer the western seaboard. Here poor agricultural smallholders supplemented their incomes by fishing, weaving or working away (usually on the mainland). Ireland was as far removed from being the 'Workshop of the World' as can be imagined. As such prospects for railways were discouraging.

The first railway opened in 1834 connecting Dublin with port facilities at Kingstown (Dunleary). Railway speculation slowed in 1836 with a bad harvest and with the establishment of a government commission to review where railways should be constructed. This attempt at a planned network faltered because the government was expected to fund construction, an unlikely prospect in the era of *laissez-faire*.

One consequence of the commission was the adoption of the broad 5ft 3in gauge for Irish mainline railways – a luxury for modest traffic that increased construction costs. In the early 1840s potato blight and famine struck. This disaster influenced government policy and thereafter to modest degree Irish railways were to benefit from measures to assist their development.

One of the first, in 1847, was a proposed government loan of £620,000 to three Irish railways (Great Southern & Western, Waterford & Kilkenny, and Dublin & Drogheda) to fund construction intended to boost employment and productivity. This was undoubtedly influenced by a sense of post-Famine guilt, but the concept of providing government funding to generate local employment was not new. It had been seen on the mainland when post-Napoleonic distress had led to the provision of some limited funds for canal and later railway building under the Exchequer Bill Loan Commissioners scheme. Irish railways though continued to struggle against low capital availability, high construction costs and poor traffic. In the 1860s legislation was passed to promote tramway building with modest success.

The Devonshire Commission set up to consider state purchase of railways under Gladstone's Act considered Ireland first. Its initial conclusions favoured state ownership in Ireland but, when Palmerstone's administration ended, the Conservatives deferred progress. Irish MPs pressed and Gladstone intervened on their side from the opposition benches. When the whole question was looked at again, on the prospect of returns on railways, Ireland seemed too thin to justify the expense. Gladstone, who had been thought by some to have effectively promised state railway purchase in Ireland in his interventions, was now satisfied that state purchase was unviable and was prepared, albeit with some embarrassment, to defend this position.

In 1883 the Tramway and Public Companies Act made it possible for tramway/railway promoters to seek government guarantees for a decent return on capital. The county authorities (Grand Juries) on approving such schemes then required individual Baronies (Districts) through which the line passed to offer a guaranteed rate of return, usually 5 per cent, to the promoters on the proportion of capital guaranteed. This return was greater than was being paid by most of the main-line companies in Ireland at the time, so marginal schemes that proved unable to meet the guaranteed rates of return were supported which then often became a burden to ratepayers. Nonetheless the measure was successful in promoting line building and creating employment in poor areas, even if the funds provided might have been better employed.

Lines constructed with support from the scheme include the Schull & Skibberbeen Tramway which had £57,000 of its £95,000 capital guaranteed, yet construction was so poor that it struggled to pass inspection. It soon ran into financial difficulties and the local authorities appointed a management committee to run the line. The Cork & Muskerry Light Railway by 1913 managed without any reliance on its guarantee. Others included the Tralee & Dingle Railway, the lines from Loughrea & Attymon and the Ballinrobe & Claremorris. Beyond Baronial guarantees, the Loughrea and Ballinrobe lines had other features in common: both entered into working agreements with the Midland & Great Western Railway (MGWR) and were built to broad gauge standards. The lines' association with a main-line railway company ultimately ensured these projects were among the more successful.

Balfour became Ireland's leading administrator in 1887. He chose to tour the western areas of Ireland and saw appalling poverty which encouraged him to act. In railway terms there were two measures of note. In 1891 he set up the Congested Districts Board. This body, funded principally from the disestablishment of the church in Ireland, had funds set aside to generate an annual income of just over £41,000 which it deployed to improve fisheries, agriculture, roads, telegraphy and steamship services amongst other things. The impact on railway traffic was indirect, but the fishery developments for example boosted railway traffic around counties Galway and Kerry. More directly his Light Railways (Ireland) Act of 1889 allowed access to central government funds to finance railway projects approved by the Lord

Lieutenant, so long as they were constructed by an established railway company. The main outcome was to fund lines that the main-line railway companies already had planned.

Much of the continued expansion of railways in Ireland in the latter years of the nineteenth and early twentieth centuries is owed to Balfour's measures and the earlier 1883 Act. The economic situation in the west meant many of the new railways were laid to 3ft gauge and would have been unfeasible without state help. The amounts deposited in Post Office Savings is an indication of improved financial position of population – they increased from an aggregate of £243,140 to £2,265,076 between 1891 and 1918 in the counties of Donegal, Galway, Kerry Leitrim, Mayo, Roscommon and Sligo. While it is a clumsy measure it does point to some real progress.

Ireland eventually achieved an impressive network of 3,442 miles by the 1920s and although when road transport developed much of it closed, there were benefits derived to the population from its existence. It was over-engineered and over-expanded in relation to real commercial needs. This reflects the government's choice of gauge, the competition encouraged early on between main-line companies duplicating services and diminishing beneficial cooperation, and later the encouragement of marginal lines in the expectation of economic benefits.

Benefits were certainly achieved, but it is highly questionable given the extent of traffic whether some of these lines represented value for money. The support for railway building offers an example of modest success against a general background of significant British policy failure in Ireland.

## Wars and Governmental Control

BRITAIN'S railways envisaged military role was to move men and equipment to preserve order at home or to reach a port of embarkation to fight abroad. The Engineer & Railway Staff Volunteer Corps formed in 1865 prepared war plans, but lacked War Office support. From 1871 'planning was based on the premise that government would take control on the outbreak of war, giving overall direction to the companies which would continue to manage the operation of their lines' under Section 16 of the Regulation of the Forces Act. In 1896 the Army Railway Council was established, hereafter railway war plans were reviewed regularly. The London & South Western Railway (LSWR) during the Boer War (1899–1902) was not placed under government control, but nevertheless embarked 520,000 troops with horses and equipment at Southampton docks.

Before the First World War the government took control of railways through the Railway Executive Committee (REC) formed in a consultative capacity in

**Railways were controlled by government but the ultimate sacrifice was made
by the railwaymen – the Great Eastern memorial commemorating its dead from
the Great War at London Liverpool Street station.**

1912. Extensive army manoeuvres conducted in the same year enabled railway
performance to be assessed, the Great Eastern (GER) acting as unlikely host.
The REC consisted of eleven general managers nominally under the chair-
manship of the President of the Board of Trade, but in practice the role of
Acting Chairman fell to Sir Herbert Walker of the LSWR (who succeeded
Sir Frank Ree of the LNWR in April 1914).

The REC controlled 21,331 route miles of 130 companies and joint committees, although not Irish railways until 1917. Within a fortnight during
August 1914, 1,408 pre-planned special trains mobilised 334,500 troops and
their equipment and stores. The British Expeditionary Force landed in France
just sixteen days after hostilities began. This involved another 689 special trains
carrying 126,496 men and all equipment prompting Kitchener's praise in the
House of Lords. Railways tried to maintain business as usual: the LBSCR ran
services to the coast in the early days while the GER managed to maintain its
Hook of Holland (via Harwich) service throughout hostilities. When capacity
was reached services began to suffer degradation.

The railways' challenges included supplying the Grand Fleet at Scapa Flow. Overall 13,630 'Jellicoe specials' ran 375 miles from Pontypool to Grangemouth to maintain the navy's coal supply and from 1917 nightly departures left Euston for Thurso carrying naval personnel. Railways, despite handling more traffic than in peacetime, also provided their quota of men for military service (in the end 49 per cent of railway staff of military age), many roles backfilled by women.

Equipment, especially locomotives, were requisitioned and carriages converted for use as ambulances. Railway managers also saw wartime service coordinating non-railway activities. Examples include Sir Sam Fay (Great Central) working at the Department of Military Railways and Sir Guy Calthrop (Caledonian) as Controller of Coal Mines. Railway works made armaments. New ordinance works often built in remote areas required new rail connections and generated dense traffic.

Many dining cars were withdrawn, although sleepers were maintained with the justification of allowing government officials a good night's sleep. Carriages were adapted to black-out conditions to avoid Zeppelins and their bombs.

Railways suffered mainly superficial war damage, an exception being damage to the North Eastern around Hartlepool caused by naval bombardment in December 1914. There were twenty four wartime rail worker fatalities. Incompetence more than enemy action disrupted services, such as the failure to return empty wagons quickly. Some lines were used as sidings for wagons holding equipment in case of shortage. The stress on the system is revealed in part by accidents; the multiple collisions at Quintinshill on 22 May 1915 cost at least 227 lives, ostensibly caused by the carelessness of signalmen during their shift change, but wartime operational strain was a background factor. Heavy traffic and the lack of workshops caused by munitions work left some 20 per cent of British locomotives in need of repair by the war's end.

Preparations for the next war began in earnest in 1937 when a special committee was established. In 1938 plans addressed civilian evacuation and removal of cultural artefacts – by 1939 the consideration was train operations in blackout conditions.

In 1939 a Railway Executive Committee consisting of the general managers of the 'Big Four' companies and a representative from London Transport again began to control the railways. The Minister of Transport was usually absent, so Sir Ralph Wedgwood (Chief General Manager at the LNER) acted as chairman, followed from August 1941 by Sir Alan Garrett Anderson. Fast services quickly vanished, many ordinary services were withdrawn and trains became crowded.

First class was abolished and towards the end of the war dining cars were withdrawn completely. Railways excelled in the war's early stages especially the success transporting the British Expeditionary Force's 338,000 men, many injured, after Dunkirk. The worst air-attacks were in 1940–1 and 1944–5, the more serious included the downing of the Southern's Southwark Street Bridge on 19 April 1941 which crippled eight running lines. Overall damage was not as severe as it might have been: some 484 locomotives were damaged but only eight written off; however 637 carriages and 2,685 wagons were destroyed. Disruptions were of short duration; after the big Coventry raid in November 1940, lines were restored within a week.

Railways coped with civilian evacuation. Twelve armoured trains carrying anti-aircraft guns were deployed around the south coast. In Kent several spurs were built to handle rail-mounted guns, troops even worked on the 15inch-gauge Romney Hythe & Dymchurch Railway. American and Canadian military needs, especially for D-Day, generated enormous traffic. Railways again gave up men and equipment, although there were essential reserved railway occupations. Around 100,000 railwaymen saw military service, while 298 steam and forty five diesel locomotives were provided for use overseas.

Again railway works made armaments. The LMS alone made 642 tanks at Horwich and Crewe. Ludendorff had concluded in 1918 that 'there comes a time when locomotives are more important than guns'. Britain's railways demonstrated clearly the insightful nature of his statement. During the war some 538,559 special trains were ran, of which 258,624 carried troops and 279,935 freight.

Common to both wars was the harsh financial treatment of the industry. After the First World War, Transport Minister Sir Eric Geddes was slow to make compensation payments. Consider the North British (NBR). A disputed claim in 1920 was first referred to the Railway & Canal Commission whose decision was later reversed by the Court of Session. Only after much legal wrangling did the government meet £9,790,545 of the £10,681,243 claimed by the NBR. During the Second World War the government reduced the agreed compensation payments. In the end the government paid the railways, including London Transport, £43million per annum during the war years and war damage was not fully compensated. All earnings above that figure were taken by the government (in 1942 this amounted to more than £45million and in 1943 £62million). 'Thus railways [helped] to pay for the war they sustained.' *

---

* Ellis, *British Railway History*, Vol.2, p.380

Another common factor was expectations around nationalisation; indeed nationalisation probably appeared more likely in 1914 than it did in 1939. In the aftermath of wars the government had to wrestle with essentially the same problems; the consequences of failing to resolve them between the wars made for even greater challenges after 1945.

## Regulated Regional Monopoly: Interwar and the Big Four

RAILWAY nationalisation was expected. The creation of the Ministry of Transport appeared to be a stepping stone, yet the return to Parliament of more Conservatives in the 1918 election changed the political balance. Instead the Transport Act (1921) formed four regulated regional monopolies as the 120 extant railway companies were merged creating: the London Midland & Scottish (LMS), an enlarged Great Western (GWR), the Southern (SR) and the London & North Eastern (LNER). Overlapping networks preserved some competition; many population centres had more than one company providing services, but promoting competition was no longer a priority. Britain was also no longer the leading industrial nation. Regional mergers along American lines might enable scale economies yet preserve private enterprise.

The 1921 Act strengthened railways' obligations in the face of stronger road competition. Railways remained common carriers obliged to publish tariffs which hauliers then used to undercut them. A new system of rates introduced in 1928 proved as inflexible as the system it replaced. The companies were impotent in the face of rate and fare controls (not increased from 1920 until 1937) while deteriorating industrial relations increased costs. All this occurred against a background of serious economic depression. Treating the railways as a regulated monopoly was outmoded by this changed environment, yet government priorities were to avoid unsettling wider commercial interests that were struggling in difficult economic times.

In 1928 railways obtained the power to run road services, passenger duty was abolished in 1929 and regulatory measures were extended to buses (1930) and road haulage (1933). These changes did not improve railway finances as railways had entered the road transport business themselves. By 1931 railways were associated with about 47 per cent of the buses and by 1938 they owned around 10,000 goods vehicles. Regulating road transport was probably counter-productive impacting efficiency and offering the railways some insulation from the need to modernise. Rail-owned road transport did increase coordination, especially for passengers, but did little for costs.

---

\* Derek Aldcroft, *British Railways in Transition: The Economic Problems of Britain's Railways since 1914*, 1968, p.85 cites R. Brady, *Crisis in Britain*, 1950, pp.264–5

Efficiency might have been improved had roads taken the traffic off the least cost-effective routes perhaps enabling railways to lose a third of their route mileage, Aldcroft estimates.* It is therefore little surprise to note that even as the general economy improved the railways' operating ratio for the period 1934–8 stood at 81 per cent and the average revenue earned was some 35 per cent below the 'standard revenue' of £51,395,095 laid down in 1921. Railway ordinary shareholders were left with little to please them.

Another government priority was tackling unemployment. It fell back on an old device. It made loan guarantees available under the Trade Facilities Act (1921). Under Section 3 the Treasury might guarantee loan capital and interest up to a maximum aggregate value of £25million, this covering principal and/or interest. Loans guarantees were provided in conjunction with finance privately raised for capital projects where the scheme concerned promoted employment within the UK and the loan concerned could not be raised without state assistance. The Act assisted with construction of the LNER and Metropolitan Railways' branch to Watford, started in 1922 and completed in 1925. Also the London Electric Railway and City & South London Railway Companies used the scheme to improve and extend their lines for example from Hampstead to Edgware, and in constructing depot facilities at Chiswick. This was the beginning of a pattern in London as the Piccadilly line extensions (1930–3), the New Works Programme (1935–40) and even the Victoria Line (1964) benefited from this type of finance arrangement. The Southern Railway's electrification schemes were another major beneficiary, its constituent companies applying for guarantees for funding prior to the amalgamation, albeit deciding on the standard electrification system and other administrative factors arising from the grouping delayed progress.

Government reports were numerous but actions few. Unification of the transport system in Britain was advocated by the Balfour Commission in 1929 and the Boscawen Commission in 1931 – in the latter case a minority statement in favour of nationalisation was included. In 1931 the Weir Committee recommended railway electrification but noted that a nationwide main-line scheme would cost around £261million, while offering a return on capital of just 7 per cent. The Inter-War financial crisis, then at its deepest, ruled out any such scheme.

Various government schemes 1929–35 allowed the 'Big Four' to borrow at below market rates of interest to finance employment creating projects, effectively a small subsidy. Railways benefited from relief on around three-quarters of its local tax burden in 1929. The Southern Railway made good use of £32million which had become available under the New Works Programme to continue electrification.

The Railway Companies' Association in 1938 launched its 'Square Deal' campaign seeking freedom for the railways to set rates and fares like the road competition. The hauliers, who now had nearly 500,000 lorries (compared with 100,000 vehicles of all types on Britain's roads in 1914), hit back with 'Give the Railways a Square Wheel'. By the time of the outbreak of war nothing had changed. In many ways management and the government can both be criticised for their failure to tackle the performance of Britain's railways during the interwar period:

> The big four effectively became government tools of wider macro-economic policy since they were a huge source of employment and found themselves at the mercy of government whims, which were not necessarily in the railways interest. They were encouraged to undertake inappropriate investment because of the government's desire to protect jobs when a carefully drawn up programme of culling the most uneconomic branch lines and several duplicated longer routes might have given them a more stable financial basis.*

Special mention should be made of the London Passenger Transport Board (LPTB), one notable innovation achieved by government which came into existence on 1 July 1933. Herbert Morrison, when Labour transport minister, was its architect and he established the London Transport (LT) brand. London might have ended up with a regulated private monopoly; transport co-ordination had reversed in the mid-1920s as the Underground Group, which ran most bus services, found itself up against many small competitors who creamed off traffic on busy routes at key times. Transport coordination across London was advocated by the Conservative peer Lord Ashfield (Albert H. Stanley). In 1924 he wrote that coordinated transport, such as bus connections to the stations, was necessary to increase the catchment area to make underground railways in London's suburbs viable. Until persuaded by Morrison, Ashfield favoured the private sector to achieve this:

> LT marked the beginning of much tighter state control over the capital's transport ... it was the first example of how a public body could be invested with commercial as well as social responsibilities, and carry out both aspects successfully...it is almost impossible to exaggerate the high regard in which LT was held during its all too brief heyday.*

* Christian Wolmar, *Fire & Steam*, p.250

* Wolmar, Subterranean, p.255

LT's success relied on the partnership of Ashfield (Chairman) and Frank Pick (CEO). LT did everything it could for itself including food production, train and bus design and engineering. Work was secure and perks included high relative wages and even the prospect of a retirement home. Pick expected discipline but was prepared to pay for it. The workforce was always highly unionised. In 1935 the government, employing Keynesian economic ideology to reduce unemployment, embarked on the New Works Programme. Pick and Ashfield presented plans under the scheme which included extending London Underground: the Northern Line was to be taken out to East Finchley and High Barnet and the Central Line would expand on its western and eastern extremities. The £45million capital needed was raised on beneficial terms with government backing saving around £330,000 in interest compared with a commercial scheme.

The interest burden of servicing the legacy of its past shareholders and these investment plans, rising wages, pensions and renewal costs began to impact LPTB; almost a rehearsal for later problems of British Rail. Ashfield appreciated the threat that the car would pose to medium distance journeys (the Underground's financial lifeblood) and warned that the quality of services would have to improve to keep LT competitive. By the mid 1940s an annual deficit of £3million was envisaged by Ashfield, but this problem was side-stepped by war. The LTPB legacy included excellent PR, brilliant poster designs, and Harry Beck's famous underground map.

## Nationalisation – The Rise and Fall of British Rail (1945–1993)

WAR had boosted traffic, and although the government received much of the wartime lift in receipts for itself, shareholders also had become somewhat insulated. Peacetime saw traffic decline sharply as military need ended. As American aid for the economy evaporated the bite of austerity took hold. The railways were in poor condition, make do and mend rather more than wartime damage had left infrastructure creaking, accidents were more common and the return to normality was delayed by nationalisation arguments around its scope and compensation. Management was in a near limbo state until Atlee's government's Transport Act (1947) established the British Transport Commission and its Railway Executive. Most road and all rail transport was nationalised. Any hopes that nationalisation was a panacea were quickly dashed.

The wartime fund set up to repair the railways could be spent, but arrears in maintenance already exceeded these funds. The locomotive shortage was addressed by building steam, the electrification that nationalisation had been expected to enable pre-war was postponed. Austerity and the currency impact of imported oil made steam appear more viable than diesel power. The underlying structural problems faced by railways remained. Traffic was lost to roads and both the common carrier requirements and excessively low railway tariffs and fares were left in place. Businesses employing their own haulage were left outside the BTC. Fair wages and government employment expectations inflated railway costs, a problem which deteriorating industrial relations in the 1950s would exacerbate. British Railways were left servicing a large debt to fund the agreed shareholder compensation. Far from generating a surplus to invest in modernisation, railway finances deteriorated sharply and began to be a drain on government coffers. Unanticipated, there was no rehearsed argument of social service obligations to fall back on.

Regionalised management and de-nationalisation of medium distance haulage were the measures implemented by Churchill's government. Both created new problems. The latter increased the intensity of road competition impacting railway finances. The former ensured that the Modernisation Plan, a laudable but excessively ambitious scheme that the Conservative administration also introduced, was hamstrung by colloquialism and over-bidding.

The Modernisation Plan ran quickly over-budget and had no discernible impact on the current account deficit. Inter-union rivalry and the desire to either maintain or close pay differentials achieved its triumphal folly in the settlement following the Guilbeau Report ensuring that railway costs continued to rise. Motorway building further boosted the efficiencies of road haulage. Users were not paying the full cost of road infrastructure unlike the railways who funded maintenance from receipts rather than taxation.

Motorway building was a highly effective subsidy to road users. The combination of these factors undermined railway finances and caused alarm in government. This set the stage for the entry of one of the industry's most controversial figures, Dr Richard Beeching.

Beeching was scientifically educated and became Technical Director at ICI. He joined the committee led by Sir Ivan Stedeford, the MD at Tube Investments, to restructure the British Transport Commission. He became principal architect of the new structure, wound down the BTC as its last chairman and was appointed British Rail's first by motorway builder Ernest Marples when he served as Transport Minister. Beeching's brief was to resolve the railways' financial problems. This is what the (first) Beeching Report set out to address.

Beeching applied scientific methods to his analysis and his report identified where railways had comparative advantages over roads and where they did not. His solution for the industry was for railways to concentrate on what they were

**Dr Richard Beeching with his first report.**
Part of the National Railway Museum collection

good at and withdraw from other areas. Hence express passenger services between principal towns and bulk goods handling were promoted. Beeching's analysis revealed that much of the network and its passenger and goods stations contributed little to revenue.

Unproductive services, lines and stations should be considered for closure and, encouraged by Marples, his report detailed proposals to curtail services. Many commentators have through hindsight's lens picked holes in Beeching's proposals and it is fair to say that at a detailed level some of his recommendations can be criticised.

This misses the point. Beeching admitted later that he probably should have resisted Marples encouragement to publish what was effectively a large closure list because this focused public hostility on protecting their local line. Given the deteriorating state of railway finances and the failed promises underlying the Modernisation Plan it would have been almost impossible for BR to attempt to resolve its problems through vague operational efficiency commitments. 'Jam tomorrow' would not wash. Beeching delivered what was necessary at the time and it is wrong to vilify him. He simply tried to address the consequences of forty years of political procrastination which had left the railways hamstrung as the economic world changed.

**Travellers Fare MaxPax coffee as served in InterCity buffets in the early 1980s.
Travellers Fare was an early candidate for privatisation.**
Part of the National Railway Museum collection

Even Beeching's draconian steps did not restore BR's finances. Beeching's second report proposed to go further, but this was too far for the new Harold Wilson administration which ended Beeching's secondment from ICI acknowledging his difficult role with a peerage. In Beeching's name the railway network was shrunk, yet his proposals were not implemented without modification. Revisions, for example to avoid closures in marginal constituencies were made, while other closure proposals were added. Investment in railway modernisation continued, intermodal services were introduced and the blue-grey InterCity brand launched, west coast electrification was completed speeding services and boosting passenger usage and diesels continued to rapidly replace steam, in many cases before the life expiry of these locomotives *(see plate 12)*. Nonetheless closures and cuts remain synonymous with Beeching's name.

Barbara Castle's Transport Act of 1968 removed the break-even burden established in Marples' era. Services became divided: commercial ones which should pay for themselves and social ones warranting subsidy. The accumulated £153million debt was wiped away; innovation was encouraged on commercial routes, while the six Passenger Transport Executives created in the main conurbations with subsidised funding successfully developed traffic.

**East Coast electrification was one of BR's later acts.**
**Leeds station was rebuilt a decade ago and it needs expansion again but this**
**Saturday afternoon service to Manchester is yet to promote much interest.**

*The Times'* leading article of Tuesday 22 October 1968 is revealing: while reserving judgement to a degree on the overall measure the editorial clearly considers Castle's approach with enthusiasm:

> Something had to be done about the railways, which at the time
> Mrs Castle took over were plunging virtually out of control
> towards a deficit of £200million a year and the reorganisation on
> the railways remains the outstanding contribution of the Bill.
> If the railways situation continues to deteriorate it will be in spite
> of rather than because of it.

However the decline in the railways' importance is clear from a later section in the same editorial:

> If the 1968 Transport Act does end up being a burden on the
> economy it is most likely to do so because of the additional costs
> and inefficiencies it imposes on road transport, which is far more
> important to British industry than the railways can ever be.

Philip Payton writing of British Rail in the 1970s observes 'the celebration of railways as the cutting edge of modernity had been replaced long-since by a nostalgia which saw in the rural cross-country routes and branch lines a "timelessness" which was itself the epitome of England and Englishness'.* This view explains some of the vociferous opposition to closures and the lasting reputation of Beeching. Rail closures slowed to a trickle after the 1968 Act, by 1977 closures were effectively complete.

Although BR's financial woes were never far away during the 1970s and early 1980s, Castle's Transport Act began a period of greater optimism. The 1970s witnessed the development of the diesel High Speed Train (HST) enabling sustained 125mph running and improving services and passenger numbers on the Great Western and East Coast routes. Less successful, but perhaps more representative of the new optimism was the electric Advanced Passenger Train. Revolutionary tilting technology was to have enabled high speed running on the more geographically challenging West Coast main line, but early proving-runs revealed teething problems which the press reported widely. Short of funds and wary of further adverse publicity the project was dropped. Tilting Pendolino trains made in Italy now form the mainstay of services on the West Coast.

Margaret Thatcher was a Prime Minister with little time for railways. Nationalised industries were set for privatisation, but the poor state of railway finances especially in the aftermath of the recession of the early 1980s ensured that railways as a whole were not prioritised. The Serpell Report, prompted by recession and the resulting deterioration in railway finances proposed dramatic network downsizing, but this was seen as too radical and was ignored. Elements of the BR business were sold off including catering, hotels, ferries and engineering. Joint ventures were considered, although rarely progressed. BR management was generally positive in terms of working with private capital throughout the period. BR restructured its remaining core business into sectors: for passengers there was InterCity, Regional Railways and Network South East; for freight were the Railfreight and Trainload sectors. This focus on sub-markets and general economic recovery led to BR's financial performance hardening and in 1987/8 a record low level of subsidy was paid by the government of just £495million. BR's productivity was the highest in Europe.

1988 witnessed tragedy at Clapham Junction when a double-collision caused by a faulty signalling installation led to the deaths of thirty-five people. The accident heralded a thorough review of safety procedures, a management

---

* G. Letherby & G. Reynolds, *Train Tracks :Work, Play and Politics on the Railways*, 2005, p.77, cites Philip Payton, 'An English Cross-country Railway: Rural England and Cultural Reconstruction of the Somerset and Dorset Railway' in Colin Divall (ed.), *Railways Place and Identity:Working Papers in Railway Studies No.2*, 1997, p.19

**Semaphore signals survive on many routes. The box at Abergele & Pensarn on the ex-LNWR route to Holyhead still controls upper quadrant home signals, albeit the distant signals are colour light.**

distraction at the time the government were contemplating full privatisation (*see plate 13*).

Right-leaning academics had been considering how railways might be privatised. Private sector management it was hoped would lead to railway industry subsidies being minimised, even eliminated. By the time the Conservative government's privatisation programme got to BR, several models for potential privatisation had been developed. In the end there were two main choices. BR favoured becoming a PLC and floating as a whole in the same way as telecoms and gas. The Treasury, influenced more by the new thinking, and hopeful of driving out more benefits through competition, preferred separating infrastructure from operations. EU directive 91/440 (1991) opening railways to inter-European competition further influenced thinking at the Treasury and this appeared in the white paper 'New Opportunities for the Railways' (July 1992) and later formed the basis of the Railways Act (1993).

The choice of privatisation approach was radical and influenced by economic theory: letting franchises for fixed time periods would ensure the incumbent felt the threat of competition – another operator might run the service and pay the Treasury more (or receive less subsidy). The proposal is not far removed from Gladstone and Laing's thinking nearly 150 years earlier. While not originally intended to occur quickly, it was the decision to privatise the infrastructure provider Railtrack which became most contentious.

## Privatisation – The First Ten Years (1993–2003)

*(see plates 10, 11, 15, 16 and 17)*

SEVERAL private national freight companies have entered the market with some success and the freight business has grown, focused generally on bulk handling and inter-modal containerised services. Passenger franchises were let and if necessary re-let. There is tension between railway investment which has long-term rewards and short-term franchises. Rather than award long-term franchises, government has preferred to manage investment and determines for example the timing and allocation of new rolling stock.

Franchise holders have little opportunity to develop their business and adopt strategies aimed at short-term profit maximisation. Improvements in subsidy never materialised. Services have generally not improved, certainly that is the conclusion of much of the media; there are exceptions like Chiltern Railways where an innovative investment programme continues to deliver benefits to the company and its customers alike *(see plate 14)*. Passenger numbers have nonetheless grown steadily. The passenger model has left the government with a free hand to pull the strings while having train operators to blame for any resulting problems. The scapegoats, who need to ensure success in the next round of franchise letting, generally appear to demur.

Most controversial is the story of Railtrack. Most economic theory around franchising railway operations placed the infrastructure owner in the public sector. At its creation the organisation was, but its leader Bob Horton, former CEO at BP, was keen to make it private and encouraged the government. The 1992 white paper gave the government powers to privatise the infrastructure company, but its tone is suggestive of this being something that would take place at some future date when all other changes had settled down. Instead, and it has been suggested that the need to provide funding headroom for promises to aid the government to fight the 1997 General Election was a factor, Railtrack was offered for sale in 1996 and at an attractive price.

In the months that followed, Railtrack's ordinary shares performed well. However this masked fundamental factors underlying Railtrack's business. Its income was pretty fixed, reliant on access charges paid by train operators. This in turn was dependent on government subsidy. Railtrack lacked engineering expertise on the board. It embarked upon a just-in-time maintenance strategy that was only viable if Railtrack had access to a database detailing asset quality. Wear and tear could be modelled and maintenance might be made more predictable.

The problem was that it embarked on this strategy without any such database. Its problems were compounded by its desire to maximise use of sub-contractors in railway maintenance and capital projects to drive down costs. The multifarious contractors and sub-contractors and their sub-contractors in turn created communications difficulties. Roles and responsibilities could become confused and messages about the condition of assets might be misunderstood or ignored altogether. Railtrack's shortcomings were highlighted by a spate of bad accidents around the turn of the millennium when poor maintenance and communication were laid bare. The final straw came at Hatfield in October 2000 when a rail fractured under a 115mph King's Cross to Leeds express causing most of the train to leave the rails with fatal consequences.

Serious concerns were raised about Railtrack's infrastructure and in the absence of reliable data it was obliged to impose probably the most expansive (and unnecessary) set of speed restrictions since the war. Delays were widespread and Railtrack had to meet the compensation bill that resulted.

Also the West Coast main line modernisation scheme, promised as part of the Virgin franchise, was seeing costs spiral. Railtrack was simply running out of time and money. The government restructured its finances in 2000, but this was insufficient. In 2001 it posted a huge loss of £530million as a result of Hatfield, yet still Railtrack's board proposed a healthy dividend to its shareholders. The government realised that Railtrack was no longer a viable business and used its powers to put the company into administration. Its successor, Network Rail, is a not-for-profit enterprise owned by the state, but ran as far as possible on private sector principles. The jury is still out on the effectiveness of this organisational structure, certainly thus far it seems to have managed to avoid the pitfalls of its predecessor. Railways are certainly enjoying a continuation of the resurgence that began at towards the end of BR.

The industry now seems set for a further shake up arising out of the McNulty Report highlighting that costs on Britain's railways are amongst the highest in Europe. This perhaps is a function of the industry's post-privatisation structure which is complex and where clear responsibility seems often lacking. The growth in subsidy seen, and the poor industry cost performance, appear at odds with the objectives of railway privatisation at the outset and seem to mark a deterioration from BR's last days.

# Conclusion

THE railway industry's birth coincided with fashion for small government and free markets. The pre-existing political-cultural norms for turnpikes and canals were naturally extended to railways. It took time to understand railway economics' peculiarities and any intervention that might be proposed had to struggle against ideology and emerging industry opposition. Gladstone's talent was enough to secure a framework the government might have used to take greater control, but the opportunity offered by Equivalents was simply misunderstood by Peel's cabinet, a situation which was fuelled by malicious gossip. Gladstone's state purchase provisions were however, despite his best efforts, watered down to the point of futility. In 1867 they might have been implemented. The benefits were essentially thought to be the enablement of lower rates achieved via lower debt-servicing costs obtained by substituting consuls for commercial paper. This benefit was too tenuous and the risk too great for this bold step to be taken. More recent experiences, with franchises and infrastructure companies, suggest that had state-purchase occurred, the boundaries of nineteenth-century administrative capability would have been stretched.

The safety regime of the market, 'Crash and Tell', failed to incentivise railway companies to act on 'brake, block and interlock'. Injuries and fatalities might have been avoided; instead it took multiple child mortality at Armagh to shake the government to make these sensible safety measures obligatory, albeit better late than never. Cheaper, safer third class travel was more successful as a social measure and perhaps accelerated the discovery of the profits offered by mass transit. Later in the nineteenth century workmen's fares formed a successful component of suburban redevelopment which improved the lives of many. In Ireland extending the political cultural norm of loan guarantees and then state assistance made a real difference to the poor of Ireland's western seaboard. These latter aspects represent a more positive legacy of nineteenth century government action around the railway industry.

Attempts at economic regulation began in the 1880s lacked subtlety. True, the haste required by the Board of Trade to implement new rates in the early 1890s was compounded by industry arrogance in moving immediately to maximum rates, but the bureaucratic apparatus thereafter worked by the Rates Tribunal left the industry incapable of increasing prices even when costs rose. Competitors in road transport began to eat into railway traffic.

Commercial interests, now buffeted as never before by global competition, hoped that railway nationalisation might enable efficiencies to further force down rates still further and campaigned for it. Labour interests expected the same benefits could improve pay and conditions. Railways opposed national-isation until some began to realise that modernisation, such as electrification, might only be feasible with state help. Wartime dilapidation, recurrent interwar depression and the threats of internal combustion left a regulated regionally restructured railway industry teetering on the brink.

The government like Nero fiddled, leaving the industry perhaps not yet ablaze but certainly smouldering. An exception was the LPTB which provided respite in the capital, reversing traffic declines, coordinating as never before the different modes of transport, and like the Southern, tapping into government loan guarantees to improve its network. Rehearsing in its microclimate some of the features of nationalisation to come, by the time war arrived LPTB finances were becoming stretched.

War delayed financial crisis for the whole industry, and although the govern-ment siphoned off extra receipts, railway shareholders were generally well rewarded by war. The combination of further dilapidations and the sudden decline in traffic left the industry in need of a post-war rescue which national-isation was expected to provide. In 1948 the British Transport Commission took control. Nationalisation changed ownership, but resolved little else.

There was no clear social agenda: the industry was left as a commercial enterprise at arm's-length, continuing the political-cultural norm, but it was in a wretched state. It was accident prone, debt-ridden yet lacking adequate capital and facing the same structural problems as before, but with less resilience. Deficits began and then spiralled, unions pursued their own agendas, while government preferred motorways to what modernists saw as a Victorian relic. Railway modernisation was first delayed and then launched hurriedly and carelessly leaving government still unconvinced of the industry's place. Such long neglect required particularly bad tasting medicine to restore confidence and Dr Beeching was its administrator.

His cure was certainly not fully effective, but it was in some ways cathartic, in demonstrating that the industry did have a place handling bulk freight and express longer distance passenger traffic. Castle's reforms in the later 1960s set the industry on a new more optimistic journey. Financial problems remained and flared periodically, but the principle of social subsidy was accepted. With non-core assets hived off, as Thatcher's premiership drew to its end the industry was in good shape, ready for inevitable sell-off. Ironically, after the Railtrack era, government direct control over the industry has actually become stronger despite the arrival of multiple private operators. Traffic declines have been reversed, but subsidies have grown while passenger franchise holders have been left by the Transport Department/Treasury with little wriggle room to develop their business.

Government has nearly always seen railways through a commercial lens, the dominant long-term political cultural norm. Railway users are expected to pay the full price, usually higher in Britain than elsewhere. Social obligations come and go, but the current debate around the HS2 route shows that railways do have a long term future in Britain, despite the many players in the privatised industry worsening the industry's comparative efficiency levels. Five years is the interval between general elections, yet that is barely time to complete an order of new rolling stock. Railway time is much slower than political time and this perhaps explains most why repeatedly government actions have tended to cause difficulties for the industry. Jack Simmons, the well-known British railway historian, should perhaps be left with the last word. 'Politicians,' he argues, 'have always been cynical about railways, either overtly or covertly. They have treated railways as a "passing opportunity" in politics rather than as a long term public service.' *

*This chapter is partly based upon a dissertation written for MA History of Britain course at Birkbeck College, University of London. Thanks are due to many in the History department at Birkbeck, but special mention must go to Dr Mike Berlin who supervised my dissertation.*

## Further reading

See Selective Bibliography on pages 220–222.

* Jack Simmons, *Railways: an Anthology*, 1991

# CHAPTER 7

# Railways as Employers

*Andrew Jones*

As the railway network in Britain grew so did the numbers employed on it. There were barely 2,000 at the 1841 Census but over the 70 years thereafter the numbers grew almost exponentially. By 1850 there were over 50,000, and this had doubled by 1856. By the 1880s the figure exceeded 300,000 and then doubled again over the subsequent 30 years. At its peak, during the years of the First World War, the railways were employing somewhere in the region of 650,000 people. Although the numbers would reduce slightly during the depression years between the wars there were still some 629,000 employed at nationalisation in 1948.

For over a century, the railways as an industry were only outdone by mining as the largest private employers in the country. Railway company employees didn't just number those who ran the trains, maintained the tracks and staffed the stations – the railways also had to man their hotels, shipping and ferry services, docks and harbours, warehouses, and all manner of activities directly and indirectly connected with the conveyance of goods and passengers around the country both on and off the rails.

Being such major employers placed the railway companies in the position of being a primary force in shaping and directing employment practices across the country, for good or ill. For many the railways became a family business with successive generations working for the company at any one time. The companies supported their employees with housing, education, social and health services long before these were offered to everyone by the state. In many cases the arrangements and models developed by the railways provided a template for the services offered by other employers and, in due course, the Welfare State.

After the Second World War nationalisation and the coming of the Welfare State, the position of employers, railways or otherwise, changed dramatically. Individuals no longer had to rely on their employers for the provision of healthcare and housing. The relationship between worker and manager changed and the old certainties of a 'job for life' and a 'career' path began to disappear. Workers, and employers, began to expect greater flexibility, the days of the railway family were numbered.

## The earliest years

THE first railways had to recruit such workers with such skills as they could find to staff their new enterprises. In order to do so they sought individuals skilled in similar areas and, in many cases, offered them better wages and conditions to entice them to the new, otherwise unknown, industry.

The first railways were constructed by engineers who had formerly built roads, or were miners and canal navigators 'navvies' many of whom found their skills readily transferable and much sought after. Once built, their operations required managers, drivers, mechanics, guards, constables, signalmen, clerks and porters. Again the new companies sought to fill their new roles with existing experienced and trained men. The managers might be ex-army officers, of whom there were many after the ending of the Napoleonic Wars. Drivers, mechanics and engineers could be recruited from the mines and factories. Guards, constables and signalmen were often ex-army or ex-navy men. Clerks would frequently be youngsters of reasonable education put forward by members of the company's board. The more menial roles, such as porters, could be filled from the many displaced agricultural labourers across the country.

With a high proportion of management and supervisory grades coming from a forces background it is hardly surprising that railways were run in quasi-military fashion. The hierarchies and management structures were very rigid with a strict set of rules covering all aspects of the job. For the first time a civilian body, railwaymen, wore a uniform identifying their role and rank whilst at work. Once the railways were established vacancies could be filled from within and promotion became an opportunity for many. A career ladder had developed with youngsters starting as lowly porters, clerks or cleaners and progressing through the ranks by diligent hard work to become firemen, stationmasters, mechanics and even senior managers of the company.

In order to attract and keep the necessary quality and number of men, the railways had to offer rates of pay higher than that elsewhere. This, together with the comparative security of employment on offer, the availability of housing in some cases, and even the provision of uniform clothing made railway work a much sought-after job.

# Pay and conditions

FOR the first decades of the railways' existence the rates of pay offered compared favourably with those available elsewhere. In the 1840s a railway porter could expect to be paid more than double that on offer to a farm labourer, and an engine driver a good third more than a skilled engineer. In addition railway employment, for those who obeyed the rules, was generally more secure and came with fringe benefits – uniform, free or discounted travel, health care, social clubs, housing and some provision for old age. It's no wonder that competition for jobs on the railways was so intense with many more applicants than roles available.

At the end of the nineteenth century, once railway companies had become well established, wages remained almost static, in some cases actually being cut as a result of economic conditions, and increasing hours of work were commonplace.

Throughout the first century of railways there was a strict hierarchy of wages according to position and rank. Drivers were the elite of the manual grades as befitted their skill and importance in controlling the great iron beasts that literally ran the railways. Passenger porters and guards were paid less than their goods equivalent but benefited from the possibility of receiving tips from passengers as well as being issued with a company uniform. Crossing-gate keepers were the lowest paid, for some companies the provision of a rent-free dwelling was the only remuneration given.

The following table demonstrates the wages for various grades in the 1840s and 1870s:

|  | 1840s<br>Shillings per week | 1870s<br>Shillings per week |
|---|---|---|
| Driver | 28 – 43 | 30 – 45 |
| Fireman | 17 – 26 | 18 – 27 |
| Passenger Porter | 15 – 20 | 12 – 20 |
| Goods Porter | 20 – 21 | 17 – 21 |
| Goods Guard | 21 – 30 | 21 – 36 |

The rates of pay did not move dramatically in the first 30 years of railway operation, which is hardly surprising at a time of low inflation. Such was the effect of the railways on the country's economy that the prices of many essential commodities actually fell during this period.

Clerks and stationmasters were on an entirely different scale: an annual salary rather than a daily or weekly rate. For these employees the location and responsibility of their work also influenced their pay with a clerk at a large station or in head office earning more than his country counterpart – and working longer hours to boot. These managerial grades did see dramatic increases in the upper levels of pay. In the 1840s stationmasters were being paid between £50 and £150 a year. By the 1870s the spread had increased to between £65 and £300. For clerks the range moves from between £40 and £100 to between £65 and £200. These increases were driven by the increasing size of the companies and the relative changes in responsibility placed on some individuals in these grades.

The number of hours worked by an employee was not always fixed; they were more usually determined by circumstances with men often being expected to work lengthy shifts of ten, twelve or more hours with minimal breaks. Accidents and fatalities were frequently attributed to fatigue and both public and governmental pressure was brought to bear in an effort to limit working hours. The companies reluctantly responded, limiting the hours worked and setting minimum breaks between shifts but countered by arguing that hours should be measured by actual activity and not include any periods of waiting, such as between trains. A move to reduce the length of the working day to eight hours was met with reactions suggesting that this was 'an impossible practicable minimum' and not a 'panacea for all ills in the industrial world'.

With no legal requirement to give paid holidays, the railways did permit annual leave, without loss of pay, depending on the grade of the worker. In the early 1900s a stationmaster would be entitled to 14 days a year, inspectors 10, porters and signalmen 6, and 'lads' only 3 (or 4 after they had completed five years service). At least with cheap or even free travel on the company's trains they might have the opportunity to actually go away, even if only for a day's outing.

The provision of uniform clothing was also a great benefit. An entitlement could be: a cloth coat or jacket and vest (waistcoat), and a serge coat or jacket and a vest in alternate years; cloth trousers, serge trousers and a cap once a year; and an overcoat or mackintosh and leggings every two years. It may not sound like much but the financial saving in not having to provide work wear himself could be a respectable addition to the wages on offer.

From the end of the nineteenth century wages would increase in response to general inflation, but the response was often too slow for the employees and their families. During the First World War various 'war bonuses' were paid because of general price rises affecting everyone, even so by the end of 1918 wages were slightly *below* their 1914 equivalents in real terms. In late 1919 there were various strikes resulting in new rates being agreed, after government intervention with the unions. The existing relationship between the various grades was maintained.

*Old Lady.* "PORTER! PORTER! DID I GIVE YOU THE WRONG HALF JUST NOW?"

**Contemporary 'Punch' cartoon.**

Government involvement in railway matters was not unusual and they fixed the tariffs and fares that the railways could charge as part of the 1923 Act grouping the railways into the 'Big Four' companies. These rates were based on 1913 activity and intended to allow railways to be profitable without unduly impacting the wider economy they served. No notice had been taken of the effects of increased road competition on the business and the railways were left at a disadvantage. Such problems in profitability were frequently felt by the employees trying to maintain their living standards.

In the late 1920s there was a 2.5 per cent reduction in wages across the board, though this was matched by a reduction in the cost of living in the years immediately after the war. The depression of the 1930s worsened matters and there were further cuts between 1932 and 1937.

During the Second World War, 'war bonuses' were again paid, increasing pay by over 60 per cent. This compared favourably with other industries where the increases averaged about 45 per cent but is explained in part by the fact that before the war, railway pay lagged well behind other industries. By 1945 railway pay had reached a comparatively favourable position.

1945 also brought changes to the way Sunday working was paid (increasing the rate from $1\frac{1}{2}$ to $1\frac{3}{4}$ times the weekday rate) and increases in holiday entitlement. With labour in short supply, railways once again found it necessary to make their terms attractive to attract and keep those needed to operate the network.

For the first seven years after nationalisation the railways paid their way, but after that they were once again loss making and finding it difficult to keep their pay rates in line with similar occupations and, in 1954–5, the National Union of Railwaymen gave notice of strike action. The government set up a committee to look into the matter of railway pay. In their report the Cameron Committee observed: 'The nation has provided by statute that there shall be a nationalised system of railway transport. Having willed the end the nation must will the means'. Wage increases were quickly agreed.

By 1960 there were again problems and a further committee of inquiry reported that pay was 10 per cent below comparable industries. Pay increases were again agreed.

By the late 1960s thoughts and discussions had moved on to include productivity in discussions of pay. The established system of rigid grades and job roles were felt to be hindering matters. The Penzance Agreement between the Unions and the employers swept away the old grades and ushered in a much more streamlined pay structure. As an example forty-one old grades were replaced by one new one of 'railwayman'. There was still a need to reduce costs and there were many redundancies. For those that remained pay was once again at a comparable level with other industries.

Railway employees' concerns about their pay levels continued. With privatisation in the 1980s and '90s the train operating companies were once again operating to make a profit whilst working within the constraints laid down by government through the regulator. Workers' concerns about wage comparability remained, now not only between the railways and other industries but also between the separate companies.

## Housing

FROM the earliest days the railway companies recognised the need to directly provide housing for at least some of their employees. Staff required to work in remote locations needed to be on the spot, especially at isolated crossings where the gates had to be manned or at signalboxes far removed from habitation, and nearby housing had to be provided for men and families.

Whole new communities were created by the arrival of a railway. Towns, such as at Crewe, grew up where there had been nothing more than a village before. Small isolated groups of houses appeared to support the railway and some, such as Riccarton Junction on the NBR, were accessible only by rail.

Usually developments grew up on the edge of existing towns, 220 houses for the GNR on the edge of Peterborough, or the 200 dwellings adjacent to GWR's works in Swindon.

At their peak the railway companies acted as landlords for over 27,000 homes. These houses were often better designed and built than their contemporaries though an 1863 survey by the NER of its stock of over 1,090 houses produced a catalogue of defects shocking to today's ears. Many were in need of a clean water supply, whether from the mains, a pump, a well or just something other than the local river. Others were in need of good, or any, sanitation. References to dampness, whether through flooding or a hole in the roof, were common. At least one tenant requested that a fence be installed at the front of the cottage to prevent the children from straying onto the railway line.

The same survey provides an insight into the nature of the accommodation provided. Over a fifth of the properties had only one bedroom, two-thirds had two, whilst there were twelve properties with no bedrooms at all, and one with a grand six bedrooms.

Initially the companies provided these homes rent-free. For some crossing-keepers the rent-free house was the only payment received for their services. (Though it seems to have been understood that the man of the house, ostensibly the employee, was free to take work elsewhere as long as there was someone left, wife or child, to operate the gate as and when required). Rent was charged by the GWR from the outset and by the 1840s it was commonplace. Rents were usually set on a strict commercial basis with the companies seeking to earn a suitable return on their capital expenditure. Even when paying rent most tenants found they were better off in a railway house than elsewhere and would be loathe to leave.

Building of new houses by the railway companies gradually tailed off across the late nineteenth and early twentieth centuries. The GWR virtually stopped in the 1850s and by the 1920s the SR was the only one still actively building new houses although the need was still there across all the companies.

As an alternative to being a landlord some companies preferred to assist in a more indirect way. In July 1923 motions were passed at the Railwaymen's Conference in Crewe praising the GWR for its involvement in schemes to construct affordable houses for sale to their employees and for offering them cheap mortgages, or underwriting building society loans.

The GWR used two schemes: The first was one of individual loans. The company would advance up to 90 per cent of the property's valuation (at a time when most building societies would only go to 80 per cent), over a period not exceeding 20 years, at an interest rate of 5 per cent per annum (building societies were charging 6 per cent and more). These loans were made directly by the company or, in Swindon, by the company lending £20,000 to the Swindon Permanent Building Society, and underwriting the additional 10 per cent being advanced to their employee. Between 1922 and 1925 the company assisted 1,778 employees through this scheme.

The second scheme used Public Utility Societies, an arrangement established by government to help encourage the construction of houses across the country. Under this scheme the GWR bought land, constructed roads and sewers and then leased the sites to the society for 99 years at Ground Rents equal to 4 per cent of their capital expenditure. The Societies, a form of friendly society, made up of railway employees, then constructed homes on the plots for rent – the construction being funded by loans from the company repayable over 50 years at 4 per cent per annum. Schemes were set up in London, Plymouth, Truro, Newport, Penarth, Barry, Caerphilly, Llanelly, Swansea, and at Severn Tunnel Junction.

Although both schemes were well received by many, at least one trade unionist objected on the grounds that 'houses should be provided for people as citizens, and they should not be liable to the risk of having to leave railway houses if they give up their employment'. And the GWR's loans direct to staff, fixed at 5 per cent, came under attack in 1936 when the prevailing building society rate fell to 4.5 per cent.

The provision of housing by the railway companies, or assisting with finance to those purchasing, was always one of practicality. The houses were necessary so that their employees would be on hand when they were needed;

good quality affordable housing was desirable to remove workers from bad company in undesirable areas of town; provision of housing as part of the job ensured a greater degree of loyalty and discipline.

Railway houses continued to be a feature of the industry well into nationalisation days but, with changes in wider society, the stock was gradually sold off – either to sitting railway tenants or to new owners. By the early twenty-first century railway houses were virtually unheard of and, with further changes in the economic situation, railway employees once again find it difficult to find suitable and affordable family accommodation near to their places of work.

# Health

WITH accidents and injuries at work commonplace it was quite evident to railway companies and managers that provision for medical aid to employees was a necessity. Initially it fell to the individual concerned to make their own arrangements, which would often be done with assistance from workmates and even local managers.

In the mid 1840s the Grand Junction and GWR set up medical funds in Crewe and Swindon respectively. For a small deduction from wages employees could receive treatment from the appointed surgeon. Over the following years hospitals and clinics were set-up by many companies, often quietly so as to avoid shareholder revolt at the expense. In some cases personal donations from individual managers and directors were instrumental in getting things going. (Daniel Gooch contributed half the cost of starting the GWR fund).

Once operational these medical arrangements were almost entirely funded by the men's contributions. The GWR Medical Fund Hospital in Swindon received an annual contribution of £50 from the company, its premises were provided and maintained by the company as was its gas supply, but all other operating expenses were entirely met out of the members' subscriptions.

Not only were the workers covered by these arrangements but also their dependant family and retired workers. The arrangements were a blueprint for the National Health Service, which took over all the arrangements on its formation in 1948.

As well as the health services provided to employees, many of the employees themselves provided medical aid as first aiders or members of ambulance corps. Born out of a need to help their fellow workers, and passengers after all-too-frequent accidents, many took first-aid courses through the likes of St John's Ambulance Association and served as volunteers for many years. Many received long-service medals for their efforts. Such volunteers proved invaluable during the two world wars providing assistance during and after air raids as well as to the war wounded conveyed to hospitals and convalescent homes by ambulance trains.

# Education

THE Stockton & Darlington Railway provided a school for employees' children at Waskerley in County Durham due to the remoteness of the location. The NBR did the same at Riccarton Junction. Away from these remote rural locations it was rare for the companies to be involved directly in the provision of children's education though they did support and influence schools in the vicinity of their works in an effort to ensure that the rising generation would be equipped for work on the railways.

Adult education was where the railways had their greatest impact. During the nineteenth century there was a great movement for self-improvement amongst all classes of workers. Mechanics Institutes had begun appearing from the 1820s and these were often the home of mutual improvement classes arranged for, and by, railway workers. The railway companies themselves helped set up new establishments near to their works.

In 1850 the Derby Railway Literary Institution was set up as a result of a petition to the MR to fund premises for a reading society there. In the early 1900s there was a much-respected GWR Lecture and Debating Society at Paddington. In 1943 the GWR Mechanics Institute in Swindon was operating a lending and reference library, accessible to more than just railwaymen, well before the first public library in that town.

Anyone wanting to get promotion in railway service was required to study; progression between grades often required success in examinations set by the companies. Examinations were held in such subjects as: Regulations for train signalling by block telegraph; Goods station work and accounts; Locomotive, carriage and wagon accounts and statistics; Railway and commercial geography of the United Kingdom; Railway operations; Law relating to the conveyance of goods and passengers by railway; and Railway economics.

Classes to study for examinations would be held in various institutes near to main railway centres around the country. Even so some students had to travel a fair distance, by train, to attend. Others would study by correspondence course and textbooks were published detailing all that was necessary for the aspiring railwayman to know. Self-improvement was the order of the day with study undertaken in the employee's own time, in the evenings and on rest days.

It was not until later in the twentieth century that railway companies started offering apprenticeships to suitable candidates. Initially these were in the mechanical sciences and based in the locomotive and carriage works, but eventually apprenticeships were available in just about every branch of the business.

Later still, British Rail offered both apprenticeships and university sponsorship for candidates.

## Social

IN Swindon the GWR Mechanics Institute provided facilities for both social and educational events. In 1930 it had some 15,000 members each paying between 1*s* and 2*s* 6*d* a quarter depending on their grade. The Institute boasted a reading room with the latest newspapers and magazines, a dance hall which could be used as a theatre, a smoking room, rooms for billiards and chess/ draughts, as well as other meeting rooms and the lending and reference library. The Institute was host to amateur dramatics, talks and lectures, union meetings, as well as many social events. Outside of the building there were athletic and sports branches and the managing committee was responsible for organising the annual works outing as well as the children's fete.

Although the railway companies might support these social activities in some way, like the health services they were primarily funded by the employees' subscriptions and payments. Unlike healthcare there were competing attractions outside the railway realm and not all clubs and societies prospered or continued. In Norwich the Railwaymen's Social & Athletic Club had use of a clubhouse purchased for their use by the LNER in 1924 and for which the club paid rent. By 1936 their financial affairs were such that they were petitioning the company to reduce the rent by over a third as they were making a substantial annual deficit as 'the membership of the various sections catered for by the Club has declined, and the development of housing estates some distance from the Club premises has had an appreciable effect on the receipts'.

## Further reading

Hamilton Ellis, *British Railway History 1830–1876*, George Allen and Unwin Ltd, 1954

Peter Timms, *In and Around Swindon Works*, Amberley, 2009

Adrian Vaughan, *Railwaymen Politics & Money – The Great Age of Railways in Britain*, John Murray, 1997

**Literally on the beach: Braystones station on the coastal section of the Furness Railway in north-west Cumbria, in the late 1930s.**

Cumbrian Railways Association Collection

# CHAPTER 8

# Railways in the Country

## *Gordon Biddle*

## The rural landscape

THE familiar British country landscape can be attributed to three major influences, starting in Tudor times with the creation of large estates and areas of parkland by great landowners, and continuing well into the 1800s accompanied by enclosures within hedges in the lowlands and stone walls in hill country – a process that was speeded up enormously by Acts of Parliament, forming the distinctive field patterns we know today. Between 1761and 1844 Parliament passed over 2,500 Enclosure Acts. The third influence was the railway. True, canals had to some extent already changed the landscape, but in a subtle, limited manner that in the main fitted unobtrusively into the rural scene.

By contrast, as W.G. Hoskins wrote in *The Making of the English Landscape*, the impact of the railways was massive. Far more extensive than the canals, they penetrated everywhere, with unprecedentedly massive earthworks, impressive viaducts, deep cuttings, innumerable bridges and awe-inspiring tunnels. To quote Hoskins again, they manipulated the landscape on a grand scale. Moreover, their advance soon ended vernacular building traditions, supplanting local materials by easily-transported universal brick, slate and iron. Most importantly of all, railways gave tremendous impetus to wholesale changes in Britain's way of life: the industrial revolution.

The railways ruthlessly broke up existing field patterns, keeping a direct course by cutting through enclosures, which is why there are so many occupation and accommodation bridges and crossings, the first to connect severed land and the other to cross private roads and tracks, some of which were rights of way. They were rarely provided willingly, but often as a means to overcome opposition from landowners in Parliament, without whose assent lines could not be built. What is more, the transformation of the countryside by railways happened at enormous speed. In the 30 years up to 1860 over 9,000 miles were built; by 1890 that figure had doubled.

Yet the huge disruption was not permanent. Raw cuttings and embankments soon healed and became grassed over, providing new habitats for wildlife. In some places they were deliberately planted, frequently at the landowner's insistence. Railways were quickly accepted too, admired by writers as a positive contribution to the landscape. In 1842, only two years after the Midland Counties line was opened through Leicestershire, T.R. Potter wrote in his *History and Antiquities of Charnwood Forest* that from one vantage point 'the trains of the Midland Counties Railway may be observed almost uninterruptedly from Sileby to Derby, and form a pleasing object darting across the grand panorama'.

Further, in those first 30 years or so, great effort and skill were exercised in designing new structures to harmonise with the locality or, where that was not possible as in the case of viaducts, to give them an aspect of majesty and grandeur that was intended to enhance their surroundings. Later the railway's course was marked by less prominent structures: telegraph poles, tall semaphore signals, remote signalboxes and, at closer quarters, distinctive post-and-rail fencing.

Valleys formed natural routes for railways. A valley traversed by a river and a road might require one or both to be diverted in order to provide a suitable route for the railway, as is the case in the Calder valley in West Yorkshire where the river was diverted between Wakefield and Normanton to avoid building two bridges, and at four places in the valley of the river Wenning in North Yorkshire. Where a straight road and a railway intersected at an acute angle, a double bend could be introduced into the road to enable a bridge to be built at right angles instead of a more expensive skew arch. In order to avoid excessive gradients, valley routes could only be connected by tunnelling through the watershed separating them, although in the Scottish Highlands through valleys obviated this need, which is why Scotland has so few tunnels, but at the expense of deviations, major earthworks and viaducts. The Callander & Oban Railway through Glen Ogle and Glen Dochart is an example.

## Viaducts, bridges and tunnels

THE grand concept of the lofty viaduct was the most readily accepted intrusion in the landscape *(see plate 18)*. *The Midland Counties Railway Guide* of 1840 contains a description of the line over the Avon near Rugby that is typical, crossing the river on 'a magnificent viaduct of nine arches, which does not in the least destroy the scene along the valley'.

Very conscious of the transformations they were making, the engineers of the day were careful to design in what we would now call an environmentally-acceptable manner. The engineer J.U. Rastrick had to take the London & Brighton Railway across the valley of the river Ouse at Balcombe in Sussex. It is to his credit – and, of course, the railway's directors – that in 1841 the thirty-seven red-brick arches of his great viaduct were decorated with delicate balustrades and eight charming pavilions, four at each end, in Heddon stone brought by river and sea from Northumberland. These were men driven by a desire to enhance the verdant valley, and the London architect David Mocatta was commissioned to design embellishments that were inspired by the same urge that motivated the owners of eighteenth-century parks and gardens to 'improve' the landscape by creating vistas containing ornamental bridges, Greek temples, mock ruins and similar follies. The result at Balcombe was one of the most elegant viaducts in Britain.

Robert Stephenson displayed a very different but equally sensitive sense of place in his Royal Border Bridge at Berwick-on-Tweed, where twenty-eight stone arches rely on simplicity to complement the broad river in its shallow valley, their only adornment being arcades of small rounded dentils that emphasise the low parapets immediately above. Likewise, the plain stone Ribble-head viaduct on the Settle & Carlisle line stands in perfect harmony with the empty Pennine moorland and drystone walls. Admittedly, it was built in 1875–6 when the desire for the 'picturesque' had gone and cost was the prime consideration, but the fact remains that anything more elaborate would have been completely out of place. Yet only a few years earlier there were localities where the romantic movement was still strong. In 1864 Henry Robertson completed one of Britain's most picturesque viaducts at Knucklas, where Shropshire meets Wales. Probably inspired by the Welsh border castles, its rugged masonry is almost overwhelmed by crenellated parapets, turrets and mock-cruciform arrow slits; possibly demanded by the Pryce-Greens, powerful local landowners.

Evidence of the same need to satisfy insistent landowners can sometimes be found upon bridges on railways crossing country estates. One in Shugborough Park, Staffordshire (now a National Trust property) has among its adornments Ionic columns, ornamental balustrades, a seahorse, a lion and the Earl of Lichfield's armorial device and crest. Not far away, a bridge at Sandon displays the arms of the Earl of Harrowby, while near Kenilworth in Warwickshire a mere accommodation bridge connecting two fields carries the separate arms of Lord and Lady Leigh of Stoneleigh Abbey, one on each side, unseen except from a passing train.

On the same line a few miles away, in what is now a suburb of Coventry, their neighbours the Gregorys of Stivichale Manor (long demolished) had their arms displayed on the appropriately named Coat-of-Arms Bridge over a public road; perhaps an example of Victorian one-upmanship. Two bridges on the Bolton–Blackburn line in Lancashire have turrets above Tudoresque arches, all to satisfy a wealthy cotton spinner, James Kay of Turton Tower, while the medieval-looking gateway to Guthrie Castle in Angus, Scotland, carried what was the Caledonian Railway main line to Aberdeen, the tracks being laid between crenellated parapets and turrets above the porter's lodge. Here it was partly paid for by the Guthries, who had lived there since 1468.

Up to the 1860–70s railway bridges, both under and over, were built of brick or stone with three main types of arch: semicircular, segmental or semi-elliptical. The first two were very common; the third less so, although I.K. Brunel designed some very dignified semi-elliptical arched bridges over his railways. Least common were graceful 'flying arches' over deep rock cuttings; flattened segmental arches springing directly from the rock without any need for abutments. The first apear to have been built by Robert Stephenson over deep cuttings at Blisworth and Coventry on the London & Birmingham Railway in 1838, followed by Brunel on the Bristol & Exeter and Cornwall Railways.

With the development of wrought iron and later steel, flat plate and lattice girder bridges became very common, cheap and easy to build but generally lacking the appeal of arched bridges. There were exceptions. Some wrought-iron arched bridges were very attractive, like Ouseburn and Willington Dene viaducts at Newcastle on which the spandrels replicate the delicate lace-work of their wooden predecessors; likewise decorative cast-iron arches such as those on the Nene viaduct at Peterborough and the Belvidere Bridge over the Severn near Shrewsbury. Having said that, there are iron and steel bridges and viaducts that are internationally acclaimed for their daring engineering, which by their sheer size and form have become majestic additions to the landscape, notably Brunel's Royal Albert Bridge at Saltash, the Runcorn Bridge over the Mersey and, above all, the Forth Bridge. Brunel was a great exponent of timber trestle viaducts on his lines in the West Country and South Wales but, while structurally they were unique, in general they were no adornment to their surroundings and eventually had to be replaced by more conventional structures.

In the mid-twentieth century reinforced concrete was increasingly used for bridge structures, occasionally to striking designs but more generally flat concrete beams as uninspiring as their plate girder predecessors, with little regard to their locale. A notable exception is the Medway viaduct on the Channel Tunnel link, HS1.

Tunnel mouths are seldom prominent, hidden as they usually are at the end of a cutting. That some early ones had massive, highly ornamental portals

**Coat-of-Arms bridge, Coventry, bearing the arms of the Gregory family of nearby Styvechale Manor, 1985.**

is more a measure of the railways' desire to reassure anxious passengers that it was safe to travel deep under the earth in noisy smoke-filled darkness. So they were designed to give an impression of great solidity by adding turrets and crenellations. The north portal of Clayton tunnel in Sussex is an example, although here there was an additional motive: clearly visible from the London–Brighton road, it was also meant to impress passing travellers, as was the classical western portal of Brunel's Box tunnel in Wiltshire, adjacent to the main London–Bath road. In both instances the other ends were left plain, buried in deep cuttings far from public view. Indeed, many tunnel mouths were relatively plain, such as Robert Stephenson's Kilsby tunnel in Northamptonshire where the close proximity of the Holyhead Road to its north end might be expected to have attracted special treatment.

As with bridges, influential landowners could demand special treatment for tunnels through their estates *(see plate 19)*. There are instances where an unnecessary tunnel to hide the railway and preserve the landscape was the price of support for a railway scheme. The Earl of Lichfield at Shugborough secured not only the ornamental bridge already noted, but a tunnel with an Egyptian-style portal at one end and Norman at the other. Similarly, Lord Braybrooke got not only unusual ornamental portals to Audley End and Littlebury tunnels in Essex, but on the former his coat-of- arms as well. Neither tunnel was needed; they simply hid the railway from his view.

# The coast

ONE of the most obvious changes to the landscape made by railways is along the coast, where it afforded the most direct route or where inland routes were too hilly, in some instances taking to the shoreline. Best known is the spectacular 4½-mile stretch along the south Devon sea wall and cliffs between Dawlish Warren and Teignmouth. The three miles along the foot of the cliffs between Dover and Folkestone are less dramatic because nearly two miles are in tunnels inside the cliffs. Much of the railway mileage following the Cumbrian coast is along or close to the shore, particularly beside Morecambe Bay where a total of seven miles of embankments between Ulverston and Arnside enabled some 20,000 acres of salt marsh to be reclaimed. The converse happened in the broad estuary of the river Kent upstream of the viaduct at Arnside, which changed flow patterns – and still does – creating 900 acres of new salt marsh and significantly changing the shore line. The viaducts across the Loughor and Mawddach estuaries in Wales and the mouth of the Montrose Basin in Angus had similar effects.

Extensive land reclamation took place elsewhere, too. When the Chester & Holyhead Railway was built along 24 miles of the North Wales coastline between Flint and Colwyn Bay, for instance, apart from eight miles slightly inland between Talacre and Kinmel Bay, the railway hugged the shore on a low embankment, allowing the land behind it to be reclaimed. It opened up the coast to holidaymakers, too, producing the resorts of Prestatyn, Rhyl, Abergele and Colwyn Bay, the last two on the landward side of the railway which effectively cut them off from the sea. Beyond the peninsular on which Llandudno stands – a planned resort indirectly owing itself to the railway – the line regains the sea for five miles from Penmaenbach to Llanfairfechan, much of it at the base of cliffs and again separating communities from the sea. But nowhere on this coast is the railway nearly as great an intrusion as the late twentieth-century dual carriageway of the North Wales Expressway. Beyond the Lleyn Peninsula the Cambrian Railways' line clings to the edge of Cardigan Bay, some nine miles of it along the shoreline between Fairbourne and Tywyn. More than two miles of track, near Friog, are on a shelf cut in the cliff, heavily reinforced including a 200ft-long avalanche shelter built after rock falls caused accidents.

The North Yorkshire coastal route from Scarborough to Redcar tended to keep more inland. Where it encountered deep valleys it made great loops towards the coast, there to cross them on lofty iron trestle viaducts where they narrowed near the sea, becoming notable landmarks at Robin Hood's Bay, Sandsend – where the viaduct was virtually on the beach – Kettleness and

Staithes. After closure they were all demolished, except the tall, red brick Larpool viaduct that crosses the Esk 1½ miles upstream from Whitby.

In Scotland the railway at Carnoustie, north of Dundee, traverses the flat shoreline as far as Arbroath, where it cuts inland, briefly touching the coast again near Montrose. Thereafter it sweeps inland once more, then rejoins the cliff-tops for most of the way from Stonehaven to Aberdeen, much of it in cuttings interspersed with dramatic views out over the North Sea. Nearly all of the 17 miles of the Highland Railway between Golspie and Helmsdale in north west Scotland, and the 7¾ mile Dornoch branch, took advantage of raised beaches.

At Cullen on the Moray Firth, the Great North of Scotland Railway ran on a high embankment containing three viaducts, behind the old town and the harbour, cutting them off from the new town laid out in 1820–30, and dictated by the Earl of Seafield's refusal to allow the line through the grounds of Cullen House. An ornamental bridge over the main road into the town today is a bottleneck for traffic but is prized for its scenic value.

Estuaries also provided easy, level routes for railways, such as along the Stour in Essex; both sides of the Exe in south Devon; the Camel estuary from Wadebridge to Padstow in Cornwall; and along the Towy between Kidwelly and Carmarthen in South Wales.

## Country stations

DURING the first three decades of railway construction companies made great efforts to erect country stations that blended in comfortably with their surroundings *(see plate 21)*, partly to provide homely and familiar buildings that would encourage a hitherto static rural population to travel by the new mode, and partly from a sense of place that lingered on from the age of enlightenment. Architects were engaged to produce appropriate designs, some of them local men but many of them well-known figures like Sir William Tite, William Tress, Francis Thompson and, in the north east, Benjamin Green. They worked closely with the engineers, busy men willing enough to leave building design work to others. Some formed close relationships, at times including a contractor as well, such as that between the eminent engineer Joseph Locke, the great contractors Thomas Brassey and William Mackenzie, and Tite who, as part of the consortium, designed well over a hundred stations on lines they built in England, Scotland and France.

Many country stations of this period were not only seemly but in some cases were also cost-effective inasmuch as they introduced a measure of standardisation. For instance Brunel, who was his own architect, produced two designs for wayside stations, one Tudor and the other Italianate, both sharing common characteristics. He took care to employ local materials that varied from district to district, thereby combining homogeneity with the vernacular.

For stations on the Lancaster & Carlisle Railway Tite submitted four different-sized designs based on local farm and cottage buildings. Three were adopted and, although they have common characteristics, minor modifications and the use of local stone avoided giving the impression of uniformity. Even Sir Gilbert Scott, who later became the leading architect of his day and was no friend of Tite, remarked on how well they fitted into the landscape. Tite used similar designs on the Caledonian and Scottish Central Railways, acknowledging their locale simply by adding Scottish-style crow-steps to the gables. Otherwise they were the same as their English counterparts, yet none the worse for it.

This concept of a 'line style' was quite widely adopted by others. Tite himself and his partner Edward N. Clifton used several stock station designs for the London & South Western Railway for over 20 years, but with careful modifications to avoid repetitiveness. John Livock adopted a charming Tudor or Jacobean theme that imparted a unified quality to the stations, good sheds and cottages on the London & Birmingham's Northampton–Peterborough line and also on the Trent Valley Railway between Rugby and Stafford. Unfortunately only a handful have survived.

Conversely, other designers preferred greater diversity in style. Francis Thompson's exquisite stations on the North Midland Railway from Derby to Leeds were all different, while William Tress produced two basic designs, Italianate and Tudor, for his stations in Kent between Tunbridge Wells and Hastings, yet with differences in detail that gave each one a distinctive character. Conversely, his stations at Appledore, Aylesford, Cuxton and Warteringbury in the same county are delightfully varied in style.

Of course there were exceptions. In their haste to open lines and begin earning revenue some railway companies constructed mean wooden stations, quick to build and often stated to be temporary but destined to become permanent. Throughout its 51 years' independent existence, the South Eastern Railway gained a reputation for cheap wooden stations, about which the best that can be said is that they represented the Kentish clapboard tradition, yet no expense was spared on Tress's contemporary work for the same company.

Although I.K. Brunel designed some excellent series of small stations on the Great Western and its associated railways, he also produced a standard design for a small wooden station that he used quite widely, together with his unattractive wooden train sheds that were built at larger places and were dismissively nicknamed 'Brunel's barns'. They were forerunners of a growing standardisation on all railways from the mid-1860s onward, beginning a

**Hatfield Peverel station, Essex, c.1900; a typical Great Eastern Railway design of 1878.**
From an old postcard

fashion for distinctive corporate architecture widely adopted by other large commercial and public organisations that lasted for a century. It was applied to work in all materials – brick, stone, iron and, in the twentieth century, concrete – and for all kinds of purposes, from stations, goods sheds, houses and signal-boxes to smaller items like mass-produced mileposts and signals, all in distinctive designs that clearly identified their owners and, in the case of buildings, regardless of location.

Consequently railway buildings became the antithesis of the sympathetic treatment accorded to their earlier counterparts. For example, in the late 1880s standard buildings began appearing all over the Great Western system in bright-red brick from Ruabon or Bristol brickworks, embellished with Staffordshire blue brick trimmings, usually standing out with complete disregard to other buildings in the vicinity. Likewise, the London & North Western Railway adopted uniform designs for virtually everything, including prefabricated timberwork from its workshops at Crewe and red bricks from its own brickyard there. Consequently, near-identical wooden stations made from standard components and singularly ugly red-brick houses appeared on all its widespread lines, from London to Carlisle, Holyhead and Swansea to Leeds.

All the other large companies produced their own standard styles, changing them from time to time, some of them being quite elaborate. One or two, like the Midland and the North Eastern, to their credit tended to soften the environmental impact by using local stone instead of universal brick, where it was appropriate.

The location of a station was important to the company and the community it was intended to serve, although not always in the same way. The company needed to assess a locality's traffic potential to justify a station for a single village or, if not, whether one station could be conveniently (more or less) provided to serve two or more. For the community, a station bearing its name became something of a status symbol, even though it might be some distance away, as many were. For instance, Kirkby Lonsdale, a small country town in Cumbria, was 1¾ miles from the station, as Bradshaw's timetable was at pains to point out. Some railways, notably the Great Western, added the suffix 'Road' to the station name to indicate that the place served was some distance away. There were four in Cornwall alone: Bodmin Road, St Columb Road, Grampound Road and Gwinear Road, to which can be added the London & South Western's Port Isaac Road. In the case of Llanbister Road on the London & North Western Railway's Central Wales line, Llanbister was a full six miles away.

Confusion could arise if a branch to the destination place was opened later, as happened when one did open from Bodmin Road to Bodmin, where the LSWR also had a station named Bodmin. It was left to British Railways to differentiate them and, later, to rename Bodmin Road 'Bodmin Parkway'. It was only slightly less confusing at Berkeley Road on the Midland's Gloucester–Bristol line when a station was opened at Berkeley itself on the Severn & Wye branch to Sharpness and the Severn Bridge.

Scottish railways tended to ignore the device. There, 'Road' generally referred to the name of a road, as in the case of urban stations on both sides of the border. Neither did they much use double-barrelled names, unlike on English and Welsh railways where it was a favourite device to indicate that a station was intended to serve two places. Often the first named was the place furthest away, as at Puxton & Worle station in Somerset, villages respectively two miles and one mile distant. Great confusion could afflict a newcomer to Hope in North Wales, which enjoyed three stations bearing its name. Hope & Pen-y-fford was actually in Pen-y-ffordd on the LNWR's Chester–Mold line two miles from Hope, which in any case had its own station named Hope Village on the Great Central line from Wrexham to the Wirral. The third, Hope Exchange, was an interchange station where the two lines crossed. To add even more confusion, there was also a separate Pen-y-ffordd station on the GC line. Southam, a small south Warwickshire country town, enjoyed both styles: the GWR's Southam Road & Harbury and the LNWR's Southam & Long Itchington. Both were stations two miles from Southam but only three quarters of a mile from the other two places.

The accommodation at a country station depended on its size. Typically the main building would contain a booking hall, a ticket office combined with the stationmaster's office if he did not have a separate one, a porters' room, a waiting room heated by a fire, a ladies' room and a 'gents'. The opposite platform might also have a heated waiting room, or just an open-fronted waiting shelter, according to the station's importance. The stationmaster's house might also be included in the same range or be a separate building nearby. The goods shed in the yard would have its own office, with a weighbridge close by, and the yard would also provide accommodation for private traders such as the local coal, builders' and agricultural merchants, and other local businesses reliant on the railway for bulk supplies.

## The rural economy

IN order to build a railway it was necessary to incorporate a company by Act of Parliament which, among other powers, authorised the compulsory purchase of land. It has been estimated that the average area required per route mile was eleven acres. The country's most powerful people, the large landowners, at first opposed the early railways and, if they could not deny them land, determined to extract the maximum price. Frequently their demands were excessive and if no agreement could be reached recourse had to be made to a statutory form of arbitration which vendors used to maximum advantage.

As time went on landowners began to realise that railways could increase land values, from about 10 per cent to as much as 20 per cent near stations. After the London & Birmingham was opened through Leighton Buzzard the value of a 200-acre farm rose by 30 per cent. In Scotland it was less marked. Once the main framework of trunk railways was in place by the mid-1850s and the benefits to agriculture had become evident, landowners 'joined the club' and began seeking railway expansion into rural areas by helping to promote secondary routes and branches. The Improvement of Land Act 1864 allowed landowners to subscribe to railway companies' capital and charge it to their estates. Competing trunk lines also contributed to this infilling of the railway map; the steady expansion of the London & South Western into the West Country, territory that the Great Western considered its own, is a good example. Rural communities benefited from both types of infill, so that by 1900 there were few places in England that were further than five miles from a railway.

As a result, the power of English landowners was reduced by the coming of the railway, although less so in central Wales and much of Scotland where railways were thinner on the ground. Only one area of the rural economy was unaffected. The parish system of local government remained intact with its taxation system based on annual land values. The railways learned to mitigate their effect by negotiating long-term agreements, from which both parties benefited. The parishes secured a guaranteed annual fixed income, and the railways could rely on a fixed annual expenditure.

To fill gaps in the system the Light Railways Act of 1896 was intended to encourage the construction of lines to a lower standard than the conventional railway: cheaper to build, with lower speeds, limitations on weight and, most importantly, authorised by a Light Railway Order issued by the Board of Trade, saving the cost of a parliamentary Act. Although common in many continental countries, they failed to succeed in Britain. They were still relatively expensive to build – unnecessarily so – and local authorities, which were empowered to lend financial support, were unenthusiastic. The main-line companies on which light railways relied for connections and co-operation in services were equally disinclined to take a positive attitude. The few that were built were isolated and scattered, and there was no attempt at a uniform system like those in France.

Within a few years the railways faced a new competitor: the internal combustion engine and the motor bus. Several companies began to operate country bus services, the first being the Great Western, from Helston in Cornwall to The Lizard, together with motor lorry delivery services. In 1913 the GWR had 99 buses and 67 lorries, the London & North Western 41 and 43, and the North Eastern Railway 50 and 23 respectively. Of the other companies, only the Great Eastern ran significant bus services, but in that year sold them to a local operator. Steam railcars were tried by a few railways in an effort to reduce the cost of rural services, again led by the Great Western, but after a few years they were generally replaced by what became known as push-and-pull trains; a small locomotive attached to a single trailer coach fitted with a driving compartment at one end from which the driver could control the train when it was being propelled, thus avoiding the need to uncouple the engine and run round at the end of each journey. Sometimes a second coach was sandwiched between the engine and trailer, or as many as four with the engine in the middle and a driving trailer at both ends. The GWR in particular went in for push-and-pulls, or auto trains as it called them, on its branch lines, of which it had a great many. In the 1930s it also led the way in successfully using single diesel railcars of a strikingly streamline design, but its fellow main-line companies did not follow.

Railways played a major part in the era of agricultural improvement. Indeed, it is no exaggeration to say that in the nineteenth century they transformed farming practices, providing quick and easy transport for livestock and produce to markets and, by return, goods such as fertilisers, coal and cattle feed, all at reduced cost.

By 1920 the railways were carrying 12 million tons of agricultural products and 2½ million tons of fertilizer annually. Cattle droving quickly became extinct as carriage by train in purpose-built cattle trucks took over, enabling beasts to be moved quickly and without losing condition. Every country station had its cattle dock. Railways also contributed to the decline of markets by encouraging their concentration at large trading centres at the expense of small local markets. To prosper, a market now had to be close or next to a railway; some large ones had their own private sidings. Others might move to a new site closer to the railway, as happened at Kirkoswald in Cumbria which moved a mile away to Lazonby when the Settle & Carlisle line was opened in 1876. Some were new, like the auction mart opened alongside the railway at Gisburn in north Lancashire.

The grain trade, too, changed greatly. In corn-growing districts granaries were built close to stations, on occasions by the railway itself, such as the large four-storey pair at Sleaford, Lincolnshire; and maltings such as those at Ware in Hertfordshire, where the Great Eastern Railway built a large granary in the goods yard.

One of the greatest changes the railways brought to agriculture was in the milk trade. Whereas previously milk was supplied to small towns from nearby farms or, in the case of large cities, by cow-keepers who kept their animals literally in their back yards in unhygienic conditions, milk could now be brought in quickly and in quantity by train from further afield. Large-scale dairy farming replaced arable farming, notably in Berkshire, Wiltshire and the West Country and these sources became the principal suppliers to London, considerably improving the health of the capital. It was the same in other large urban areas. Large dairies and milk-processing factories were set up next to country stations in milk-producing districts, providing cream, butter and other dairy products.

The railways also brought about a revolution in horticulture, not only enabling market gardens to provide fresh fruit and vegetables to the towns but giving rise to rural food processing plants producing tinned foods and jam. The effect of railways on other rural industries like corn milling could be to concentrate production at a single large mill or factory near a station, or a brewery such as the one built opposite the station at Leeming Bar in North Yorkshire.

The extractive industries – brickmaking, quarrying, mining and lime and cement works – were also encouraged by the railway to be absorbed into larger units, but by their very nature remained country-based, dominating rural economies and landscapes. Growth was stimulated by a combination of high demand for building materials and minerals during the rapid industrialisation of the national economy, and the ability of the railways to carry them. Small country brickyards producing hand-made bricks were supplanted by large mechanical works close to a railway. Dotted about the country, some exploited local clay deposits discovered during railway construction; others in areas with extensive deposits formed large groups of brickworks, such as those whose tall chimneys dominate the landscape in the Bedfordshire brickfields alongside the east coast main line south of Peterborough and the cross-country line from Bletchley to Bedford.

Quarrying and mining similarly grew at the expense of small local workings, requiring their own branch lines or tramways, often with rope-worked inclines, to connect them to the nearest railway. Frequently they were quite lengthy. The 2½ mile long Corncockle mineral railway near Lockerbie in Dumfries-shire was relied on by Glasgow for much of its building stone after local supplies ran out. As with so many others up and down Britain, its course is still visible. Such lines were generally built and operated by the mine and quarry owners, although there were several run by main-line companies. For example the Great Northern company opened two quite extensive series of mineral lines to serve the ironstone field in north Leicestershire and adjacent Lincolnshire, and a number serving quarries and china clay deposits in Cornwall came into Great Western ownership.

The same combination of high demand and readily available rail transport led to the demise of small country limekilns, replaced by large lime and cement works, dominating the landscape in lime and chalk-bearing areas such as north Derbyshire, north Kent and around Dunbar in East Lothian, invariably along-side a railway. The output of slate from the quarries of North Wales, and the huge waste tips that completely transformed the landscapes of places like Blaenau Festiniog and Bethesda, would not have been possible but for the development of the narrow-gauge railways that uniquely served them, able to penetrate the mountainous area more easily and cheaply than standard gauge lines.

The fastest growth in mineral extraction was, of course, coal. Railways and coal mining were mutually dependent. Small local pits were supplanted by large groups as rural areas rapidly became industrial, marked by pit-head gear and slag heaps, and criss-crossed by colliery railways, many, but not all, built by the railway companies and sometimes carrying passengers as well. The Londonderry Railway, for instance, which was built to serve the Marquis of Londonderry's collieries in County Durham, ran passenger trains through a district that in a few places was surprisingly rural.

Physical changes occurring at a village following the opening of a railway depended on the location of the station. If it was close by, expansion would often take place to fill the gap between them, while some villages expanded into small towns. The aim of the Kendal & Windermere Railway, opened in 1847, was to reach Ambleside but local opposition forced it to terminate at Birthwaite, a hamlet nearly two miles from the lake itself. The station was named Windermere. Its name was adopted by the small town and resort that sprang up next to it, creating confusion that remains today. Ambleside never got a railway and Birthwaite is now forgotten, even though it was the birthplace of popular tourism in the Lake District.

Scottish tourism, too, can be attributed to railway expansion as lines were opened through the glens, bringing growth to small communities. When Callander, a small weaving village in Perthshire, saw its first railway in 1858 its population was about 1,750. It gave tourists access to The Trossachs and began to expand, while the railway slowly crept westward, finally reaching Oban in 1880, by which time Callander was growing into a small town, had become a junction and, three years later, had a new and larger station. By 1921 it had 2,215 inhabitants. When the railway reached Strathyre, 9½ miles towards Oban, there were just a few cottages. Although it did not grow to anything like the extent of Callander, by 1894 it merited a mention in Murray's *Handbook* as 'a place of summer resort'. Yet Dalmally, a scattered community further west at the foot of Loch Awe and reached by the railway in 1877, by 1890 had barely grown at all and had no village as such.

Railways did not always increase prosperity in popular scenic areas. Neither did they in agricultural districts. They enabled small businesses to amalgamate and concentrate elsewhere, taking employment with them, as happened at Abbotsbury in Dorset after the railway arrived in 1885. Local employers began to move to Dorchester and Weymouth, reducing the population by half during the next century. The railway, never profitable, unsurprisingly closed in 1952. Lavenham, Suffolk's largest village, likewise lost out when the railway reached it in 1865. Business declined, the population of 1,800 was only 200 more in 1901, and by 1961 had actually fallen to 1,300. The railway closed four years later. In the same county the population of Framlingham fell from 2,450 to 2,000 over the century following the opening of a railway in 1859, making it easy to travel the 16 miles to Ipswich.

## The social impact

RAILWAYS changed rural lifestyles in a number of ways; lifestyles that contained a great deal of poverty. Although the 'tied cottage' system had no legal backing, in practice most agricultural workers lived in a house that went with the job. If they sought better paid work elsewhere they lost their home. The new railways now offered them new opportunities. Labouring on railway construction was better paid than in agriculture, and although most of it was done by itinerant groups of navvies, a significant degree was performed by local labour.

In turn, the railways greatly encouraged migration to the towns, or even overseas, in search of better prospects and a higher standard of living. There was a negative aspect in that it weakened traditional family ties and local relationships. In 1851, 50 per cent of Britain's population were urban dwellers; by 1881 it had grown to 70 per cent, but the overall effect for those who stayed was a gradual improvement in agricultural wages, most noticeably in districts directly served by a railway, less so in others. Railways also provided great impetus to seasonal itinerant labour, especially at harvest time. Beginning in 1856, special trains were run in September to the Weald of Kent by the South Eastern Railway and its successors, right up to 1960, for the annual exodus of London east-end families for several weeks' hop-picking, their only form of holiday. In the 1930s over 33,000 hop-pickers were carried from London annually by the Southern Railway, and there was a similar but smaller migration from the Black Country to the hop fields of Herefordshire and Worcestershire, in trains comprising the Great Western Railway's oldest carriages.

Village life became less insular. In 1838 railways were required by law to carry mails, closely followed by the penny post in 1840. Villages began to find themselves in rapid and easy contact with the outside world as mail arrived and left daily by train. Carriage of newspapers coincided with mail services, so that national papers were delivered to stations the next day. The electric telegraph made communication even faster, pioneered by the railways' own systems which usually were available for public use at stations. Private telegraph companies were set up, using railway routes for their poles and wires, providing another option. They were placed under Post Office control in 1869. Railways made it easier for farmers to move from one holding to another, often at a considerable distance. A special train would be assembled to transport an entire farm – livestock, implements, machinery, household goods and family – with stops for watering and feeding the animals and even milking cows.

Because so much village activity revolved around the station, the station-master was a person of importance, ranking after the squire, the parson and the doctor in the local hierarchy. Respected as the representative of the organisation upon which so much village life had come to depend, he was often the recipient of favours from important local people and leading customers. He was not always the most popular figure though, representing as he did a large, remote and usually monopolistic undertaking, bound by rules and regulations that often seemed uncompromising. Moreover, his job could be rather lonely. Promotion meant moving to another station. A good man would be transferred every few years, giving him and his family little time to become assimilated into the community.

Field sports were greatly stimulated by the railway, on which they increasingly relied. Hunt meets could now be held further afield. Horseboxes that included a compartment for the rider or groom could be attached to a passenger train and easily taken from one side of a county to the other or beyond, both occupants arriving fresh for the chase. It also broke the hold of the landed gentry on hunting, enabling the wealthy middle classes from the towns to join in. Shooting in particular benefited from the railways, bringing influxes of parties to country estates and moors. Grouse shooting was among the most popular, especially in Scotland, and at the beginning of the season lines from the south were busy with special trains carrying whole families with their servants, dogs and equipment.

Railways also gave access to the countryside for simpler pleasures, such as an outing for town dwellers on a whole- or half-day excursion to a beauty spot, while country people could make visits to the town or the seaside, unheard of before railways enabled them to travel more than a few miles from home. It was the beginning of mobility for all.

## Railway villages, enclaves and settlements

A rural railway junction could create economic growth at an existing village or, quite often, at a place where there was little or nothing before. Llandudno Junction is an example of the latter. The Chester & Holyhead Railway opened a branch to the growing resort of Llandudno in 1856. It built a station at the junction, followed by a few railway houses and a small engine shed. A branch down the Conwy valley followed, then a larger shed, and in 1897 a new larger station, all increasing railway employment which in turn stimulated growth until Llandudno Junction was a village that in character today is large enough to resemble a small town.

The same happened on a smaller scale at Craven Arms in Shropshire, where there was only a coaching inn at a cross roads when the railway arrived in 1852. It became the junction for the Central Wales line in 1866, with an engine shed, a carriage shed, forty-six railway houses and other developments following, and by 1881 it had grown into a sizeable village.

The new life that a railway brought to a village frequently showed in the form of an enclave of railway houses. When Woodford Halse in Northamptonshire became an important junction on the newly-opened Great Central

Railway in 1898–99, it was accompanied by an engine shed, repair shops, a small marshalling yard and 170 houses built by private builders and leased to the railway. Although the railway closed in 1966, leaving little trace, Woodford and its twin village Hinton continued to grow into a commuter village. The junction settlement at Hellifield in North Yorkshire was quite separate from the village, comprising distinctive rows of houses near the station, built by the Midland and the Lancashire & Yorkshire companies for their staff there and at their respective engine sheds and yards.

The same happened at Tebay in Cumbria, where the London & North Western and North Eastern companies each built their own terraced houses, forming a distinctive colony half a mile from the original village which is now known as Old Tebay. Today the station, junction, engine shed and yards have gone, leaving only the railway settlements prominent in the landscape alongside the busy west coast main line.

In Scotland in the mid-1700s–1800s, landowners built planned villages, mainly to re-house displaced families during the agrarian revolution. Several of the later ones were built at stations, such as Newtyle in 1833, Washington, a few miles away in 1835, and Dyce – now a suburb of Aberdeen – in 1865. Where the village was a distance from the station, a separate village might be established next to it, taking its name as at Thornhill Station in Dumfriesshire; place names that have been perpetuated to the present day, long after the stations or even the railway itself have closed. Ferryhill Station and Bedlington Station in Co. Durham, Uphall Station in West Lothian, Widdrington Station in Northumberland and Otterham Station in north Cornwall are examples.

The suffix 'Junction' has also been perpetuated in the names of places no longer having a station, in the case of Horbury Junction in West Yorkshire lost as long ago as 1927 when it was replaced by Horbury Millfield Road, itself now gone. Most of the closures were in the 1960s Beeching era. Verney Junction in rural Buckinghamshire, a railway creation which never had more than the station, a hotel and seven houses (even now there are only nine more) is still prominently signed on approach roads. Seaton Junction, an equally small place in east Devon, is similarly well identified. In Somerset, Chard Junction promoted a little more development, but Yeovil Junction, on the same line, did not give its name to the locality at all because it was on the edge of the village of Stoford. Each of these three junctions served a branch line to the town after which they were named, a practice which was fairly widespread. Today there is not even a railway at Halwill Junction in north Devon; only the village's name is a reminder.

In the late 1850s a Scottish paper suggested that railways could generate commuter traffic by building their own villages outside large cities. The

Edinburgh & Glasgow Railway modified the idea by offering free season tickets for a limited number of years to anyone building on open land near the railway. The most successful initiative was at Campsie Junction, an isolated station near Kirkintilloch, where the residents chose the name Lenzie for their new village. In 1867 the station took its name, and in 1891 the population had reached 1,600.

The same idea was adopted by some other railways or by groups of their directors, generally in attempts to create coastal resorts, with limited success. The Cambrian Railways tried it along Cardigan Bay, the Hull & Holderness Railway at Withernsea, and the Scarborough & Whitby at Robin Hood's Bay and at Ravenscar. Like the Furness Railway's ambitious scheme at Seascale, none of them succeeded. As late as 1929 the Southern Railway collaborated with developers to promote Allhallows-on-Sea in Kent, including a branch line, but it failed.

Some railway settlements attracted no development, staying as railway colonies, usually because of their remoteness. The Stanhope & Tyne Railway, a waggonway of 1823, built a village at Waskerley on the Durham moors, complete with shop, two chapels and a school. Now it is largely abandoned. Riccarton Junction in the Scottish Borders was completely remote. The station served only for changing trains and the railway was its only means of access. There were thirty houses, a school and recreation hall, and a shop and post office on the station. Everything and everybody went in and out by rail. After closure in 1969 nearly all of it was razed.

In the same area, Riddings Junction comprised only a few railway cottages; on the Settle & Carlisle line Hawes Junction, now named Garsdale, still does – twenty-two in all. Low Gill in Cumbria comprises an attractive row of Lancaster & Carlisle Railway cottages and a school, still beside a main line but its junction and station long gone. At Battersby Junction, a colony of railway houses in North Yorkshire and now only a reversing point on the Middlesbrough–Whitby line, the station is still open, half a mile from Battersby village.

On Scotland's scenic West Highland line the isolated Rannoch Moor station had a few railway houses and a school which also served the signal-men's children from Gorten, a crossing loop seven miles away. In the far north, remote stations like Altnabreac and Dalnaspidal were built as much for operating purposes as for any local traffic, but still required railwaymen's houses.

At Builth Road in Central Wales, the London & North Western and Cambrian Railways had adjoining stations at the point where their lines crossed. The Cambrian establishment comprised only three houses and a mission hall, but the LNWR had a small engine shed and engineers' yard, requiring thirty red-brick houses, mainly terraces, looking strangely out of place in the open landscape.

In 1890 the same company built a large engine shed at Mold Junction alongside the Dee near Chester, and a large red-brick terraced village of over 120 houses, a school, a shop and a three-storey lodging house for enginemen working away from home, all at that time quite alien to the area. At Oxenholme, the junction for the Windermere branch, in 1882–98 the LNWR erected in open country two colonies of its standard terraces a short distance apart, one for station and signalling staff and the other for the locomotive department. From the 1920s onward, private housing began filling the gap between them.

These houses were built to several standard designs that were repeated singly, in pairs or in terraces at rural level crossings and signalboxes all over that company's system, in raw red brick regardless of location. Of all the uniform house styles adopted by the main railway companies the LNWR's were the most easily recognised, uncompromisingly severe. Other companies' designs, although still distinctive, tended to be less harsh, often using local materials.

As with most railway buildings and stations built from the 1860s onward, company houses were the product of evolving corporate designs. Before then there was much greater individuality and respect for local styles in station houses and crossing cottages, lending them considerable charm and character. Many still stand today *(see plate 20)*.

Now we consider four railway villages that did develop, becoming towns, beginning with Carnforth at the northern extremity of Lancashire. When the Lancaster & Carlisle Railway opened a small station there in 1846 the place was little more than a hamlet of less than 100 people. Within 25 years it had become a junction with two other railways, all three companies built their own engine sheds, and the station underwent successive enlargements. In 1864 an ironworks was established, and the population had grown to over 800. When the ironworks closed in 1929 Carnforth was a town and Urban District with a population in excess of 3,000. It is still a junction, although of lesser importance, and the long-closed locomotive depots have been replaced by a rolling stock company, maintaining a railway influence although much reduced. Residential and industrial developments have increased the population to nearly 7,500.

Westbury in Wiltshire was a parallel instance. It had a population of 350 when the Great Western Railway opened a station in 1848. It became a junction, the station was enlarged, an engine shed was opened and, as at Carnforth, an ironworks was established from 1857 to 1925, by which time Westbury was a small town and Urban District of 4,000 people. The third example is also on the Great Western, Didcot, then in Berkshire but now

Oxfordshire, where a junction station and engine shed were opened in 1844. A small railway settlement grew close by, separate from the old village. The railway installations were steadily enlarged and by 1932 the population of the combined villages was 2,200. After the engine shed closed in 1965 it became a highly successful railway heritage centre, thus, like Carnforth, maintaining a railway connection apart from the main-line railway. But it was post-war development rather than the railway that made Didcot into a small town although, as with Carnforth and Westbury, the railway was the genesis.

Lastly, a place where the opposite happened. Melton Constable in Norfolk was an insignificant village of 118 people where four secondary lines made a junction in 1882. It was a convenient location for railway workshops and it became the headquarters of the Midland & Great Northern Joint Railway. By 1911 the population had risen to 1,157, Melton had the amenities of a small town and the new houses, with their red pantiled roofs, gave it a little more character than the average railway settlement. After the railway closed in 1964 the population declined to 650 and today recognisable evidence of the railway is almost non-existent.

## Abandonments

AFTER the so-called rationalising of the railways of the 1960s old railway alignments became a familiar sight, their overgrown cuttings, embankments and bridges rapidly assimilating themselves into the rural scene. Many disused viaducts were listed for preservation, both for their historical value and because they had become an integral part of the landscape. But these were not new features; railway abandonments have occurred since the first part of the nineteenth century, usually the result of over-ambition by their builders. The remains of old curves and spurs that once connected adjacent lines are widespread, as, for instance, at each end of the cross-country Bletchley–Oxford line at Bletchley and Wolvercote; and at Clifton near Penrith, where a south curve once linked the west coast and Eden Valley lines.

A surprising number never saw a train, such as a projected line in the Ouse valley in Sussex; an inexplicably isolated 300yd cutting in a field at Hurst Green in the Ribble valley of north Lancashire, the remains of a scheme to build a new trunk line into Yorkshire; and a few earthworks marking the start of an ambitious endeavour to shorten the Furness Railway's route up the Cumbrian coast by building a viaduct across the Duddon sands. More tangible remains exist in the eleven arches of Tadcaster viaduct, intended to be part of a new line from Leeds to York in 1847, but never used except for a siding to a factory.

Near Llangurig in North Wales there are remains of one of the largest unrealised projects, the grandly-named Manchester & Milford Railway. The three miles that were opened before the money ran out in 1864 only saw an occasional goods train, and the track was removed in 1882.

Here and there post-World War Two abandonments have been used for new roads, although generally even a double-track railway is not wide enough for a modern main highway. Significant sections of the Merthyr–Abergavenny line were used for the Heads of the Valleys road in South Wales, and part of the North Wales coast line was slewed sideways to make room for the North Wales Expressway. Several short lengths of the Gilling–Pickering line in North Yorkshire have been used to straighten the A170, while one of the longest stretches is the 5½ miles of the Tebay–Barnard Castle line used by the A685 trunk road between the M6 at Junction 38 and Newbiggin-on-Lune.

The Beeching era saw the near-extinction of the country railway, but within 20 years there was a growing realisation that some closures had been over-hasty. Stations began to be reopened, such as New Cumnock and Sanquhar in Dumfriesshire and stations on the Settle & Carlisle line, a trend that steadily gathered impetus, including some new stations.

Passenger services have been restored between Blackburn and Clitheroe and on South Wales valley lines, and more recently in Scotland the closed Airdrie–Bathgate line has been reopened, while work is progressing on reopening the old Waverley route between Edinburgh and Galashiels. Calls for more have been led by rail revival groups, aided by the setting up of Community Rail Partnerships and, more recently, by regional local authority groupings. One of the largest schemes is to reinstate the direct rail route between Oxford and Cambridge by relaying the disused section between Oxford and Bletchley, long closed to passengers but still *in situ*; using the existing line onward to Bedford; and restoring the abandoned remainder eastward, including a section of entirely new railway. The country railway is returning, an integral part of a modern rail renaissance.

# Further reading

J.H. Appleton, *The Geography of Communications in Great Britain*, 1962

Gordon Biddle, *The Railway Surveyors*, 1990

W.G. Hoskins, *The Making of the English Landscape*, 1955

Francis Pryor, *The Making of the British Landscape*, 2010

Michael Robbins, *The Railway Age*, 1962

Jack Simmons, *The Railway in Town and Country, 1830–1914*, 1986

Jack Simmons and Gordon Biddle (eds), *The Oxford Companion to British Railway History*, 1999 edn

David St John Thomas, *The Country Railway*, 2011 edn

# CHAPTER 9

# Railways as a Business Enterprise

## David Hodgkins

RAILWAYS are rightly regarded as Britain's first modern big businesses. The forms of organisation they adopted and the techniques they developed often pioneered the way for other businesses to follow. This chapter examines these aspects and then goes on to consider the impact railways had on the economy and society. A number of statistics are taken from a variety of sources. Some, particularly rates of return on capital, are estimates for which other figures are available calculated on slightly different bases. They are included to show the direction of change.

Railways did not first become big businesses when the four big companies were created in 1923, though all four were among the six largest companies in Britain in 1934–5. The LMS employed 220,000 workers while the largest manufacturing company had 60,000. From the start, in comparison with firms in other industries, the railway companies were giants both in terms of capital employed and of numbers of employees. In 1825 there were only eight firms with a capital of more than £1million – four canals, two docks and two insurance companies. By 1840 sixteen railway companies had more than £1million authorised capital and the London & Birmingham (LBR) had £5million.

By 1851 the LNWR had raised nearly £30million. The railway industry was highly concentrated in a relatively small number of firms. As early as 1850 the fifteen largest railway companies accounted for 75 per cent of gross traffic revenue and 61 per cent of paid-up capital in the industry. By 1870 the four largest (LNWR, Midland, GWR, NER) accounted for 44 per cent and 38 per cent respectively.

The industry as a whole was employing 275,000 or 3.3 per cent of the country's entire male labour force. The seven largest companies were all railways.

197

By the beginning of the twentieth century it might have been expected that the growth of manufacturing firms aided by consolidation and conversion to limited liability status would have rivalled the railways in size, but in 1904–5 the ten largest companies ranked by market value of their shares were all railway companies. The largest manufacturing company, Coats (J. & P.) Ltd was twelfth. Only the General Post Office had more employees than the biggest railway companies. The Midland and LNWR were probably the world's second and third largest corporations at that time.

The size of the early major railway companies, and the distances covered presented unprecedented challenges to management. The negotiations for land were complex before construction started. There was little directly relevant experience, and no generalised management expertise or principles had been developed. Industries had developed their own management structures to suit their particular needs. Railways therefore had to a large extent to devise their own systems of management.

There was no overnight revolution. The practices of canal and coach companies was drawn upon to an extent. The Stockton & Darlington Railway not only contracted out the construction of the line as railway companies continued to do, but initially opted for a public right of way for non-mineral traffic. In 1833 it subcontracted the operation of the railway, a practice which lasted until it was taken over by the NER in 1863. It also subcontracted the maintenance of the permanent way, locomotives and rolling stock. The limited geographical area which the railway served, and the concentration of traffic on relatively few commodities enabled the close supervision of the contractors' standards by a few managers and directors.

In another respect the SDR was also an interim development. Its capital was drawn largely from local sources or from the close-knit network of Quakers, so the management was closer to the personalised or partnership form of firm widely found in industry at the time. Other railway companies developed a form which soon saw a divorce between ownership and control. The railways had large volumes of plant, both mobile and fixed, and a huge workforce spread over an extensive area, but requiring high levels of control to secure efficiency and safety.

The first main-line railways were highly profitable concerns. However the 1830s and 1840s saw the exposure of major problems as well as pointers towards their solution. This initial period saw little by way of development of techniques to deal with the control of a complex and large-scale organisation or problems such as depreciation. This contributed to the high capital cost of construction and to over-optimistic forecasts of future traffic. In 1844 the Board of Trade estimated that the average cost per route mile in Britain was substantially higher than in other countries. Much of this was due to the procedure adopted. Parliamentary expenses were not paralleled abroad. Legal costs were much higher, as was land and compensation. Earthworks, bridges and other engineering works also tended to cost more in Britain, and stations markedly so. The result was a permanent addition to the capital burden.

Early railwaymen were well aware they were breaking new ground. On the formation of the LNWR George Carr Glyn, the chairman and a City banker with extensive experience in insurance and docks, emphasised the success of the constituent companies and the difficulties with which they had to struggle in carrying out what, in the first instance, had been nothing but an experiment on the largest scale. Glyn himself had given some thought to the problem of management. As a member of the LBR board he had urged that each department should be directed by an officer responsible to the committee or the board and the details of management should be left to him.

The board however would need a confidential superior officer to generally superintend the working of the system. This in essence was the genesis of the general manager, and approximated to the position occupied by Mark Huish in the LNWR after 1846. However in practice the management system was less clear cut with executive duties and responsibilities not well defined or not followed. Initially the primary executive lead was taken by secretaries, traffic managers, or engineers or others. By 1847 there were only two general managers and even by 1870 the position was still not universal, though most major lines had such a post. There was no ready-formed body of managers. Several were recruited from carrying firms. Others had substantial business experience, like Henry Booth of the Liverpool & Manchester, Creed (LBR) and Saunders (GWR) and some were ex-naval or army officers, like Moorsom (LBR), O'Brien (NER), and Huish.

The roles of shareholders and directors were more substantial than they became later. Shareholders were highly influential. There were 170,000 railway shareholders in 1855. They nominated the directors and were quick to put forward people who represented their interests. The clearest examples were rich Liverpudlians who fought hard to obtain what they regarded as adequate representation on several of the boards of the principal companies. In the 1850s and 1860s committees of shareholders played important parts at crucial moments in the history of the West Midland, GWR and GER, bringing about a change of management in ways that were rarely seen after 1875. Their interventions were however generally defensive designed to prevent a further deterioration in the company's finances, exemplified by the campaigns in many companies to close the capital account in the 1850s.

Nevertheless there were the beginnings a divorce between ownership and control, unlike in most manufacturing firms of the period. It was a form which was denoted in the twentieth century as managerial capitalism. The managers tended to keep dividends at a level which would avoid shareholder revolt but they were more interested in furthering company growth and extending their own power than they were in maximising returns to the investors.

Structurally the railway companies were generally of the centralised, departmental or functional type with departments headed by specialist managers, responsible for operations, goods, accounts, legal affairs, etc who were coordinated by the general manager. The geographical spread of the larger companies meant that responsibility had to be delegated to district specialist managers but who reported to the specialist managers.

This departmental system was the norm until after the formation of the Big Four in 1923. This did not mean that the general manager could always be more than a co-ordinator. Responsibilities for traffic and trains were not necessarily brought together. Because in-house production of locomotives was usual and because the locomotive superintendents enjoyed a high professional status, technical merit rather than financial criteria could be the basis of decision making.

By 1905 there were 620,000 shareholders in railways, but the proportion of shares held by board members averaged only 1 per cent, giving railway directors less voting control than in any other industry. There were no British parallels to the moguls who held financial sway over their companies' fortunes in the USA, such as Gould, Vanderbilt, Huntingdon or Harriman. As Terry Gourvish has put it, large railway companies remained for several decades the only places where managers could operate in a bureaucratic environment divorced from the persistent intervention of owners.

The railways did much to establish the status of the business executive, as seen in the prestigious figure of the general manager. A few like Fay (Great Central) and Pole (GWR) moved to other industries. The managers were however almost entirely career railwaymen though a proportion had experience in one or more other railway companies. Watkin (Manchester, Sheffield and Lincoln-shire (MSLR and SER) and Forbes (London, Chatham and Dover (LCDR)) became chairmen and so were encouraged to act as a managing director on the lines of an American railroad president, as did Scotter (LSWR), Thompson (Caledonian) and Granet (Midland) in the early twentieth century.

The internalisation of management did not mean that recruitment and training was entirely ignored. The MSLR began a special apprenticeship training scheme for managers in 1855. In an era when management training was virtually unknown, Acworth, the railway economist, lectured on railway

**Chief Officers of the LNWR, 1869.**
National Railway Museum, Science & Society Picture Library

economics at the London School of Economics in the 1890s, where a Railway Department was formed in 1904 with railway money and in 1897 the NER began its traffic apprentice scheme which was carried on by the LNER.

The creation of the Big Four in 1923 might have been expected to lead to new systems of decentralised management to cope with the much larger units. The response of the companies varied. The GWR continued with a centralised system, while the LNER adopted a decentralised system based on divisions corresponding to the constituent companies. The Southern started with three general managers, soon replaced by a single general manager with a number of departmental heads. Only the LMS introduced a system of general management in which a president and four vice-presidents, each responsible for a defined area of management, acted as a co-ordinating and policy-making executive. By 1938, particularly on the LMS, a more sophisticated style of management had been introduced with better cost control and the introduction of scientific research with the establishment of a research department with laboratories at Derby. In the other companies there were merely meetings of chief officers so that it was not easy to take an overall view against the specialist departmental heads.

The degree of consolidation in the 1840s and 1850s referred to earlier was achieved by the major companies allying with local interests, putting up money, appointing directors and often leasing or purchasing the line, sometimes at exorbitant cost, coupled with amalgamations. This process together with the Railway Mania in 1845 revealed shortcomings in accounting, audit, fraud and the muddling of revenue and capital. Practices to which many in the

Mania had turned a blind eye or with which they had connived were less acceptable in the post-Mania depression.

Before 1845 only the LBR had produced a general balance sheet. It also devised the double account system. Other improvements followed, some brought about by legislation or the threat of it. The LNWR decided in 1848 to issue more comprehensive accounts, an example which was followed. Standard formats for the accounts of railway companies had to await the Regulation of Railways Act of 1868. Nevertheless the needs of this large new industry provided the basic features of all company reporting and generated principles of account-ancy of more general application. Auditing was at first in the hands of share-holders elected for that purpose, but gradually a class of professional auditors emerged who carried out the regular half-yearly auditing of railway accounts. Price, Holyland & Waterhouse, and Deloitte, first made their mark in railways, the latter in unravelling the consequences of the Redpath frauds on the GNR.

Railways provided much work for lawyers, though it was 1861 before a railway company employed its own solicitor. Surveying was another profession which developed as a result of the railways: fifteen of the twenty founder members of the Institute of Surveyors in 1868 were railway surveyors.

The railways made a rapid impact on the country. Links were quickly established between the major cities. Liverpool was linked with Manchester in 1830 and by 1840 they and the other four largest English cities (Birmingham, Sheffield, Leeds and Bristol) were all linked to London. The trains offered substantial savings in time and comfort over coach travel. Manchester was reached from London in 18hr 30min in 1836, but in 7hr 45min by train in 1844. By 1850 it was possible to travel by rail from London to Plymouth, Holyhead, Glasgow, Edinburgh and Aberdeen.

Even in the 1830s the railways north of London saw themselves as an end-on connecting system. Arrangements had to be made for through fares and rates and the subsequent sharing of payments on an agreed basis. Bilateral arrangements were gradually replaced by the mechanism of the Railway Clearing House (RCH) set up in 1842 with the LBR in the lead which then handled all traffic to and from London and the Midlands and the North. It was the end of the decade before the RCH took on the more difficult task of dealing with inter-company freight traffic. Gradually most companies joined and by the early 1870s it dealt with 38 per cent of UK freight traffic and 17 per cent of passenger traffic on the 92 per cent of UK route mileage owned by its members.

The establishment of through routes was followed by the amalgamations as early as the mid-1840s to form the Midland and the LNWR. There were serious attempts to make a mega-merger involving two or more of the LNWR, GWR, LSWR and Midland. Far from aggressively competing, the railway enterprises soon started pooling schemes whereby receipts were divided between the companies in agreed and fixed proportions between certain routes and specified companies.

The first essays led by the LNWR were designed to preserve the primacy of the west coast route to the northwest, Yorkshire and Scotland. The company also negotiated secret 'Confederate' traffic agreements by which traffic and rates were regulated. Although some types of agreement were ruled illegal, pooling from 1861 was regarded as within the law and in principle and practice was to remain a feature of the railway business, though the application of such agreements to new lines was always a source of weakness, and in 1866 was ruled *ultra vires*. Thereafter pooling agreements continued with limitations but the tendency to direct competition away from fares and rates was enhanced.

This did not stop the development of new lines. Railway building increased in the 1860s. The Midland reached London and then, in 1876, Carlisle to open up its own route to Scotland, but much of the new construction was of more lines in the London area, or extensions in the more rural parts of the kingdom where the companies would find it hard to justify investment or raise the necessary money themselves. Thus finance companies and contractors came to play a bigger part, both in floating new schemes and in the financing of construction. When the contractors got into difficulties in 1866 through over expansion, the companies which were most closely bound to them, the LCDR and the GER, found themselves in the hands of receivers and other companies including the GWR and SER were hard pressed financially in the 1866 crash.

The years from 1870 to 1914 can be regarded as the golden age of British railways, but in this period railways were hardly dynamic institutions run by thrusting entrepreneurs. The top ten companies share of the market was virtually unchanged. No new entrants made it into the top fifteen, and there were no amalgamations of the larger companies, though they did absorb many smaller companies. The railway companies themselves saw value in further consolidation, but in the early 1870s the Government effectively killed off pro-posals for a merger between two lines which were competitive in Lancashire (the LNWR and LYR) and the end-on merger between the Midland and the GSWR.

The most radical marketing initiative by a company was taken by the Midland. In the 1840s and 1850s on many lines, passengers had to pay more to travel by express train. From 1859 the Midland had abolished express fares and its competitors were generally forced to do likewise. The same company went further in 1872 when it admitted third-class passengers to all trains, including expresses, and three years later abolished the second class and charged first-class passengers the old second-class rates.

These moves were greeted with dismay by some other companies, particularly those like the LNWR which had a larger proportion of first-class passengers, but its competitors followed, eventually even the southern companies which were not in competition, though the LSWR maintained the second class until 1918. This revolutionised the market. There was a very big rise in third-class passengers and a large, but proportionately smaller, increase in receipts compared with small falls in first-class passengers and receipts.

Rising incomes and other factors brought a greater demand, and the accompanying increased industrial activity was met by the railways with better and often cheaper facilities. The number of passengers carried rose from 322 million in 1870 to 1,265 million in 1912, and freight carried from 166 million tons to 513 million. Moreover the system expanded with a rise in line mileage from 13,560 to 20,260 and gross receipts from £43million to £124million. However this was on a much larger capital base – £502million in 1870 grew to £1,085million and was accompanied by higher costs.

There were examples of unprofitable expansion which included many branch and feeder lines. Some would not have been built but for pressure from the local community. Lines, which had been originated by a loss-making local company, had to be taken over by the main-line company. Some branch lines, for example those with heavy mineral traffic, were clearly profitable but, as a study of the NER's network of branch lines concluded, the best that could be said was that in cash terms the drain on the company's finances was not great in this period and there clearly was a social return in terms of service to the local communities by providing access to markets, and cheaper products such as coal. Nevertheless as early as 1897 the financial position was entirely negative on all but a few lines in the NER sample. There is nothing to suggest that this was not replicated in other parts of the country.

Much of the building was to keep up with the demand for transport at key points in the system with the provision of sidings, additional lines for suburban traffic and cut-offs on main lines. The last were to shorten routes of which the Severn Tunnel and the Tay and Forth Bridges, and in the first decade of the twentieth century the GWR's Westbury and Bicester cut-offs, were the prime examples. Such developments were often regarded by the public as signs of a fully mature industry running at the height of its powers and the railways were still providing a reasonable return to investors. Improvements however were expensive and in what was now a mature industry the law of diminishing returns set in. The early 1870s saw a peak in the profitability of railways in Britain followed by a slow decline until 1904 with a slight revival to World War One. The percentage of working expenses to gross receipts rose steadily from about 50 per cent in 1860–80 to 63 per cent in 1900–12. The rate of return on paid-up capital fell from a peak of 4.41 per cent in 1870 to an annual average of 3.42 per cent in 1905–9.

How far the fall in the rate of return in this period resulted from a deterioration of the operating performance of the railways from lack of enterprise or external factors, has been a matter of some controversy among historians. Despite the move on the third class, the general practice on fares and rates was conservative. The select committee of 1882 found that no general principle or system of fixing rates had been adopted: the charge was what the company thought the traffic would bear, having regard to competition both of other means of transport and of other districts or markets.

The managers told them they could not determine with accuracy the cost of carrying any particular goods between two stations. Acworth believed rates had become customary, citing the fact that the first-class fare from Oxford to London had remained at 11*s* for 30 years. A superintendent of one main line consulted his colleagues about whether to issue all-in excursion tickets to a London theatre. Controversy arose because traders disliked the practice of offering cheaper rates for large loads over long distances, particularly as it was often applied to imports. American cheese or meat brought into Liverpool was conveyed to London at half the rates for which Cheshire products were conveyed. Similarly worsted manufacturers in Bradford paid less per mile than for wool from Oxfordshire. The courts held that proportionately lower rates on longer distance traffic did not constitute an undue preference. A large load from a fixed point to another fixed point incurred lower costs and was perhaps also necessary to ensure the trade continued.

The traders' campaign was one of the principal reasons for the government's intervention by the Act of 1894 prescribing maximum rates at the 1892 level. However companies could not necessarily act unilaterally. Though the Scottish pooling agreement ceased in 1869, it was replaced by the English and Scotch Rates Conference and there were similar pools for other traffic. An attempt at a complete pool for the companies north of the Thames failed in 1886, but the move was indicative of attitudes. The trend towards a less competitive railway system was accelerated after 1900 by a wave of pooling and similar agreements which meant that the country was divided into six oligopolistic groups if the NER's territorial monopoly is included.

The Clearing House and pools meant that in an attempt to maintain and increase their share of the traffic competition between the companies concentrated on faster and more frequent trains, better carriages even for third-class passengers, and more convenient stations, and offering greater regularity and speed for goods traffic.

There were competitive routes from London to Birmingham, Manchester, Leeds, Edinburgh, Aberdeen, Exeter and Dover and on steamer crossings, particularly on the Channel short sea route and the Clyde. The Midland introduced Pullman sleeping carriages in 1874, the GNR dining cars in 1878, and by 1891–2 the corridor train was introduced.

Such carriages were however not only more expensive to manufacture, but markedly heavier: from 1875 to 1885 the average weight of main-line carriages rose from 15–20 tons to 25–30 tons. This meant construction of more powerful locomotives, sometimes of several types to cope with increasing weights and the demand for speed, exemplified by the two races to Edinburgh and Aberdeen by the West and East Coast routes in 1888 and 1895. This led to favourable publicity for the companies, prestige and extra passengers, but higher costs.

Contemporaries were concerned at the performance of British railways, particularly in comparison with the United States, a view shared by historians. Dorsey in 1885 thought that English railroads, in economical workings and appliances had apparently remained stationary for the last 30 years while the United States reduced operating expenses by 50 per cent. By 1896 British managers were visiting the US to see for themselves. Amongst them was the NER which subsequently stripped the passenger and goods departments of their operating functions and made the general superintendent responsible for handling traffic. Both commercial and traffic managers reported to a general traffic manager with the general manager left free of day to day administration and able to concentrate on wider policy issues. The NER improved methods of train working, assisted by fewer trains, more powerful locomotives and larger wagons. The average train load on the NER increased by 61 per cent from 1902 to 1913 and receipts per freight train mile improved by 87 per cent on the NER. Others made smaller but substantial improvement in the operating efficiency of freight trains, but what has been called the institutionalised obsolescence of the small privately-owned wagon was not overcome.

In 1914, 90 per cent of the general merchandise consignments of the GER were of one ton or less, whilst 70 per cent were of 3cwt or less. The improvement was not paralleled on the passenger side where train receipts per passenger mile decreased somewhat. Another comparison with the USA could be made in office efficiency. The revolution in the use of office machinery hardly affected British offices. This was particularly true of the Railway Clearing House where, as late as 1911, there appears to have been no calculating machines and only two typewriters for a staff of 3,000.

On the railways as a whole labour productivity, which had increased between 1860 to 1880 by 1.59 per cent per annum, only rose by 0.17 per cent per annum from 1880 to 1910. The railways attempted to squeeze costs by cutting wages and working longer hours but this led to the Railway Hours Act of 1893, and later the establishment of a conciliation scheme at the request of the railways themselves when faced with the prospect of a strike in 1907. In 1910 the Government had to intervene to avert a national strike. In the following year a Board of Trade Committee set up by Winston Churchill concluded that 'active competition between railway companies of an extensive kind hardly any longer exists'. It was this view, reinforced by Government control in World War One, which was to set the scene for the 1921 Act and the creation of the big four companies.

The first railways were dedicated to the carriage of minerals but, following the example of the LMR which attracted a surprisingly large passenger traffic, until the late 1840s freight traffic was less important. This was in part because the concentration on first- and second-class passenger traffic proved remunerative, but also because it was easier to arrange for the through traffic to use other lines for passengers than for freight.

Traffic managers were perhaps slow to see the potential of freight particularly coal. However by 1849 the LNWR had a contract with the Clay Cross Company to bring 45,000 tons a year to London. Companies developed an enormous traffic in coal which was widely used domestically and for locomotive firing as well as in industry. The GWR had substantial long-range hauls from the South Wales coalfields to London and to Birkenhead, the latter largely for the use of steamships. The Midland not only conveyed coal to other parts of its network, but also to Peterborough for onward transmission to the eastern counties and to Kew for the LSWR and SER.

Products such as iron and steel demanded quantities of raw materials. In 1870 the carriage of materials for the making of pig iron represented some 32 per cent of the total sums received by the railways for mineral traffic. When the Staveley Company began to work its own iron ore in Northamptonshire, half a million tons of ore per year left there for Derbyshire. In the mining areas numerous branches were built to serve individual collieries or groups. More extensive lines were also built to serve them – the Barry Railway in South Wales and the ambitiously named Lancashire, Derbyshire and East Coast Railway, both inspired by the local colliery owners.

Large brickworks grew up alongside railways and areas, with more suitable clays, sent bricks long distances, for instance Accrington and Ruabon and later Fletton bricks near Peterborough and Calvert in Buckinghamshire.

There was an extensive traffic in livestock, amounting to 3 per cent of total goods traffic by value in the 1860s. By the 1880s refrigerated vans had been developed which enabled New Zealand lamb to establish itself throughout the country. New traffic was established with perishable foodstuffs. From the

1860s milk became an important traffic. By 1890, 84 per cent of London's liquid milk was brought in by rail, much of it from the West Country and the Midlands. There was a large traffic in fruit and vegetables. These developments contributed to a rise in living standards.

On the passenger side, while the legal requirement to provide third-class travel in 1844 marked a breakthrough which much reduced and then wore away the concentration on first and second class, the companies still for some years restricted third-class travel to a number of slower trains. Moreover even the penny a mile parliamentary fare was not initially much help to the poor. Though faster and cheaper than coach travel as Jack Simmons pointed out the journey between Lancashire and London would cost the semiskilled or unskilled worker ten days wages. This did not prevent 50 per cent of passenger journeys being made at the parliamentary rate or less by 1850. Excursion trains of which there were a growing number tended to be cheaper. As described in Chapter Four (Railways and the Leisure Revolution) the railways from a very early date set out to cater for cheaper excursions for certain special groups: for example Sunday School and factory outings, race meetings and later football matches. The introduction of Bank Holidays in 1871 gave excursions a big boost, and later the growth of annual holidays led the railways to introduce additional trains at summer weekends to cater for the traffic. It is not clear how profitable the excursions were but they furnished 10 per cent of the LBSCR's passenger receipts in 1901–09.

Suburban traffic was another defined market at which many of the railways aimed, particularly with the companies running south and northeast of London and many of the lines, built in the last quarter of the century in and around London, had commuters in mind. Between the wars workmen's and season tickets, both of which began to be widely used in the 1870s, would account for over a third of all passenger miles.

It is more difficult to be sure who travelled for longer distances on the main lines, holidaymakers apart. The railways certainly wanted to encourage business travel. When the Trent Valley line was opened providing a service to the north-west which avoided Birmingham the LNWR's publicity pointed out that those needing to do business in Manchester or Liverpool and return to London the same evening would have four hours in Manchester rather than 2¼. This meant leaving London at 6.15am and arriving back at 10.30pm. Later in the century, the Saturday to Mondays at great country houses enjoyed by Gladstone and other notables were only feasible because of the railway, as was the trek to Scotland for the Glorious Twelfth.

At all levels of society the railways gave an opportunity for greater mobility. Whether for business or pleasure the number of passengers showed a steady growth from 25 million in 1842 to 73 million in 1850, 163 million in 1860 and 322 million in 1870. This was in a period when two other developments in communications made possible by the railway rendered travel apparently less necessary. In 1838 the railways were required to carry mails and it was rapid carriage by rail which enabled the success of the penny post introduced in 1840. Traffic increased from 76 million items in 1840 to 863 million in 1870.

The second was the electric telegraph which was largely routed by the telegraph companies along railway lines and used for railway purposes but, with over a thousand offices, open to the public by 1868 with telegraph offices on many stations.

Railway structures and facilities quickly became part of the urban and rural landscape. The railways attained national coverage. By 1914 no town in England and Wales with a population of 3,000 or more was not within three miles of a railway station. Stationmasters were important figures in the locality. Many villages had stations, often with their sidings for coal and other wagons, a cattle dock, waiting rooms, parcels and telegraph office. Traffic was often heaviest on market days, encouraged by cheap market day tickets.

Such stations changed little over the years. Substantial though this impact was, the companies owned 7 to 10 per cent of the land in major cities compared with about ¼ per cent in the main agricultural counties, though the proportion must have been far greater in the coalfields.

In towns landmarks such as the dominant viaduct at Stockport and architecturally fine stations such as St Pancras and Huddersfield hit the eye. However large tracts of urban land were given over to goods stations and sidings. While St Pancras passenger station involved the demolition of many houses, the goods station built a few years later demanded further clearances. The GWR even had a goods station next to Smithfield, accessed by the Metropolitan Railway.

The railways affected development in other ways. The department stores were attracted to Kensington High Street by the Metropolitan railway station. Northampton lost its lead in shoes and boots to Leicester in part because the latter was much more accessible by rail. Vauxhall Motors were attracted to Luton by its position on the Midland main line. Rail was not the only reason why brewing was concentrated in Burton, but it was an important factor. Manchester became the headquarters of the Co-operative Wholesale Society because of its excellence as a distribution centre. Chivers, the jam manufacturer, developed his orchards at Histon near Cambridge as the village station was served by two railway companies. Bulk conveyance of food and clothes and other articles meant generally cheaper goods, but a greater uniformity in what was available in shops throughout the country.

As the main-line railways tended to converge on London, it meant some decline in the relative importance of provincial centres, exemplified by the conveyance of newspapers produced in London to much of the rest of the country and triumph of railway time (Greenwich Mean Time) over local time.

The exact boundaries of the railways' business varied from company to company and from time to time. Railways soon conceived of themselves as serving their customers by providing facilities additional to the railway itself, sometimes directly by the company, sometimes by associates in a separate undertaking. These included the provision of facilities for the delivery of goods – the railways had 26,000 horses in 1914. The first of many railway hotels was opened at Euston by the LBR in 1839 and was soon paying a steady dividend of 6 per cent. By 1913 there were ninety-two hotels in cities and resorts with a capital of some £8million returning about 7 per cent.

The railway routes were soon extended by steamer services to the European mainland and to Ireland. The SER bought and then improved Folkestone Harbour and soon formed a separate steamship company. The SDR was linked to Middlesbrough by 1830 and the town and docks were soon developed by parties allied to the railway, which secured a profitable traffic.

These were often peripheral activities and the success or failure of the enterprise did not depend on them, though providing revenue and underlining the railway's image as a provider of service to the public. The investments involved were far from negligible. By 1885 the docks and associated works at Grimsby accounted for nearly 10 per cent of the capital of the MSLR. Fresh fish was conveyed by rail in special trains from Grimsby, Hull and Yarmouth to be sold cheaply in Manchester, London and elsewhere, enabling a broadening of the city dwellers' diet. Southampton Docks were in decline when purchased by the LSWR in 1892. It was the capital that the railway injected which enabled it to become one of the chief passenger ports in Europe.

The railways were also manufacturers of locomotives and rolling stock and in some cases steel rails. These activities led to the establishment of new company towns such as Wolverton and Crewe and later Eastleigh, and the domination by the railway of older towns such as Swindon and Doncaster with the provision of houses and schools by the paternalistic employer. Locomotives were built for the early railways by a number of specialist and other firms, but in the 1840s, first the Grand Junction and then the GWR and the Manchester & Leeds, built locomotives at their own works and by 1853 the practice was generally established. By 1914 railway company workshops employed 50,000 men. It was difficult to secure locomotives from outside companies when order books were full at a time of rapid expansion and manufacture was a natural extension of facilities for the maintenance and repair of locomotives.

**Wagon Shop at Wolverton Works, c.1928.**
National Railway Museum, Science & Society Picture Library

How far this policy was justified has been a matter of some debate by historians. It is argued it led to a culture of dominance of the company by the locomotive engineer, 'the technical master of the board', and often a proliferation of types due to the failure to adopt standardisation or replacement policies. On the other hand the LNWR under Ramsbottom and Webb, and later the GWR under Churchward did much to standardise locomotive types.

What was the overall effect on the economy? Dudley Baxter in 1866 suggested that, had the railway traffic of 1865 been conveyed by canal and road at pre-railway rates, it would have cost three times as much. There was thus a saving of £72million, the equivalent of 9 per cent of the net national income. Present day economic historians have made much more complex calculations of the effect of the railways on the economy, notably G.R. Hawke, but his conclusion is not substantially different. The savings after 1870 were probably considerably greater.

In World War One the Government guaranteed to the companies the net revenue of 1913. This had been a good year, but there was no opportunity for the companies to do well out of the war. Indeed they did rather badly as the need to transport troops and munitions even to the far North of Scotland for the naval base at Scapa Flow and the considerable substitution of long-haul coal traffic for sea-borne traffic meant that the plant, both fixed and moving, deteriorated. Immediately after the war costs rose faster than gross receipts and the government had to top up the revenue to the guaranteed level.

The Transport Act of 1921 resulted in a radical reduction of the number of companies from 120 to four, but the consequences were less fundamental than might have been expected. It was assumed that amalgamation would lead to more economic working by consolidation of staff and facilities. To some extent this happened, but much had already been achieved in this direction in the War. The Royal Commission on Transport reviewed the matter in 1930 but was unable to decide how far alleged economies could be attributed to the consolidation or to the fall in input prices.

The 1921 Act was a return to private enterprise with price control governed by a standard revenue supervised by the Railway Rates Tribunal, but its purpose was to eliminate wasteful competition. Competition for revenue was however limited by pooling. Some of the longstanding arrangements were confirmed by the 1921 Act. Others were introduced in the 1920s and by 1933 the Ministry of Transport had approved schemes which covered about half of the traffic receipts of the four companies. They were intended to be four regulated regional monopolies, but overlapped to a considerable extent except for the Southern, particularly in services between major towns. Fifty of the sixty-six towns, with over 50,000 population served by more than one company before grouping, were still so served, but such rivalry was increasingly tempered by pooling arrangements.

Instead competition came from outside the railway industry. The biggest challenge the railways had to meet in this period was from road transport. Tramways apart, before 1914 this was not a rival. The road haulage industry grew rapidly after 1918 primed by the purchase of war surplus vehicles. The prescribed system of regulated monopoly prescribed by the 1921 Act could be undermined by unregulated road hauliers, mostly small firms who competed with each other for traffic, so driving down prices and gaining traffic from the railway. They operated door-to-door services, avoiding trans-shipment and the new industry rapidly improved its technology with diesel engines and other technical advances, so reducing its own operating costs.

How did the companies respond? Railway managers have been criticised for putting more emphasis on the technical problems of railway operation than on the commercial problems of competing for revenue, but on many fronts their hands were tied. The railways had a continued obligation to accept traffic, publish charges, provide a reasonable level of service, avoid undue preference

**Whitemore Marshalling Yard, showing wagons and coal stacks.**
National Railway Museum, Science & Society Picture Library

in their dealings with customers and were also subject to government regulation of wages and conditions.

Railways could and did offer exceptional rates but, on account of the flexibility of road rates, found it impractical to draw up revised scales. They were therefore inclined to blame the operating environment and the fact that in the 1920s the road licensing system raised little towards the cost of providing and maintaining roads while the railways were responsible for their own tracks.

Changes in favour of railways were made in the 1930s in local authority rates, railway passenger duty and in the taxation of petrol and motor vehicles, but did not go as far as the companies wished. The railways responded to some extent with express freights, timetabling of freight trains, and in the 1930s containerisation and by taking over road haulage businesses. Pickford's and Carter Paterson could not however compete with their independent rivals.

The threat from road transport was made more serious by other changes in the environment. The railways had been very reliant on precisely those regions and heavy industries which were in decline in the interwar period. Only the Southern, in much of whose area the population continued to grow and which derived some three-quarters of its revenue from passenger traffic, was exempt

213

to any extent. The newer industries were more inclined to turn to road transport and coal was vulnerable to coastal shipping.

The shareholders, unlike their nineteenth-century predecessors, were not organised and their interest in greater distributed profits was not accompanied by proposals for measures likely to bring that about. An 8-hour day and 48-hour week had been introduced during the period of government control in the war and in 1921 national negotiating machinery was established.

Wages accounted for 36 per cent of total cost in 1913 but 56 per cent in 1931, and had increased much more on the railways than in industry generally. The companies were only able to secure a modest reduction in wages in 1928 with a further reduction in 1931. Meanwhile traffic had been hit by the General Strike and the continuing coal strike which meant that the railways did not have sufficient coal to run their full service with consequent loss in revenue. The GWR had to take almost £1million from reserves to maintain the dividend, and did so again in the years of the depression, 1930–35.

Nevertheless the management, if not capable of changing these factors, did much to modernise their systems. The productivity of labour improved substantially, the number of employees falling from 735,000 in 1921 to 588,000 in 1939. The locomotive stock was improved and very necessary reductions in the number of types were made. Manufacturing, repairs and servicing were rationalised. Fuel consumption was reduced and improvements were made in the speed of trains.

Major schemes of main-line electrification such as that recommended by the Weir Committee were not feasible because of the capital required, but an extensive network of suburban lines on the Southern system where the density of traffic was great and the journeys short was electrified, and from 1929 was extended to Brighton, Portsmouth, and Eastbourne. New marshalling yards were built, and docks facilities improved. Main-line traffic continued to grow. Faster trains were introduced, some with streamlining and the achievement of the world steam record by Mallard in 1938 gave valuable publicity. The introduction of cheaper tickets in the 1930s boosted traffic but helped bring about a demand on summer Saturdays by holiday makers which could put great strains on the system. Though there were improvements in the freight business, the few attempts to tackle the fragmented ownership and low capacity of wagons met with little success, though increasingly private wagons were pooled.

By the time war broke out the revenue of the four companies was down to £33million, 35 per cent lower than the standard revenue of £51million set in 1921. The operating ratio had risen to 81 per cent; the net rate of return on capital had fallen to 3.16 per cent.

In World War Two, the railways were again taken over by the government and operations managed by a committee of railway managers with a guaranteed net revenue of £43million. The railways succeeded in carrying the greatly expanded wartime traffic – in 1944 the ton mileage of freight carried was 50 per cent higher than in 1938 and passenger traffic 67 per cent higher. However wear and tear on equipment increased with no adequate provision for replacement and renewal. The Treasury retained much of the earnings and rates rises fell well behind rising costs. When traffic generated by wartime needs ceased, net earnings fell from £62million in 1945 to only £32million in 1946. The railways share of passenger transport, down to 27 per cent in 1938 was temporarily back to the 1935 level at 31 per cent.

There were huge backlogs in maintenance and renewal of permanent way and rolling stock, and increases in the average age of fixed and moveable assets. The larger receipts for the increased wartime traffic had however allowed higher dividends and shareholders benefitted even more in 1946 and 1947 when the highest dividends for a decade were paid. On nationalisation shareholders were consequently bought out at rates which were affected by the abnormal wartime profits and based on assets falling in real value.

Nationalisation of the railways had its advocates even in 1921 and attracted growing support in the 1930s. In 1947 it was proceeded with as part of the Labour government's policy of public ownership in basic industries, including the railways. It was seen that the system was severely run down and its future under private control would be problematic and nationalisation could help develop inter-modal transport coordination.

In the first decade of the new regime, despite changes of organisation, there was little improvement on the railways, and like many in Austerity Britain they were slow to get back to pre-war standards. The British Transport Commission (BTC) was created and made responsible for overall policy with the Railway Executive (RE) charged with operational policy and losing responsibility for docks and inland waterways, and hotels which went to separate Executives as did road transport and London Transport. This did not work well.

The BTC never effectively co-ordinated different transport modes, and it tended to interfere with RE's role of operational management of the railways. In turn the RE tended towards a centralised approach which reduced the role of the regional managers. In 1953 the RE was abolished. The chairman of the BTC therefore became effectively the chief executive of the railways, and integration with other modes ceased to be an aim. However the management structure proved to be cumbersome with the lines of authority less clear cut.

In 1955 the BTC published the report 'Modernisation and Re-equipment of the British Railways' which envisaged a 15-year investment programme of

£1,240million on electrification, diesel locomotives, passenger rolling stock including diesel multiple units (dmus), freight services, particularly wagons and marshalling yards.

The BTC estimated that this expenditure would ultimately bring a return of at least £85million a year, £60million from freight. Despite some scepticism of this optimistic and not clearly articulated estimate, the government accepted the plan. Investment increased, much of it going on diesel locomotives and dmus, though the introduction of diesel locomotives was initially beset by teething problems, and the modernisation plan was slow to make any impact.

Meanwhile the road haulage industry was growing and private motoring was increasing. The end of the decade saw the beginnings of motorways and the launch of the Mini which made car ownership more affordable. The railways share of passenger traffic began to drop sharply and there was a major decline in freight traffic.

The railways were now failing to cover costs and the deficit was rising. The reasons were complex – not only the decline in freight particularly after the 1958 recession, but also stickiness in passenger fares because of fears of losing traffic and the government's price freeze. From 1958 BR attempted to win back merchandise traffic without success; its new charges system for merchandise came too late to stem the loss of traffic to road hauliers.

While it recognised that much of the delivery to rural areas was unprofitable, BR thought the public interest demanded a reasonably adequate service and failed to appreciate fully the extent of the loss-making areas. Only slow progress was made with the closure of unprofitable lines. The rise in costs was spearheaded by wages which rose over 6 per cent per annum from 1953 to 1962, though less than earnings in manufacturing industry. However BR was able to secure modest gains in both labour and total factor productivity.

At the same time the Government was trying to establish clear economic and financial objectives for all the nationalised industries, and emphasis was put on the need to concentrate on commercial objectives with improved accounting and investment appraisal. The white paper, the 'Financial and Economic Obligations of the Nationalised Industries (1961)', declared that managements should achieve a break-even position over a five-year period and attain defined rates of interest of return on investment. By then the Modernisation Plan was being reconsidered in an attempt to reconcile the obligation to break even with the cost of running and improving the existing network.

Beeching from ICI was appointed chairman of the BTC in 1961 and, on its abolition in 1963, of British Railways (BR) with a much more centralised management structure. Beeching was deliberately brought in because of his industrial and commercial background, and he brought in others at senior levels. His plan the 'Reshaping of British Railways' was based on substantial analyses of the costs of each line and station and their receipts. It recommended closure not just of small branch lines and wayside stations, a process that had started in the 1930s depression and had gathered pace after the war, but of other lines – in all some 2,000 stations and 250 train services. This included the cutting of major lines, for example virtually the complete system in the Scottish Borders. While substantially implemented it aroused considerable public opposition in the areas affected and a number of lines, particularly in Wales and Scotland survived the closure process.

The many debates did however lead to a clearer understanding of the limits of a purely commercial railway in meeting social needs which resulted in the institution under the Transport Act of 1968 of a system of specific grants for unremunerative but socially necessary services, replaced in 1974 by a lump sum grant known as the Public Service Obligation. The 1968 Act transferred to a new National Freight Corporation both the loss-making small consignments of freight traffic and the recently started and expanding Freightliner company. It also created Passenger Transport Authorities in the major provincial conurbations with power to make agreements with BR for local train services and to make subsidy payments where necessary.

The 1960s saw more physical changes in the railway business than any other decade. A slimmer network was introduced. 45 per cent of the 4,300 passenger stations and almost a third of the route miles open in 1962 had closed by 1973. In 1968 steam haulage ceased. By then steam had largely been replaced by diesel alongside the electrification of the line from London to Birmingham, Manchester and Liverpool in 1967, more suburban lines, the two lines to the Kent coast and to Bournemouth.

Novel attempts to halt the decline in freight traffic were introduced with Freightliners (fast timetabled container trains) and merry-go-round coal trains to power stations which discharged without stopping. Moreover excess stock had largely been eliminated – wagon numbers were 22 per cent of 1948 and passenger carriages about 40 per cent. All these developments led to a considerable fall in staff numbers and a rise in productivity, with single manning of electric and diesel locomotives and the abolition of guards on continuously braked trains.

The 1970s were a period of greater stability in organisation. In 1976 high-speed diesel trains entered service on the Western Region, and later on the East Coast and Midland main lines and there was further electrification. By 1976 an operating surplus had been achieved though attempts to capture the freight market met with mixed success. Bulk traffic held up with increasing emphasis on the fleet of private owner wagons, but Speedlink, the high-speed scheduled freight services using air-brake wagons started in 1972, struggled to survive until 1991.

The return of a Conservative Government in 1979 led to the privatisation of BR's hotels and shipping services, and the manufacturing side of the railway workshops by then operating as British Rail Engineering Ltd. Within BR in 1982 clearer objectives were set by the government and business sectors were created (InterCity, Freight, London and South East, and Other Provincial Services (later Regional Railways)), each under a director who produced a business plan for execution by the regional management and was responsible for monitoring it. Sub-sectors were created.

Area managers were given increased responsibilities and regional head-quarters downplayed until, apart from ScotRail, they were abolished in 1992. These developments were carried further in the early 1990s with the introduction of 'Organising for Quality'.

The business and engineering functions were integrated. Decentralised businesses were created with financial responsibility and asset ownership. The 1980s saw a rise in passenger traffic and the stringent investment limits set by the Government were to an extent offset by the boom in property values. The East Coast mainline was electrified, and there were substantial further reductions in staff levels with more single manning of locomotives and cuts of station staff. The number of staff in the core rail business fell from 223,000 in 1973 to 115,000 in 1994.

The 1990s saw by far the biggest change in the nature of the railway business since it first started. Not only were the railways returned to private ownership by the 1992 Act, but there were massive changes in the structure of the business. BR was broken up into about 100 companies. Responsibility for the track, operation, rolling stock and maintenance was split. While the first was given to a single business (Railtrack), train operation was made the responsibility of twenty-five train operating companies (TOCs) to which short-term franchises were granted. They rented rolling stock from the three rolling stock operating companies. This complex business model clearly has many more interfaces, both in daily operation and the longer term, often of a contractual nature, than a single business. There is also an elaborate regulatory apparatus.

While many aspects have changed since its introduction, the general scheme has been maintained, though Railtrack, privatised in 1997, went into administration in 2002 after it failed to deal adequately with the maintenance and repair of the track through contractors, and was replaced by Network Rail, a non-dividend paying company. In 2012 the Government held out the prospect of unified track and train control in areas where there was one dominant TOC. Although there has been substantial private investment into the system, in recent years it has only amounted to about 10 per cent of the Government finance which has sustained unprofitable lines and made possible new projects, such as the upgrading of the West Coast main line and the first high-speed line catering for both Channel Tunnel and commuter traffic. From 2005–6 to 2010–11 total government support averaged £5 billion a year and has far exceeded previous levels.

The privatised system has been subject to substantial criticism not just from those who favour public ownership, but from those who point to the fragmented nature of the various functions and the discontinuities this entails with associated costs both in operating the system and in the renewal of franchises. Nevertheless the operating results have been impressive. Traffic has seen large and sustained increases.

Passenger journeys have increased since 1993–4 from less than 800 million to 1,350 million in 2010–11, a level previously only reached in the 1920s, and passenger miles from under 20 billion to 33 billion. Since 2003–4 freight traffic, now almost entirely bulk cargo, has averaged over 12 billion tonne miles – much more than in the nadir of 1994–5 (nearly 9 billion) and the highest (about 13.6 and 9.7 billion tonne miles) since the 1950s. With the Channel Tunnel open since 1994 freight trains now run to the Continent, for example, from the Midlands to Italy. While the London commuter market has been responsible for much of the growth of passenger traffic, long-distance journeys have also increased substantially, with regular interval services now the norm. Road congestion has assisted demand, and been met by improved train services both in quantity and quality, refurbished and new stations, more car parking, further links to airports, cheap off-peak tickets and purchase through the internet.

# Further reading

Derek H. Aldcroft, *British Railways in Transition*, 1968

Michael J. Freeman, *Introduction – the age of the railway*; T.R. Gourvish, *Railways 1830–1870: the formative years*; P.J. Cain, *Railways, 1870–1914, the maturity of the private system;* all in Michael J. Freeman and Derek H. Aldcroft, (editors), *Transport in Victorian Britain*, 1988

Jack Simmons, *The Railway in Town and Country, 1830–1914*, 1986

# Selective Bibliography

## General texts

These cover railways generally during the period considered. Jack Simmons was an outstanding academic historian of Britain's railways; try his *The Railways of Britain*, 1968, for an overview and *The Oxford Companion to British Railway History*, 1997, co-edited with Gordon Biddle is a comprehensive reference aid. Cuthbert Hamilton Ellis, *British Railway History from the accession of William IV until the Nationalisation of the Railways, Vols 1–2*, 1953 and 1959, is an older text and Michael J. Freeman, *Railways and the Victorian Imagination*, 1999, provides a more recent view of the nineteenth century.

I also recommend Philip Bagwell, *The Transport Revolution from 1770*, 1974, and T.C. Barker & C.I. Savage, *An Economic History of Transport in Britain*, 1974.

More recently Adrian Vaughan, *Railwaymen Politics and Money*, 1997 and especially Christian Wolmar, *Fire & Steam: A new history of the Railways in Britain*, 2007.
Frank Dobbin, *Forging Industrial Policy: the United States Britain & France in the Railway Age*, 1994, provides international comparison of government policies in the 19th century. Randy Kostal, *Law and English Railway Capitalism 1825–1875*, 1994 is the best on railways and the early-mid Victorian legal system.

On the history of nationalisation more generally E.E. Barry, *Nationalisation in British Politics – the Historical Perspective*, 1965 is good and for accidents/safety, Tom Rolt, *Red for Danger* (first published 1955).

## Early Years (1830 to around 1870)

Henry Parris, *Government and the Railways in Nineteenth Century Britain*, 1965 is a must although you can see much of the same abbreviated in 'Railway Policy in Peel's Administration 1841–6' in *Bulletin of the Institute of Historical Research*, 33, 1960.

Terry R. Gourvish's contributions: 'Railways 1830–70: the formative years', in D.H. Aldcroft & M.J. Freeman (eds), *Transport in Victorian Britain*, 1988 and his small book *Railways and the British Economy 1830–1914*, 1980, are useful.

Consult J. Prest, 'Gladstone and the Railways' in P.J. Jagger (ed.), *Gladstone*, 1998, for an insight into Gladstone (also useful for some of the debate about Ireland).

A more academic view on the idea of *laissez-faire* is found in J. Bartlet Brebner, 'Laissez Faire and State Intervention in Nineteenth Century Britain', *Journal of Economic History*, Vol.8 Supplement, 1948, pp.59–73.

Grahame Boyes, 'Exchequer Bill Loan Commissioners as a source of Canal and Railway Finance 1817–1842', *Journal of the Railway & Canal Historical Society*, 24/3, 1978, pp.85–92 gives an account of the modest financial help offered by the government to the railways in their early years.

## Railway Maturity (1870 to 1914)

P.J. Cain, 'Railways 1870–1914: the maturity of the private system', in D.H. Aldcroft & M.J. Freeman (eds), *Transport in Victorian Britain*, 1988 is a short overview.

R.J. Irving, *The North Eastern Railway Company 1870–1914: An economic history*, 1976 is written from one company's perspective.

M. Le Guillou 'Freight rates and their influence on the Black Country iron trade in a period of growing domestic and foreign competition' in *Journal of Transport History*, 3, 1975 brings out railway customer concerns.

## Railways in Wartime

Christian Wolmar, *Engines of War: How Wars were Won and Lost on the Railways*, 2010 is a good and recent text. Also Michael Robbins, *The Railway Age*, 1962 covers railways' role in war.

## The Grouping (1918 to 1939)

Derek Aldcroft, *British Railways in Transition: The Economic Problems of Britain's Railways since 1914*, 1968, pp.83–7, and Gerald Crompton, '"Good business for the nation" The railway nationalisation issue, 1921–47', *Journal of Transport History*, 20 (20), 1999, pp.141–59, cover the interwar era.

## Nationalisation to Privatisation (1948–93)

Terry Gourvish's very comprehensive works, *British Rail 1948–1973: A business history*, and *British Rail 1974–1997: From Integration to Privatisation*, stand out.

For a sympathetic view of Richard Beeching read Richard Hardy, *Beeching – Champion of the Railway?*, 1989).

For some different aspects try two articles by J.E. Allen: 'Railway Compensation Examined', *The Economic Journal*, Vol.58, March 1948, pp.125–8 and 'Railways or Roads?', *The Economic Journal*, Vol.69, March 1959, pp.180–2.

## Privatisation Era (since 1993)

Gourvish, *Britain's Railways 1997–2005*, 2008, covers the period well.

The government white paper is also a good start to understand how privatisation was initially foreseen: 'New Opportunities for the Railways: The Privatisation of British Rail', HMSO, CM2012, July 1992.

Useful too are: Philip Bagwell, 'The Sad State of British railways: the rise and fall of Railtrack 1992–2002' in *Journal of Transport History*, 25/2, 2004, pp.111–23 and Gerald Crompton & Robert Jupe, 'Network Rail – Forward or Backward? Not-for-profit in British Transport' in *Business History*, 49/6, 2007, pp.908–28.

## London

For London start with T.C. Barker & M. Robbins' two volumes: *A History of London Transport*.

On the underground railways specifically I would start with Christian Wolmar, *The Subterranean Railway: How London Underground was built and how it changed the city forever*, 2004, and Stephen Halliday, *Underground to Everywhere: London's Underground Railway in the Life of the Capital*, 2001.

## Ireland

Tom Ferris, *Irish Railways*, 2008 is an overview.

From a governmental/legislative perspective invaluable is Tim Moriarty, 'History of Railway Legislation 5, Irish Tramway and Light Railway Law (Part 1)' in *Irish Railway Record Society Journal*, 164, 2007, and subsequent parts.

Padriag O'Cuimin's book, *The Baronial Lines of the Midland & Great Western Railway: Loughrea and Ballinrobe*, 1972, is insightful as is our editor David St John Thomas, *The Country Railway* (covers more than Ireland). Although neither is a railway specific book congested districts and the policies pertaining thereto are explored in depth in Ciara Breathnach, *The Congested Districts Board, 1891–1923*, 2005 and William L. Micks, *An account of the constitution, administration and dissolution of the Congested Districts Board for Ireland from 1891 to 1923*, 1925.

## Primary sources

Primary sources should not be neglected although they can be extremely long. Try 'Fifth Report from Select Committee on Railways', Parliamentary Papers (PP), 24 May 1844 and both 'Final Report of the Royal Commission on Railways', PP, 7 May 1867 and the 'Royal Commission on Railways 1865–7: Report of Sir Rowland Hill', PP, May 1867.

The early case for the government to have a greater role in the railway industry is stated by Sir Edwin Chadwick, *Address on Railway Reform presented to the National Association for the Promotion of Social Science*, 1865 and William Galt, *Railway Reform: Its Importance and Practicability considered*, 1843, and his updated version in 1865.

Herbert Morrison, *British Transport at Britain's Service*, Labour Party Publications Dept, 1938, is also a good presentation of pro-nationalisation arguments in the interwar period. Don't ignore newspapers and railway journals.

# Index